Autocracy and Democracy

AUTOCRACY

and

DEMOCRACY

AN EXPERIMENTAL INQUIRY

RALPH K. WHITE
Chief, Communism Analysis Division
Office of Research and Analysis
United States Information Agency

RONALD LIPPITT
Research Program Director
Research Center for Group Dynamics
University of Michigan

GREENWOOD PRESS, PUBLISHERS
WESTPORT, CONNECTICUT

Library of Congress Cataloging in Publication Data

White, Ralph K
    Autocracy and democracy.

    Bibliography: p.
    1. Social groups. 2. Democracy. 3. Leadership.
I. Lippitt, Ronald, joint author. II. Title.
[HM131.W45 1972]   301.18   71-138137
ISBN 0-8371-5710-2

Originally published in 1960 by Harper & Brothers Publishers,
New York

Reprinted with the permission of Harper & Row, Publishers

Reprinted by Greenwood Press,
a division of Williamhouse-Regency Inc.

First Greenwood Reprinting 1972
Second Greenwood Reprinting 1976

Library of Congress Catalog Card Number 71-138137

ISBN 0-8371-5710-2

Printed in the United States of America

Contents

IV Implications

Preface

THIS is the report of an inquiry into the psychological dynamics of democratic, autocratic, and unorganized social situations. In collaboration with our senior partner, the late Kurt Lewin, we conducted these experiments in an attic at the University of Iowa in 1938.[1] Since then, after writing our technical report of the studies, we have gone our separate professional ways, one of us focusing his research interests on international relations and the behavior of nations, the other continuing to work at understanding behavior and growth in the classroom and the family. We have found ourselves returning frequently, with a sense of incompleteness, to this earlier point of collaboration to review and extend the insights that emerged from these observations. Some aspects of the data have never been reported. Our notions about the meanings of our findings have changed and clarified; and the nature of events in our rapidly changing society have kept reinforcing our belief that the attitudes and methods of scientific research can be applied to the study of democracy by those who are trying to live it and extend it. Also we discovered we are a bit ashamed of ourselves for not having been willing to "stick out our necks" in our early reports by putting into print some of our speculations about possible relations between our limited inquiry and the broader aspects of life in a democracy.

[1] Readers of previous partial reports of these experiments (e.g., 1939) are familiar with the authorship sequence "Lewin, Lippitt and White." They may wonder why the name of Lippitt came first in earlier publications while White comes first in this one. The answer is that Lippitt's name was put first before in recognition of the fact that he conceived the initial experiment and carried it out under the general direction of Lewin. White joined the team a year later, and took part in the second major experiment. White is identified as senior author of this book because he did the greater part of the writing.

Kurt Lewin is no longer actively with us, but the image of his willingness and eagerness to speculate, to suggest tentative extensions of interpretation from what we know to what we are not yet clear about, is still strongly with us. Also very much with us is his passionate concern for the survival, the growth, the fruition of democracy as a way of organizing personal and collective life. In 1943 he jotted down some notes about his orientation to the scientific study of democracy. Here were some of his thoughts at that time which seem just as relevant to us today:

Democracy—people are fighting for it, people are dying for it. It is the most precious possession we have.

Or is it but a word to fool the people? An invisible bird is sitting high up on the top of the flagpole. Everybody is pointing with his finger in that direction and everybody is talking about it. Well, maybe that is the only reason why you and I have finally gotten to believe in "it." Are we really sure that it is more than ballyhoo, more than a word? Is there really anything there?

Have you noticed the peculiar mixture of desperate hope, curiosity and skepticism with which the newly arrived refugee from Fascist Europe looks at the United States? He has had to live in an atmosphere where democracy was considered identical with decadence, softness, inability to act, chaos, and—above all—as a big bluff. He hates Fascism with all he has. He is more than eager to believe in this "haven for the oppressed," to see with his own eyes a people who have the Statue of Liberty standing at the gateway of the country and "equality of men" as its law. Still, he cannot but hesitate at every step; he can't help but have his heart filled with the anxiety of a person who thinks that he soon will find out whether the world and its history has meaning aside from the eternal fight between hunter and hunted: is democracy more than an empty proclamation, is it more than a phrase for politicians? Is democracy something "real"? Is there anything behind democracy but a word? Is the bird on the flagpole alive? If it is not a perfect bird and not as much alive as it should be, is it at least real?

Historians have written many and excellent volumes about democracy, about ancient Athens, about the modern Jefferson and Lincoln and about every phase of United States democracy. The political scientists have explained the administrative details of democracy. Educators have given vivid accounts about various forms of democracy in schools and homes. But one who has watched the student at Harvard or Columbia, at Iowa or Berkeley, during the years preceding the war could not help feeling strongly that somehow or other all this did not suffice to make democracy something real, clear or tangible for these young people. . . . Maybe it is only because these young people are growing up in a comparatively democratic setting and do not have a chance for comparison, that democracy does not become real to them.

If Science is going to help to establish the reality of democracy for the young American it cannot be a science dealing with words. It will have to be a science dealing with facts; with facts of a very tangible nature; with facts close to the everyday life of the individual person; with facts that matter. . . .

These ideas seemed important to us as students; they seem even more important today. The challenging of Western democracies by totalitarian dictatorships did not end with Hitler's defeat. It has reappeared in the form of international communism, and the challenge is perhaps more formidable, partly because communism is appealing to the uncommitted peoples, with some success, as a new and more genuine form of "democracy." Again, as in World War II, the effort to make our kind of democracy as efficient as possible, and as attractive as possible to the uncommitted countries, seems to have a real bearing on the chances of our own survival. This is the challenge on the large-group level. At the same time, on the small-group level, there are unclarities and hesitancies on the part of our students, our neighbors, our children, and ourselves as to the kind of democracy that is possible and practical.

To achieve clarity requires a more solid, more discriminating understanding of the democratic process—on every level of human interaction, from the family and schoolroom up to the nation and even groups of nations.

Of course, these levels are quite different from each other. The Law and Order Patrol is not America. A nation involves many qualitatively different things—economics, propaganda, foreign policy, a nationalistic tradition—that do not exist, except possibly in an embryonic form, in a small group of eleven-year-old boys meeting after school. But in small groups there is also much that is similar to what goes on in large groups, and by watching human reactions on this level much can be learned that throws light on large-group behavior.

How much experiments, such as those here described, actually can contribute to the kind of understanding we need is another question. Will we be able to see the bird on the flagpole a little more clearly? On that question the reader is asked to remain open-minded until he has read this book. The attempt seems worth making, however, if only because of the success of controlled experimentation in the natural sciences. Since careful, detailed, concrete observations and systematic, controlled variation of conditions have brought forth rich fruit in physics, chemistry, and biology, an application of them to the democratic process, in miniature but realistic laboratory situations, seems worth a try. The scientific job is more complex, but even partial success might be valuable in getting us started in some new directions of research, speculation, and action.

Just a word about the organization of the report. The authors take four different orientations at various points in the book: (1) part of the time they are reporting, quantitatively and qualitatively, what happened in the experiments; (2) at other times they are proposing theoretical interpretations of the meaning of what was happening in the experimental groups; (3) then later there are speculations about the possible implications of these data for understanding and carrying on life in other small groups, such as the family and classroom; (4) and finally there are sections labeled "political commentary" in which speculation is pushed into the realm of large group phenomena at the level of national life and international relations. The attempt has been made to give the reader adequate cues to identify these shifts of orientation as they occur.

Our special gratitude goes to Boyd McCandless and Dan Adler, who participated very competently as leaders in Experiment II. Acknowledgment is also due to George D. Stoddard, then Director of the Iowa Child Welfare Research Station, who at all times gave the experiment his active support; to Tamara Dembo, Sibylle Escalona, Mary Martha Gordon, Jack Kounin and Maurice Farber, who participated as observers; to Elizabeth Herzog White, who made useful editorial suggestions; and to many others who took part, in one way or another, either in the Iowa experiments or in the large number of related experiments that are briefly described in this book.

Autocracy and Democracy

1

The Meaning of Democracy

FOUR POINTS OF AGREEMENT

DESPITE many variations, there are wide areas of agreement about the meaning of democracy. Here are some of the ways in which various people have expressed it:

Government of the people, by the people, and for the people.

Governments . . . deriving their just powers from the consent of the governed.

The greatest good of the greatest number.

The rule of the people.

Submission of the minority to the majority.

Life, liberty and the pursuit of happiness.

Liberty, equality and fraternity.

The equal right of all to determine the structure and administration of the State.

Freedom of speech, freedom of religion, freedom from want and freedom from fear.

The right of the people to a dignified life, without exploiters and without exploitation.

A chance for everyone to develop and contribute according to his ability.

Respect for the dignity of the individual personality.

Shared freedom and responsibility.

The most striking thing about this list is its self-consistency; no one of the definitions is inconsistent with any other. Yet four of the statements are by well-known Americans and four are by well-known citizens of the USSR (Lenin, Stalin, Khrushchev). Of course actual behavior is not necessarily consistent with public statements, but it is noteworthy that there is in some degree a world-wide consensus as to what democracy *ought* to mean.

Four more specific themes appear, in different words, again and again throughout these definitions:

1. The original Greek meaning of the word, *people's rule*—which is still its primary meaning in our dictionaries—has lost none of its vitality: "government of the people and by the people," "the consent of the governed," "the rule of the people" (Lenin), "submission . . . to the majority" (Stalin), "the equal right of all to determine the administration of the State" (Lenin). There may be doubt and disagreement as to how directly the people should rule, and as to how mature a person needs to be before he can "rule." There may be a ruthless autocracy hiding behind a façade of majority rule. Nevertheless it seems clear that even the Communists, when they use the word "democracy," are trying to convey the idea of ultimate accountability of the leaders to the majority of the group.

2. In the Western world the idea of individual *freedom* (or its synonym "liberty") has come to have an importance scarcely less than that of people's rule. It appears in expressions such as "life and liberty," "liberty and equality," "freedom of speech and religion," "a chance for everyone," and "shared freedom." On this point the Communists are much less emphatic, but even they have acknowledged its universal appeal by writing "freedom of speech" into the Soviet Constitution of 1936.

To be sure, hardly anyone wants freedom to be completely unrestricted. In practice what most people stand for is "as much freedom as is practical." The amount that is practical for children in a family or a classroom may be a good deal less than for adults, and interpretations vary greatly as to how much is practical in various situations. Setting limits to freedom does not mean, however, that the desire for freedom is not genuine. The idea of freedom is now inextricably bound up with the idea of democracy and (at least in the non-Communist world) those who sincerely value any concept of democracy are almost sure to value some kind of freedom as one aspect of it.

3. Our quotations point up a counterbalancing emphasis on the *responsibility* of the individual to cooperate with the group and concern himself with its welfare—and this is where our interpretation begins to go beyond the dictionary definition. Democracy is

here sharply distinguished from anarchy, or every-man-for-himself. This third theme includes also the notion that leaders should be "for the people"; they should consider "the greatest good of the greatest number"; there should be a spirit of "fraternity"—that is, friendliness; the society as a whole should enjoy "freedom from want and freedom from fear"—which calls for cooperative action; and everyone should have a chance not only to develop but also to "contribute" according to his ability. In other words, a well-functioning democracy is widely seen as one in which, when cooperation is important, individuals freely choose to work with the group rather than against it.

4. Finally, there is expressed again and again, at least implicitly, a concern with the development, the welfare, the happiness or the dignity of the individual. Along with its emphasis on cooperation, the philosophy of democracy is often seen as a philosophy of individualism. "Life" is, implicitly, individual life, "liberty" is individual liberty, and it is the individual who "pursues happiness." Equality implies the right of every individual to at least a minimum of respect, consideration, and opportunity. In all of these expressions a concern with the individual is implicit, and the theme becomes fully explicit in expressions, widely current now in the West, such as "respect for the dignity of the individual personality." This, too, like freedom, is much less emphasized in Communist statements but even Khrushchev speaks of "the right of people to a dignified life."

These, then, are four aspects of the common ground on which men of good will can stand in their interpretations of democracy: people's rule, freedom, responsibility, and concern with the individual. All of these are relative to time, circumstances, and the characteristics of the people concerned. At the same time, it is a rather encouraging fact that nearly all of those who value the term "democracy" accept these four aspects, at least in theory.

Of course there are some who make no pretense of subscribing to these objectives, and there are many who, while giving lip service to them, violate them in practice. Our period of history is characterized by almost universal obeisance to the verbal forms of democracy, but not by universal observance of its spirit. Even Hitler (after 1933) proclaimed his devotion to government with the consent of the governed. The present-day Communists have gone all out to appropriate for themselves the word "democracy," and explicitly claim that the kind of democracy they stand for includes liberty as well as equality, and government by the people as well as government for the people (White, 1950). Even McCarthy claimed to stand for the purest Americanism. It is often a question whether those whose behavior is anti-democratic are rationalizing and fooling themselves or are consciously and cynically hiding their will-to-power behind a façade of democratic phrases. The striking thing, nevertheless, is that they feel the need to do so. The values of people's rule, freedom ("as far as is practical"), responsibility and concern with the individual are so overwhelmingly agreed upon by men of good will that even men of ill will have to pretend that they agree too.

SOME DISPUTED POINTS

What, then, are the actual points at issue?

One real and ever-present issue is "How much freedom is practical?" Nearly everyone wants freedom up to the point, where, in his eyes, it conflicts "too much" with other values such as law and order, hard work, or group efficiency. But when does it actually conflict, seriously, with these other values? And how much is "too much"? In thousands of concrete situations these are the real issues.

Often, of course, the appeal to law and order or to efficiency, as a reason for restricting freedom, is a cover-up; but often, too, it is valid. Abraham Lincoln, to preserve the Union, approved conscription into the Union Army. At one extreme the need for coercive measures which may be called "autocratic" is clear and urgent; at the other extreme, only authoritarian personalities or persons committed to autocratic ideologies fail to see that democratic methods are preferable. But between the extremes there is a broad zone of genuine uncertainty and legitimate disagreement.

If one listens to parents, teachers, and others talking about their working philosophies, he hears such things as these:

One parent insists that it is of great importance for children to "learn to control themselves," another emphasizes the importance of "freedom to express themselves without feeling inhibited," and a third says the most important thing is "for the parent to give security and protection while the child is immature and growing up."

One teacher believes the important thing is for the children to "learn to cooperate with each other and with the teacher." A second believes children should "get the information and discipline they need in order to adjust to the realities of life." A third wants to encourage each child to be "spontaneous and creative," and to "advance at his own rate of intellectual ability."

One community committee chairman says, "The first thing is to get enough orderliness so that the group can do its job effectively." A second chairman wants "everybody to participate instead of leaving the decisions and the work up to a few of us." A third is concerned about the waste of time and inefficiency of committees as working groups and feels the important thing is to "get everything delegated to the person who can do it best."

One personnel director feels that the decision-making process should be decentralized as much as possible and taken over by the network of work groups and departmental staffs, to insure maximum productivity and morale. A second personnel director declares just as vigorously that decision making on most problems is so complex that the decisions must be made by specialists and the results communicated clearly to everyone who is concerned.

One labor leader emphasizes the priority of getting a majority of the members of his local to participate in union meetings. A second insists that large meetings are a waste of time and boring to the membership; what is needed, he says, is an efficient executive committee that will work hard in the interests of the total membership.

One political leader maintains that it is his responsibility to educate his constituency and to try to stimulate interest on their part in expressing informed opinions to him for his guidance on all important issues. Another stresses his own decision making.

Again, there are a number of recurrent themes:

1. Some stress the importance of having the weaker, more immature members of the group cared for and protected by the wiser older heads; others emphasize decentralization of responsibility and experimentation with freedom by the younger and less experienced members. A protective attitude may conflict with an emphasis on freedom.

2. Some put major emphasis on stimulating participation and contributions by all members of the group, while others feel that efficiency of decision making and action—which is often reduced by having too many cooks working on the broth—is the first priority. Stress on efficiency may conflict with stress on participation.

3. Some feel that the welfare of the total group and the necessary discipline of the individual members to insure this are of primary im-

portance, while others feel that first attention should be given to the growth and development of members as separate, unique individuals. *Disciplined responsibility* to the group may conflict with individual fulfillment.

In part, these disagreements reflect basic differences in values, which are not likely to be changed by any amount of experimental or nonexperimental evidence. For example, those who easily let a protective urge override their belief in freedom probably, in most cases, care less about freedom than those who do not. But also, to a large extent, differences of opinion in this broad zone of legitimate disagreement hinge upon different conceptions of the facts. An appeal to experimentation therefore seems appropriate.

ADVANTAGES OF THE CONTROLLED EXPERIMENT

This book reports an attempt to bring experimental evidence to bear on some current beliefs and genuine conflicts of opinion concerning the nature of democracy, its advantages and disadvantages, and the means of maximizing its advantages.

The experiments deal only with small groups, and the results naturally cannot be applied literally to larger groups such as a nation. Insights at the small-group level are valuable in themselves, however, and also add to our understanding of political events if differences between the levels are taken into account.

On issues such as these there is an enormous amount of unsystematic, nonexperimental evidence. Almost any parent, teacher, business executive, politician, or historian is likely to feel that he has some pretty good answers based on accumulated experience, direct and indirect. Probably he does. In a sense, history and everyday experience are laboratories for the investigation of this type of question, and in breadth and variety of information they greatly surpass the experiments here reported. Even simple observations of classrooms and committees would probably yield more breadth than the experimental approach followed here. Why, then, go to all the trouble of designing and conducting experiments?

The one great advantage of the method of controlled experimentation is the same in the social sciences as in physics, chemistry, and the other natural sciences: it gives comparatively clear evidence as to what is the cause of what. In the welter of ordinary events it is very difficult to pick out any one factor and to be sure that it is *the* cause—or even a cause—of something else. Too many things are varying at the same time. A quarrel breaks out in a group that is trying to work out a problem. Why? A hundred things happened during the previous hour, and thousands of things had happened earlier, that might be related to this behavior. Which of them "caused" it? A boss makes a decision on an important question without consulting his subordinates. Months later he is troubled by their "low motivation" and slipshod work. Was his arbitrary decision one of the causes of their low motivation, or would it have been just as low if he had consulted them? There is no way of being sure, in the absence of a controlled experiment.

The word "control" is used here to mean simply an effort to hold constant all of the important factors except one, so that the effects of that one factor will stand out clearly. Suppose that factors A and B are known to be important in determining an effect E, and we are uncertain whether a third factor, C, also has an influence on E. The notion of experimental control would require that A and B and other related factors should be kept the same, as far as it is humanly possible to do so, while C is deliberately changed. Only then is it possible to have some confidence that, when a change in E is noticed, the change is not due to A or B, but to C. In the case of an experiment on group behavior this might mean, for instance, that the groups themselves and the activities they engaged in should be kept the same while the leadership methods were deliberately changed, in order to be sure that a change in group behavior was due to the change in leadership rather than to the nature of the groups or to what they were doing.

This is the method that has had extraordinary success in the natural sciences and is being increasingly used in the study of human behavior, including social behavior.[1]

There are skeptics, to be sure. Some say that the methods of the natural sciences are not appropriate in the study of anything as fluid and intangible as social behavior; the social studies must develop methods of their own. But although it has been most widely used in the natural sciences, the logic of controlled experimentation does not rest primarily on the success of its application in the nat-

---

[1] For a general orientation to the experimental study of small groups, see for example the anthologies edited by Cartwright and Zander (1953) and by Hare, Borgatta, and Bales (1955), the relevant articles in the *Handbook of Social Psychology*, edited by Lindzey (1954), and the review by Roseborough (1953).

ural sciences; it is a simple and unanswerable type of logic, applicable in principle to every type of subject matter, no matter how fluid and intangible. Naturally it is more difficult to hold key factors constant in the social sciences than in physics or chemistry, and a good deal of humility is needed on the question of how far in any given experiment—for instance, those reported in this book—this constancy has been achieved. But this does not affect the desirability of holding key factors *as constant as possible*, if there is to be even a relative degree of confidence in the results.

Other skeptics feel that a controlled experiment is necessarily "artificial," and distorts the "natural" behavior of everyday life. The experiments reported here may dispel some of this type of skepticism. In these experiments real leaders are leading real groups, and hostilities, frustrations and affections exist with "real-life" intensity.

Defining Leader Roles

If the idea of experimental control were applied crudely and directly it would perhaps mean that just one single aspect of leadership behavior should be varied, while an effort was made to keep all the other aspects of leadership the same for the groups in the experiment. For example, in one group the leader might participate in the activities along with the other group members while in another group he would not participate, or in one group he might tell the members what to do while in another group he would never tell them what to do, although in other respects he would behave in the same way. This way of setting up the experiment might *seem* more scientific, but in the planning of the present experiments the experimenters came to the conclusion that it would not be very good or productive science because it would involve cutting up total behavior patterns which naturally go together. In other words, it seemed necessary to think in terms of leadership *patterns* rather than specific leadership acts. Certain types of leadership behavior seemed to hang together as total roles or patterns which represented particular philosophies of attempting to achieve the goals of individual welfare and group achievement. It seemed that some of the really important and underlying ways in which leaders who intend to be "democratic" actually differ from each other are:

1. The extent to which the leader attempts to determine and control the goals to be achieved and the means to be followed to reach these goals by the members and by the group.

2. The extent to which the leader attempts to get the group to adopt or develop group methods or group procedures by which goals are to be determined, means to be selected, and progress to be evaluated.

3. The extent to which the leader establishes a warm and friendly, or a neutral and objective, or a hostile and aggressive relationship with the group.

It was finally decided that the first experiment would compare a leader who would exercise strong control over goal setting and careful direction of means behavior (and who would therefore keep all procedures of decision making and evaluation in his own hands) with a leader who would exercise as little control as possible over goal selection and means selection but who would make definite attempts to stimulate group procedures of goal setting, means selection, and evaluation of progress. In other words, the first two of the three factors listed above, control-by-leader and stimulation of group procedures, were allowed to vary together in the way that seemed natural: an "autocratic" pattern of high control-by-leader combined with low stimulation-of-group-procedures; and a "democratic" pattern of low control-by-leader and high stimulation-of-group-procedures.[2] However, in this particular experiment it was decided that the groups would be equated on the third factor, the emotional relationship between the group and the leader, by having the leader be equally friendly but not highly affectionate in both groups.

After this first experiment with two groups it seemed, on the basis of the different effects on the groups and individuals, that the leadership patterns represented in it were important ones, relevant to a great many situations in our society. So it was decided to continue the experiment with more groups, introducing better controls on some of the factors of group composition and group activity. Then a fortunate accident occurred that ruined some of the precision of the research design but greatly increased the insights which could be derived from the total experiment. One of the four leaders who was trying to use the technique of exercising very little

[2] Our idea of leadership that was active without domination was derived especially from Pigors (1935).

control over group goal setting and means selection, but who was supposed at the same time to stimulate the development of group procedures of goal selection and means selection, failed to carry through the second part of this role assignment. He steered away from control over goals and means, but—partly from inexperience and partly from lack of clearness about his own objectives—he was not successful in stimulating the group to develop and use group procedures for goal setting and means selection. He was a "hands off" leader in both respects. Some rather striking variations in effect showed up—quite different from the effects of either of the other two patterns in the previous experiment. As a result of this fortunate accident, the second and main experiment was continued with three leadership roles which may be summarized in this way:

Leadership Role I	Leadership Role II	Leadership Role III
1. High goal and means control	Low goal and means control	Low goal and means control
2. Low stimulation of group procedures	High stimulation of group procedures	Low stimulation of group procedures
3. Medium friendly	Medium friendly	Medium friendly

Chapter 3 will discuss more fully the patterns of leadership behavior which the experimenters were trained to keep in mind in order to carry out in actual behavior these differing objectives and philosophies.

NAMING THE ROLES: AUTOCRATIC, DEMOCRATIC, AND LAISSEZ-FAIRE

Early in our discussions of these leadership roles, we, the experimenters, found ourselves naming these roles rather than calling them "role one," "role two," and "role three." The names that seemed natural and appropriate to us were "autocratic," "democratic," and "laissez-faire."

When we began to talk to other people about the experiments and the findings, these names caused us some worry because they had so many different meanings attached to them, and so many values. And after all, one of the main points was that we were studying three different common leadership roles, all of which are frequent patterns *within* our *democratic* society. All three were roles found in the behavior patterns of many leaders of strong motivation, good will, and desire to contribute to the goals of "democracy" as defined at the beginning of this chapter: people's rule, freedom ("as far as is practical"), responsibility, and concern with the individual; and all three were roles played by persons who are, in this sense, "good democrats."

Then, as we thought about this problem still further, it seemed to be worthwhile to continue using these names in spite of the disadvantages. It seemed better to try to reduce the vagueness of these terms by attaching very specific leadership and group-behavior patterns to them. As we reviewed the basic components of our three leadership roles and the effects they appeared to create, it seemed to us that in the long run it would help communication to use the terms "autocracy," "democracy" and "laissez-faire" and to define them as concretely as possible rather than to stick to such "scientifically correct" but colorless terms as "role one," "role two," and "role three."

This does not mean that we think our definition of democracy is "the" definition, or even necessarily the best definition. Others may prefer other definitions. But by pinning ourselves down to this definition we are at least making clear one concrete meaning of democracy—much more concrete than the four ultimate objectives on which, on the verbal level, nearly everyone in our society is agreed—and this concrete meaning is the one that is important for understanding the results of our experiments.

In other words, for purposes of actual experimentation, we are adopting a definition that is narrower as well as more concrete than the four objectives of democracy discussed at the beginning of this chapter, while taking for granted these four ideas as criteria for assessing outcomes. The question of how much control the leader exerts is not, in the experiments, left to his own judgment as to how much is practical. In order to carry out the experiment properly he *has* to exert a relatively low degree of control when he is playing the role of democratic leader. The freedom element in the fourfold definition of objectives *has* to be emphasized. At the same time we are taking pains to emphasize the distinction implied by the word "responsibility" in the fourfold definition of democratic goals: the distinction between the hands-off policy of not stimulating or teaching group procedures (a policy implied by our term "laissez-faire") and the active policy of stimulating or teaching group procedures, which is definitely implied by the word "democratic" as we use it here.

To Summarize

At least on the verbal level, there is throughout the world an encouraging amount of agreement that democracy ought to mean at least four things: people's rule, freedom, responsibility to cooperate, and concern for the individual.

On the other hand there is disagreement, even within our "democratic" society, on other questions such as: How much freedom is practical? To what extent, in various situations, does a high degree of freedom conflict with other values such as protection of the immature from the consequences of their own immaturity, group efficiency, and disciplined responsibility? To a large extent these real disagreements hinge on questions of fact that can be investigated by the experimental method.

The method of controlled experimentation, adopted here, has one great advantage: by varying one factor while holding other factors as constant as possible, it gives relatively clear evidence as to what is the cause of what.

The book presents and discusses two experiments in which adult leaders of clubs of children behaved in three different ways, called autocratic, democratic, and laissez-faire. "Autocracy" here implies a high degree of control by the leader without much freedom by the members or participation by them in group decisions, while both "democracy" and "laissez-faire" imply a low degree of control by the leader. "Democracy" is distinguished from "laissez-faire," however, by the fact that in it the leader is very active in stimulating group discussion and group decisions, while in laissez-faire he plays a passive, hands-off role.

2

How the Experiments Were Conducted

THE TWO EXPERIMENTS

THIS chapter describes the design and methods of the two inquiries from which we are drawing our data and interpretations. (If the reader wants to get quickly to what went on he may wish to skim Chapter 4 and then return to this one.)

The first experiment was comparatively simple.[1] Two small groups of eleven-year-old children met after school to make masks and carry on other activities. The groups were similar in many ways —age, sex, etc.,—but not identical. They were led by the same person (Lippitt), but with one group he played a "democratic" role and with the other he played an "autocratic" role. There were five children in each group; each met eleven times. Five observers took continuous notes on the behavior of the leader and the children in each group. The results consisted of the contrasting behavior of the two groups as recorded by these observers.

While the groups behaved similarly at the outset, they rapidly became different, so that in the later meetings the contrast was striking. The differences are described in detail in Chapter 5. In brief, there was far more quarreling and hostility in the autocratically led group, and far more friendliness and group spirit in the democratically led group. The children in the autocratic group

---

[1] The first experiment was planned and conducted by Ronald Lippitt, under the general direction of Kurt Lewin. It is described in detail in "An experimental study of the effect of democratic and authoritarian group atmospheres." *University of Iowa Studies in Child Welfare*, Vol. 16, No. 3 (Iowa City: University of Iowa Press, 1940), pp. 45–195.

picked on scapegoats and showed other behavior that seemed too similar to certain contemporary dictatorships to be mere coincidence. It looked as if some psychological processes of broad significance, in politics as well as in the behavior of small groups, had been isolated in test-tube form.

It seemed, too, that a way had been found to experiment with "real life" situations, with little distorting artificiality, and yet with a fairly high degree of the experimental control—the holding constant of all factors but one—discussed in Chapter 1. In both groups the children seemed to act naturally and spontaneously, with no sign of being inhibited or made self-conscious by the observers. As for experimental control, the leader's role was the only factor that seemed to have varied enough to account for the marked difference in the behavior of the groups. The groups were similar at the outset; they were recruited in the same way; they came to the meetings with similar expectations; they engaged in the same activities (at each meeting the autocratic group was ordered to do the things that the democratic group had voluntarily decided to do at an earlier meeting); and they had the same leader. The two leadership roles, however, were different. They were planned to be equally different, in opposite directions, from another major group situation they were experiencing—the classroom. All factors other than the major experimental variable, the type of leadership, seemed to have been well equalized or held constant, so that it seemed clear that the striking differences in outcome were based on the contrasting style of leadership and nothing but the differences in style of leadership.

This conclusion could not be arrived at with complete confidence, however. For one thing, the groups, though similar, were composed of different individuals, and it seemed quite conceivable that the individuals in the democratically led group might have been "naturally" more harmonious, less quarrelsome, and more interested than the children in the autocratically led group. For another thing, the outcome had occurred only once, in one comparison between two small groups. It was decided, therefore, to try the same experiment again the following year on a larger scale, with a systematic experimental design that would rule out more completely any uncertainty as to what was causing the experimental results.

In essentials the second experiment was the same.[2] Again it involved groups of eleven-year-old children, with five children in each group, meeting after school under an adult leader and carrying on interesting activities. (This time they were only boys, instead of both boys and girls, and their clubs were "G-man clubs.") Again the one factor deliberately varied was the type of leadership, while other factors were held as constant as possible. Again a bank of observers took continuous notes on the behavior of the children (again with no noticeable inhibiting effect on the children); and again the types of leadership were evaluated primarily on the basis of a systematic analysis of these observers' notes.

The second experiment, however, was better controlled and also much more extensive. The amount of evidence obtained was about six times as great as in the first experiment. Four groups instead of two were involved, and each group, instead of having a single series of meetings under a single leader, had three series of meetings under three different leaders. This design made it possible to hold more completely constant the basic factor of child personality—the one factor that had not been very well controlled in the first experiment. It was now possible to be sure that as far as personality is concerned the autocratically led and democratically led groups were strictly comparable because they were in fact identical. Each child experienced both an autocratic and a democratic form of leadership; consequently, if the children's behavior differed markedly in these two situations—as it did—the difference could not possibly be due to personality differences in the children involved.

Actually one group experienced democracy twice (under two different leaders playing the democratic role) and autocracy only once; another group experienced autocracy twice (under two different leaders playing the autocratic role) and democracy only once; the other two groups experienced autocracy, democracy and laissez-faire (see Chapter 1, pp. 9–10). However, there was a rule in every group that each boy should be in an autocratic atmosphere at least once, each should be in a democratic atmosphere at least once, and the crucial comparisons should be made between autocracy and democracy with the factor of individual personality thus equalized or held constant. (There was also a rough equalizing of the sequence

2 The second experiment was planned and conducted jointly by Ronald Lippitt and Ralph White, under the general direction of Kurt Lewin.

factor by reversing the sequence; in some cases autocracy followed democracy and in some democracy followed autocracy, so that the results cannot be attributed to any special characteristics of the first weeks, the middle weeks, or the last weeks of the experimental period.)

With this expanded experimental design it became possible also to observe several types of facts that could not be observed with the simpler design. It was possible to study the special characteristics of transition periods (i.e., the first meeting under a new leader playing a leadership role that contrasted with the role played by a former leader). It was possible to interview the boys themselves and get their direct comparison between various leaders (e.g., which they liked better, and why); and in view of the much larger amount of information about each individual boy it became worthwhile to dig into problems of personality structure, relationships between group atmosphere and personality structure, and relationships between personality structure and home background.

"NORMAL, AVERAGE CHILDREN"

Since psychologists have often made generalizations on the basis of groups that deviate from the general average in one way or another—neurotics, delinquents, or college students—it is of some interest that the children in the second and larger of the two experiments were rather typical American children.

Being taken from the fifth grades of two ordinary public schools, they were neither above nor below the normal range of socio-economic status.[3] Living in a small city in the Middle West, with a population of about 25,000, they were neither rural nor metropolitan, and did not present any such atypical regional characteristics as might be found, for instance, in the Deep South. In the population attending public elementary schools and junior high schools they were middle in age also (eleven) with neither the special problems of the very young child nor those of the adolescent.

Finally, they were drawn from the middle and upper ranges of social adjustment. If "normal" means well adjusted to one's peers,

[3] If anything, they represented a too restricted range of socioeconomic status, with both extremes missing. In this community the extremes of wealth and poverty are largely nonexistent, and most of the parents with higher education or professional status sent their children to the university school rather than to the public schools. Probably all the boys in this experiment could be described as middle-class or as upper-lower-class.

these boys were, on the average, abnormally normal. One of the methods used in equalizing the groups at the outset, and in choosing groups of equal degrees of internal harmony and cohesiveness, was a "sociometric" questionnaire (Moreno, 1934), with questions that included, "If you happen to be in one of the G-man clubs (that is being planned), what other boys would you like to have in the same club with you? Put down the names of four boys you would like to have in the same club." "Put down the names of four boys you would rather not have in the same club with you." All the boys in each of the two schoolrooms were then ranked by the experimenters according to the extent to which they were chosen by other boys—a reliable measure of popularity, and a realistic one, since the boys had an incentive to take their choices seriously; they were told—truthfully—that their choice would be considered in determining the make-up of the clubs. Then, in selecting ten boys from approximately twenty in each schoolroom (all the boys in each schoolroom wanted to be in the clubs), the ten were chosen from the middle and upper parts of the choice range. None were selected from among the least-chosen boys, since it was believed that these least-liked boys might in many cases be misfits, exceptional in various ways, and also likely to create practical problems in the conduct of the experiments. Consequently, insofar as popularity is related to social adjustment, and insofar as social adjustment is a major aspect of general adjustment, the resulting selection of boys was presumably in the range between low-average and very good in general adjustment.

In sum, then, the clubs were composed of middle western, middle-city-size, middle-school-age American boys, largely middle-class and with middle or better-than-middle social adjustment.[1]

Equalizing the Groups

In Experiment I, in which the children under autocratic leadership were different from the children under democratic leadership, it was important that the two groups should be as similar as possible. Being chosen from the two schoolrooms in the university school (representing families that were, on the average, somewhat above the community average in socio-economic status) they were similar in age, cultural background, and socio-economic status. Per-

[1] A basic question is: To what extent do the results of the experiments hold in other kinds of groups? The evidence is encouraging; see especially the report of Misumi (below, pp. 267–268) on parallel experiments in Japan.

haps more important than any of these for the purposes of the experiment, however, was the factor of internal harmony or cohesiveness. Since interpersonal relationships were to be the main object of the study, it was essential that these should be equalized at the outset with the utmost possible care. If, for instance, one group should turn out to be much more quarrelsome than the other, with much more intragroup aggression—which actually happened in the autocratically led group—this could not be attributed to the autocratic leadership, with any confidence, unless it were known that the autocratic group was as harmonious at the outset as the democratic group, with as much mutual friendship and as little mutual hostility.

In Experiment II, careful matching of the groups was not necessary because of the plan to study the same children in different group atmospheres; nevertheless, in order to increase the comparability between groups, a similar method was used to insure that all of the groups had approximately equal degrees of cohesiveness, and of general social adjustment. In both experiments the method of doing this was, as indicated above, a sociometric questionnaire. The degree of success in equalizing groups is indicated in the following table:

TABLE I

SOCIAL RELATIONS WITHIN THE CLUBS BEFORE
EXPERIMENT STARTED

EXPERIMENT I	Autocratic Group		Democratic Group	
Attractions	4		4	
Rejections	3		3	
Indifferences	13		13	
Mutual attractions	1		1	
EXPERIMENT II	School I		School II	
	Charlie Chan Club	Dick Tracy Club	Sherlock Holmes Club	Secret Agents Club
Attractions	6	7	7	7
Rejections	1	1	0	0
Indifferences	13	12	13	13
Mutual attractions	2	1	2	2

The groups within the same experiment were similar at the outset in amount of mutual friendliness and dislike, and in both experiments there was an intermediate degree of cohesiveness at the outset, with room to change in both directions. In Experiment II, friendliness consistently predominated (i.e., attractions outweighed rejections), partly because the boys were chosen from the middle and upper parts of the popularity range, and partly because a deliberate effort was made to set up groups that would have a degree of cohesion similar to that of actual clubs or friendship groups in which the members exercise a certain amount of mutual choice. In each case one of the two most popular boys in the schoolroom was chosen as a starting point in setting up a group (Reilly was the starting point of the Charlie Chan Club, for instance, and Eddie the starting point of the Sherlock Holmes Club), and others were chosen from among those who had expressed a desire to be in the same club with him. In this way it was hoped that the groups would not only be similar in degree of internal harmony but would also be similar in type of leadership structure. Similarly in Experiment I an effort was made to equalize the two groups in leadership structure by having just one natural leader in each group; on the basis of observation on the playground and discussion with the teachers it was judged that the one real leader in the autocratic group was Tom and the one real leader in the democratic group was Dick.

In addition an effort was made, especially in Experiment II, to equalize the groups as far as was feasible in other respects: scholarship, height, weight, and teachers' ratings on a number of behavior characteristics (leading, quarreling, obedience, social activity, and so forth). However, these criteria were given less weight than the sociometric measures, and experience showed that in one highly important personality characteristic—conscientiousness or "adult-value-centeredness"—some of the groups were *not* similar. It turned out that the three outstanding troublemakers in Experiment II (Reilly, Fred, and Leonard) were all in the Charlie Chan Club. There were environmental reasons for this also (see below, pp. 110) but a re-examination of the teachers' ratings, which had been made before the experiment started, showed that the groups had not been well equalized in this respect at the outset; the average rating of the Charlie Chan Club boys in "quarreling," for instance, was 3 (on a 5-point scale in which 1 represented the least amount of quar-·

reling and 5 the greatest), while the average rating of the relatively conscientious boys in the Sherlock Holmes Club was only 1.4. The Charlie Chan Club and the Sherlock Holmes Club were similar in degree of mutual liking between the members, but the mutual liking of some of the boys in the Charlie Chan Club was that of "partners in sin," while the harmony within the Sherlock Holmes Club was almost entirely the liking of one good boy for another.

THE EXPERIMENTAL DESIGN

As indicated above, the design of Experiment I was simple: one autocratically led group and another democratically led group, the leader being the same. Experiment II, however, was necessarily much more elaborate in design, with a more systematic effort to hold constant every other important factor while varying the leaders' roles.

At the beginning, it will be remembered, before the emergence of the anarchic or laissez-faire type of group atmosphere (above, pp. 9–10), the plan was simply to compare autocratic and democratic situations. Ideally, with the four groups and four adult leaders, the best way to do this would have been to let each group have a series of meetings under each of the four leaders, two of which would be playing an autocratic role and two a democratic role. In practice this was not feasible, since a club period could not well be made shorter than six weeks (six meetings) if an adequate development of club life was to be observed, and there was neither enough time for experimentation nor enough observer help to permit four such extended club periods. It was therefore decided that each club should have just three series of meetings, each series under a different leader, as follows:

ORIGINAL EXPERIMENTAL DESIGN (later modified)

Six-Week Periods	Period 1	Period 2	Period 3
Dick Tracy Club	Autocracy Mr. Bohlen	Democracy Mr. Rowe	Autocracy Mr. Davis
Sherlock Holmes Club	Autocracy Mr. Rowe	Autocracy Mr. Davis	Democracy Mr. Rankin

| Secret Agents Club | Democracy Mr. Davis | Autocracy Mr. Rankin | Democracy Mr. Bohlen |
| Charlie Chan Club | Democracy Mr. Rankin | Autocracy Mr. Bohlen | Democracy Mr. Rowe |

This design has a number of advantages. Each group experiences autocracy at least once and democracy at least once; the main purpose of the design is therefore achieved, since four different comparisons can be made, in each of which *the same group* is observed under the two types of leadership. Each leader plays an autocratic role at least once and a democratic role at least once; four different comparisons can therefore be made in which *the same leader's* success in one role is compared with his success in the other role. The importance of the leader's personality and skill as an individual can be studied by looking at the four occasions in which *the same leader role with the same group* is played by two different individuals (e.g., with the Dick Tracy Club, an autocratic role played first by Mr. Bohlen and then, in the third six-week period, by Mr. Davis). Four transitions from autocracy to democracy and three from democracy to autocracy can be studied. The advantages (or disadvantages) of coming first are distributed equally as between the two leader roles.

The emergence of "laissez-faire" as a separate type of group atmosphere, different from both autocracy and democracy (above, pp. 9–10), added considerably to the suggestiveness of the experimental findings, but unfortunately it also added to the complexity of the experimental design and the difficulty of statistical treatment. What happened was that the Charlie Chan Club, being led by Mr. Rankin in a supposedly "democratic" manner in its first six-week club period, began to behave in such an individualistic, anarchic way, and it became so clear that Mr. Rankin was not succeeding in "stimulating group procedures"—whatever the reasons for this may have been—that the term "democratic leader role" became rather clearly a misnomer and either "anarchy" or "laissez-faire" began to seem more appropriate. The possible value of exploring this phenomenon systematically seemed so great that a virtue was made of necessity; from the third meeting on, it was agreed that Mr. Rankin should not attempt to stimulate group procedures but should relax willingly into the passive role to which the behavior of the group was relegating him. He should deliberately adopt a hands-off policy, giving the group technical information when they sought it, but otherwise, in the main, playing the part of a benevolent onlooker rather than that of an active leader or participant. At the same time, the idea that "freedom is not enough"—that fully democratic leadership is a very active thing on the leader's part—was clarified and re-emphasized in the minds of those playing a "democratic" role in the remainder of the experiment. In this way "democratic" and "laissez-faire" leadership were sharply distinguished from each other, and it became possible to investigate, at least in a preliminary way, their contrasting effects in terms of group behavior.

In order to obtain results that could not be attributed to any unique characteristics of the Charlie Chan Club, it was decided that laissez-faire leadership should be tried once again with another leader and another group; accordingly, the second six-week period of the Sherlock Holmes Club (soon to be rechristened the Law and Order Patrol) was led by Mr. Davis in a laissez-faire way instead of, as originally planned, in an autocratic way. However, since the main focus of the experiment continued to be on a thorough comparison of autocratic and democratic forms of leadership, this was the only modification made in the original design. The result was five six-week periods of autocracy, five of democracy, and two of laissez-faire, distributed as follows:

FINAL EXPERIMENTAL DESIGN

SIX-WEEK PERIODS	Period 1	Period 2	Period 3
Dick Tracy Club	Autocracy Mr. Bohlen	Democracy Mr. Rowe	Autocracy Mr. Davis
Sherlock Holmes Club	Autocracy Mr. Rowe	Laissez-faire Mr. Davis	Democracy Mr. Rankin
Secret Agents Club	Democracy Mr. Davis	Autocracy Mr. Rankin	Democracy Mr. Bohlen
Charlie Chan Club	Laissez-faire Mr. Rankin	Autocracy Mr. Bohlen	Democracy Mr. Rowe

This design includes a fairly adequate test of laissez-faire, and in addition has most of the advantages of the original design. It still gives each group at least one experience in democracy and at least one in autocracy; it still allows each leader to play an autocratic role at least once and a democratic role at least once; it still gives one group a double experience of autocracy under two autocratic leaders and another group a double experience of democracy under two democratic leaders; there are still four transitions from autocracy to a freer atmosphere and three from a freer atmosphere to autocracy; the advantages (or disadvantages) of coming first are slightly, but only slightly, on the side of autocracy. The neat symmetry of the original pattern is impaired, but it is more meaningful than before, and is scarcely less rigorous.

Factors Held Constant

To summarize: While leader role varies from autocracy to democracy to laissez-faire, the following factors are, in the total procedure of Experiment II, largely held constant:

1. *The nature of the groups*, including the personalities of the boys and their more long-term relationships to each other. Held constant by:

a) Comparing a group with *itself* under a different leader.

b) Matching groups in various ways: age, grade, sex, group structure (e.g., a single "leader"), degree of mutual acquaintance, and, most important, degree of harmony (friendship vs. hostility).

2. *Expectations* of the children about the clubs; held constant by giving just the same introductory talk to all of them.

3. *Activities* held constant by making the boys in the autocratic groups do what the boys in the corresponding democratic groups had freely decided to do.

4. *Leaders* held fairly constant by having each leader play each of the two major leader roles. It is therefore certain that consistent differences between the boys' behavior in democracy and in autocracy cannot be due to greater experience, or tact, or self-confidence, or any other traits characterizing particular leaders as individuals.

Special Test Situations

In Experiment I it was noticed that insight into certain underlying dynamics of the social situation could be gained by having the leader arrive late or leave for a time during the meeting. These incidental observations were made the basis for a series of planned "leader-out situations" in Experiment II. The leader would be "detained" or be called out unexpectedly, giving the "non-present" (psychologically speaking) observers an opportunity to record the effects.

Another type of group test situation was also developed, a "stranger" episode which always took place while the leader was out. A strange graduate student, clad and functioning as a janitor or electrician, would come in to replace an electric light bulb or to sweep up. During his task he would draw the club into conversation, first in a friendly or matter-of-fact way, asking them about their leader and what the club was about. Later he would criticize the work of some of the children or of the group as a whole. In addition to stimulating remarks about the leader, the main value of this procedure was to permit comparison of the reactions to criticism on the part of the groups in the different atmospheres. Would they turn a united front of resistance to the stranger, or make a scapegoat of one of the members he criticized, or "take it" docilely?

Another special test situation, in a sense, was the presence of another club, from another school, in an adjoining part of the room at all times during Experiment II. The purpose was to study the effects of ingroup dynamics upon outgroup relationships, and especially to test the hypothesis that an aggressive spirit generated by autocratic leadership would show itself in aggression against the outgroup as well as in hostility to scapegoats within the autocratic group itself.

THE PHYSICAL SETTING AND THE PROBLEM OF OBSERVER VISIBILITY

Experiment I required little in the way of a physical setting. Meetings of both the autocratic and the democratic groups were held, at different times, in the same project room of the university school. Since the room contained ample space, about half of it was used for the club activities. A table was arranged in the other half of the room, behind which the observers sat.

Experiment II had a more elaborate setting, chiefly in that arrangements were made so that two clubs always met at the same time in the same large attic room. Within the large, dark, raftered attic room the two clubrooms were, on three sides, largely walled off by burlap and wire. A partial boundary between the two "clubrooms" was constructed with beaverboard, while the remainder was marked off as a neutral zone belonging to both groups, within which the common tool box was located.

On the side toward the observers the wall was only table-high, and behind it, under a low sloping section of the roof, the observers sat in semi-shade, considerably removed from the children. The lights were so shaded that the main focus was on the clubroom section and away from the observer space. No attempt was made to render the observers invisible to the children. As in Experiment I, no difficulty was encountered in banishing the observers from the "psychological present" after an introductory period during which their presence was explained to the children. (Before coming to the clubroom, the leader casually remarked, "There are going to be some people there who are interested in how a good club goes. They won't bother us and we won't bother them.")

There seemed to be ample evidence that the boys took these observers casually and completely or almost completely forgot about them. They almost never talked to the observers or spoke about them, rarely looked in their direction, and showed no inhibitions of a sort that could be interpreted as due to self-consciousness caused by their presence. Most convincing of all was their behavior when the leader left the room; even then they rarely looked at the observers, and sometimes even made remarks like, "Go ahead and do it; there isn't anybody here." The records of group behavior (e.g., pp. 89–128) will convey a feeling of how fully the boys became preoccupied with their own activities and personal inter-relationships, and correspondingly oblivious of the observers.

CLUB ACTIVITIES

As indicated above, the general rule was that the autocratic group was made to do the things that the corresponding democratic group freely decided to do. To some extent, however, the availability of certain materials at certain times and suggestions made to the group by democratic leaders represented a kind of activity planning by the experimenters even in the democratic groups. An attempt was made to engage in about the same type of activity, from the stand-point of interest value and cooperation demands, in each six-week club period. The activities included:

First six-week period: carpentry (club benches and table), mural painting, decorating wall, beginning plaster-of-Paris mask.

Second period: continuing mask, painting club signs, plaster footprints, club code, crime game.

Third period: wood carving, soap carving, model airplane construction.

DEFINITION OF LEADER ROLES

The actual differences between the three major types of leadership, autocracy, democracy and laissez-faire, were not necessarily identical with the verbal definition of these roles that the leaders had in their minds at the outset. These actual differences are described in some detail in Chapter 3. The initial definition of roles, however, was as follows (including the laissez-faire definition which emerged in the course of Experiment II) and it corresponds fairly well with what actually occurred:

AUTOCRATIC (OR AUTHORITARIAN)	DEMOCRATIC	LAISSEZ-FAIRE
1. All determination of policy by the leader.	1. All policies a matter of group discussion and decision, encouraged and assisted by the leader.	1. Complete freedom for group or individual decision, with a minimum of leader participation.
2. Techniques and activity steps dictated by the authority, one at a time, so that future steps are always uncertain to a large degree.	2. Activity perspective gained during discussion period. General steps to group goal sketched, and where technical advice is needed the leader suggests two or more alternative procedures from which choice can be made.	2. Various materials supplied by the leader, who makes it clear that he will supply information when asked. He takes no other part in work discussion.

3. The leader usually dictates the particular work task and work companion of each member.

3. The members are free to work with whomever they choose, and the division of tasks is left up to the group.

3. Complete non-participation of the leader in determining tasks and companions.

4. The leader tends to be "personal" in his praise and criticism of the work of each member, but remains aloof from active group participation except when demonstrating.

4. The leader is "objective" or "fact-minded" in his praise and criticism, and tries to be a regular group member in spirit without doing too much of the work.

4. Infrequent spontaneous comments on member activities unless questioned, and no attempt to appraise or regulate the course of events.

In practice the distinctions between these three leader-roles were not extreme. All three remained within the normal range of leader-behavior in different situations in our own society.

OBSERVATION TECHNIQUES

In both experiments four types of records were continuously kept on each group:

1. *Stenographic record.* The most important type of record from the standpoint of reconstructing a full report of what occurred (see excerpts below, Chapters 4, 6 and 7, which were in large part taken from the stenographic record), and also from the standpoint of obtaining important quantitative data, was the continuous record taken in shorthand by two stenographers. As far as was practicable, one took down what was said by three of the boys in a five-boy club, and the other covered the other two boys and the adult leader. (For a discussion of technical problems and the reliability of this type of record, see Lippitt, 1940a).

2. *Running account.* This observer, chosen for experience with and insight into the behavior of children, was given a minimum of direction by the investigators. The idea was to get an interpretive continuous picture of the club life by a person who was free to be receptive to any and all aspects of the group life, who would feel no pressure to record events in terms of certain set criteria, but who

would, rather, be able to describe what seemed to be the most significant occurrences in each momentary cross section of club activity. This account proved highly useful as a way of giving continuity and context to the bare, literal facts provided by the stenographic record and the various types of statistical recording; it provided a background upon which the strands of the other observations could be integrated, and supplied many suggestive leads for interpreting the "why" of what happened.

3. *Social interaction account.* Somewhat less valuable than either the stenographic record or the qualitative running account was the quantitative record of the social interactions of the five children and the leader, in terms of symbols for directive (ascendant), compliant (submissive) and fact-minded (objective) actions, and also a category of purposeful refusal to respond to a social approach. As overlapping categories, additional symbols for friendly and hostile meaning were added to any of the above categories.

4. *Group structure analysis.* One observer kept a minute-by-minute record of the activity subgroups within the club, the activity goal of each subgroup, whether each subgroup was initiated by the leader or spontaneously formed by the children, and ratings of the degree of functional unity of each subgrouping. Like the social interaction account this one was somewhat disappointing; its abstract form seemed to squeeze much of the juice and meaning out of what occurred.

5. *Intergroup running account.* In Experiment I the above four types of record (involving five persons) were enough. In Experiment II the same four types were used again, with five observers focusing on each group; and in addition, because of the new feature of having two clubs meeting next to each other in one large room, one observer was added to keep an interpretive running account of the interactions between the two clubs. This person also served to check to a considerable extent on many of the interpretive comments made by the other two running-accountists.

One technical problem of some importance was the problem of synchronizing the various types of record so that they could later be compared, minute-by-minute, and inter-relationships between them studied. An electric clock was connected to sound a buzzer every minute. The observers were all supplied with polygraph paper ruled off in units to serve as minute segments. Each time the buzzer sounded the observers moved up one space. The spaces were also numbered so that the observers could check with each other frequently to be sure they had heard all the signals.

ADDITIONAL DATA

Leader write-ups. After each meeting the leader wrote up a brief account of incidents that seemed significant to him, from his own point of view.

Interviews with children. At the end of each six-week club period in Experiment II (i.e., three times), each boy was interviewed at school by a person who had not served as his club leader. The interviews were kept on a friendly conversational basis, but a rather carefully planned series of questions was covered in each interview. Typical items of discussion included: comparison of club leaders (after the second and third club periods), what things the boys liked and didn't like about each of them, comments on, and rankings of other club members, comparison of parents, teacher and club leader, reaction to parental and teacher discipline. These interviews proved unexpectedly fruitful in getting at individual differences in the perception of the same club leader, and in giving leads to background factors which could be related to these individual differences.

Interviews with parents. At the close of Experiment II the experimenters spent an hour or more at nearly all of the homes, conversing with one or both of the parents about the club experience of their son, explaining some of the purposes of the clubs, and covering a planned group of questions on such points as: relations with brothers and sisters, other group participation, typical after-school and evening activities, amount of time spent with parents and types of activities shared, home responsibilities and how the boy reacted to them, allowance policy, discipline policy for specific forms of misbehavior, reaction to discipline, differences between the two parents on matters of discipline, the boy's independence in planning, and how much he confided in his parents. (For illustrations of the kind of material obtained, see below, Chapters 12, 13.)

Rating of child by parents. During the interview one or both of the parents filled out a five-point rating scale on their boy covering the following items of behavior: obedience, activity or social participation, mingling with own age group, leading, teasing, criticizing, showing off, quarreling, attempts to dominate, ability to compete with others on a physical basis, and degree of physical energy. These questions served as the basis for part of the discussion with the parents, which made for a thoughtful checking of items on the part of the parents.

Rating of child by teacher. The role of teachers' ratings in equating the groups has already been mentioned. The teacher in each of the two classrooms from which the boys were selected for Experiment II checked the same items on the same rating scale as that filled out by the parents.

All of the above material was brought together in making a series of case studies of individual children, of which four are presented in this book (Chapters 12 and 13). In this analysis the most important material was provided by a sentence-by-sentence content analysis of the boy's conversation as stenographically recorded, each sentence being interpreted in the light of its social context at the moment as provided especially by the running account. The analysis was in terms of categories such as "aggression in democracy," "aggression in autocracy," "friendly," "work-minded," "work-directing," "attention-demanding," "playful." (This was also the most important basis for the statistical comparisons between group atmospheres which are presented in Chapter 5.) The picture of each boy's "club personality" was drawn in terms of all the qualitative material, supplemented and checked by the ranking of the boys on the basis of these quantitative records, and also to some extent by rankings based on the social interaction account and the group structure analysis. All of these together give a relatively varied and many-sided, qualitatively rich and quantitatively precise picture of the club personality. The other types of data, derived from interviews with the boys and interviews with the parents, are relatively meager in comparison with many other individual case studies that have been published, but these kinds of evidence provide many clues as to why the boys behaved as they did, and the combination of exceptionally full concrete data on social behavior with some background information gives a good basis for the study of personality dynamics in a social situation.

3

Leaders' Behavior

To SOME extent, the observation of what the leaders actually did was a process of discovery, both for the observers and for the leaders themselves. As we will see, some of the statistically significant differences in leaders' behavior could not have been directly deduced from our central definitions, although they tend to be consistent with these role definitions. The adult who was faced with the constantly changing problems of leading a group of actual children found himself doing things, in the new situations which presented themselves, which he himself could never have anticipated he would do. And the unanticipated things which the leader with the predetermined autocratic philosophy in the back of his mind found himself doing were different from the things which he found himself doing in the same situations when he changed to the democratic role and had the predefined democratic philosophy in the back of his mind.

ORDERS, DISRUPTING AND NON-DISRUPTING

Statistically, the chief single characteristic of our autocratic leader role, as distinguished from both democracy and laissez-faire, is also the simplest and most easily defined—the giving of orders. Forty-five per cent[1] of the verbal behavior of the autocrats, in contrast to 3 per cent in the case of democracy and 4 per cent in the case of laissez-faire, consisted of this simplest form of the imposition of

---

[1] A summary graph of leader behavior is on page 32. Percentage figures are used because they are not distorted by differences in total volume of behavior of each leader. It is easier therefore to look at the "behavior pattern" as the boys saw it. Total volume of behavior is also important and is discussed separately. All differences which are discussed are statistically significant at the 5 per cent level of confidence or better.

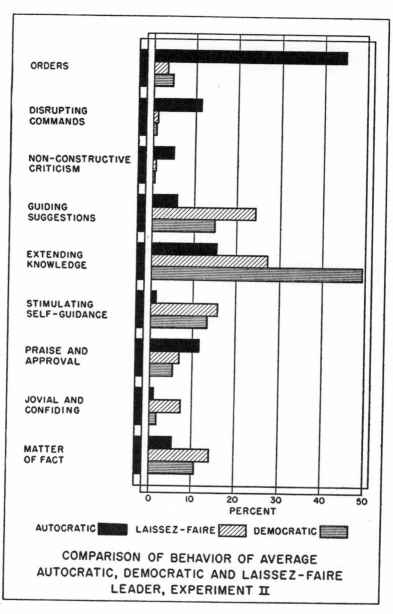

FIGURE 1.   Leaders' behavior.

one human will upon another. Many of these were direct orders or statements in the imperative form:

"Get your work aprons on."
"Vinnie, help Ben."
"All right, put your brush away."
"Each of you turn yours over and try on the back."

Many others were indirect orders, not in the imperative form, but recognizable as autocratic if given in certain contexts and in certain tones of voice:

"Now we need some plaster."
"That should be about two-thirds full."
"Today we've got to paint and letter the sign."
"Before we start there's something we have to do. That's to make work aprons."

Such orders clearly correspond to the part of our strict experimental definition of autocratic leadership which calls for "high goal and means control." An adult who gives orders is usually exerting "means control" (i.e., telling the children what they must do in order to achieve a certain end), and he may or may not be also exerting "goal control" (i.e., telling the children what end they must try to achieve). He wants to insure successful achievement, and perhaps also to set up what he feels are worthwhile and feasible goals. It is worthwhile to ask ourselves what relationship this kind of behavior has to our broader definition of the four criteria of democracy, and especially to the criterion of "concern for the individual." Is order giving necessarily a "bad thing to do," or inherently undemocratic?

In our judgment it is not. There are many situations in which the giving of orders is consistent with a realistic regard for the ultimate welfare of the individuals concerned. For instance, there are many work situations in which a work goal is genuinely desired by all or most of the people in the group, and orders by the leader are accepted as simply a necessary way of getting the job done. There was much of this attitude among the boys in at least two of our own autocratic situations, and in these situations the evidence of discontent among the boys was at a minimum. Nevertheless, the act of order giving is inherently one-sided, and it easily tends to become coercive in spirit (i.e., insensitive to the real feelings and ideas of those who are being directed). It is quite easy for an order giver to fool himself as to the extent to which his purposes are actually shared by those whom he directs. He tends to exert a large amount of "goal control" as well as "means control." Perhaps what is most feasible in most situations is a combination of order giving with the give-and-take of productive group discussion, and a limitation of order giving largely to those technical matters in which the group itself accepts the superior competence of the leader and definitely wants his direction, and where no goal of "learning to do it myself" is also relevant.

DISRUPTING COMMANDS

A more unambiguous criterion of means and end control is the giving of "disrupting commands"—commands which cut across an expressed wish or ongoing activity of a member of the group, and substitute for it some wish of the leader. Such commands represented 11 per cent of the verbal behavior of our autocratic leaders, as contrasted to one per cent or less for our democratic and laissez-faire leaders. For example:

"I want to saw."
"No, Bill, you and Hamil make another leg."

Mr. Bohlen says he wants "two fellows."
Fred volunteers, "Let Reilly and I do it."
But Mr. Bohlen appoints two others, "I'm going to let Sam and Leonard do this."

Mr. Bohlen consistently refuses to let Fred do what he wants to do —painting on the sign.

Obviously, this type of command is likely to lead to discontent, and even the efficiency minded autocrat would do well to keep it at a minimum in the interests of good morale and acceptance by the group members.

The data show that the laissez-faire leaders were consistent in restraining themselves from initiating goals and means.

NONOBJECTIVE CRITICISM AND PRAISE

A third type of behavior which was more characteristic of our autocratic leaders was "nonobjective criticism"—criticism which was adverse and personal in character, and which did not point objectively toward improvement by suggesting a reason for failure or a way of doing the thing better. Such criticism constituted 5 per cent of the leader's behavior in our autocratic atmospheres, 2 per cent in the democratic atmospheres, and less than 1 per cent in laissez-faire. For example:

> "You're not making a sack, you're making an apron."
> "No, you can't make it like that. That isn't a good job at all."
> "Who was it left the tool box on the floor again?"

Before discussing the relation of such criticism to our definitions of experimental leader roles, it will be worthwhile to mention the paradoxical fact that *praise* was also given more often by the autocratic (11 per cent) than the democratic (7 per cent) or laissez-faire (5 per cent) leaders. For example:

> Fred is doing a nice job of lettering, and Mr. Bohlen compliments him on it—the second compliment he has given him today.

> "That's the best side view there. But I think I want a front view."

> (In democracy) Bill to Mr. Rankin: "Eddie did a swell job on that, didn't he? I couldn't do as good a job as that."
> Mr. Rankin: "Yeah, it's swell."

Different kinds of praise in different contexts can obviously (like different kinds of criticism) have widely different psychological meanings. Yet it is probably significant, from more than one standpoint, that *both* praise and criticism were especially characteristic of our autocratic leaders. It is interesting, for one thing, as an indication that our autocrats were not "mean"—as some autocrats are.[2] From our present standpoint, however, the most interesting implication of the large amount of both praise and criticism is that it suggests an emphasis on *personal evaluation from the leader's standpoint*. The expression of approval and disapproval implies an emphasis on a status hierarchy, and suggests that the leader is setting himself up as chief judge of the status and achievement of the members of the group. To that extent, both are forms of means and ends control on the part of the leader. It is as if he said "I have

---

[2] The leaders were in fact aware of the possibility that they might consciously or unconsciously "stack the cards" in favor of the democratic role by being unnecessarily critical or unfriendly in their autocratic roles. They consciously tried to guard against this possibility, and the frequency of praise in the records of their behavior shows that they were at least partly successful in this effort.

decided that you deserve the reward of praise" and "I have decided that you deserve criticism." From this standpoint, then, an excessive amount of either praise or criticism would seem to be in line with a leadership policy of maintaining dependence on the leader and inconsistent with a policy of building up control by the group or by an individual over his own sources of satisfaction and his own behavior.

GUIDING SUGGESTIONS

We come now to the forms of leader behavior that were more characteristic of democratic or of laissez-faire leadership than of the autocratic role. For example, as a direct counterpart of the order giving which was characteristic of the autocratic style, we find "guiding suggestions" to be one of the two most frequent forms of verbal behavior on the part of democratic leaders. It represents 24 per cent of the democratic leaders' behavior, as compared with 6 per cent of the autocratic leaders' behavior. The line between "guiding suggestions" and the indirect type of order giving is of course sometimes difficult to draw. However, the reliability of making this distinction in the coding of the conversation was satisfactory. The way in which we defined guiding suggestions can be seen from the following examples, which were classified in this way:

"Did you ever try going the other way—with the grain?"

"That's a knife sharpener so you can have sharp knives to carve wood with."

Bill holds up his model for Mr. Rankin to see. "That's pretty weak there."

Mr. Rankin: "If you don't get it any thinner I think it will be all right."

Mr. Rankin sits down beside Van as he works. "That's good, Van, because if you leave as big a piece as that you can try again."

The distinguishing characteristic in each of these examples is that a given course of action is implicitly or explicitly related to one of the boy's own purposes. In the first case, in which the leader suggested planing with the grain of the wood, the boy was having difficulty with his planing and his desire to do it more easily was obvious to both persons. In the other cases, the end in view—to have sharp knives for carving, to avoid breaking a model of a boat carved in soap, and to have a piece of soap big enough to "try again" was clear; the leader left up to the boy himself the choice as to whether he wanted the goal in question, or simply sensed (correctly, in most cases) that he did want it. The spirit underlying such suggestions clearly implies more respect for the boy's own ideas about goals and means than "You do this because I say so" or "You do this because I think it's the right thing to do." The emphasis was put as frequently as possible on learning the reason for the improved method, "so you can do it yourself from now on."

Very similar in psychological meaning is the *clarifying of alternatives* between which the boys themselves are free to choose (which was included in this same category):

"Motion carried. Now the question is, who wants to be the G-man?"
(All speak.) "Should we choose from everybody that wants to be, or just those that haven't had a chance yet?"

And similar, too, is the giving of suggestions by example rather than by precept:

Reilly discovers that Mr. Rankin is making papier-mâché, and stops throwing to join him. He tears paper too, and so does Fred. Leonard stops throwing. The group is gathered around Mr. Rankin and is listening to him and paying attention.

Bill: "Let's get ready to go home."
Mr. Rankin (picking up a broom): "We don't have much cleaning up to do today."

It should be especially noticed that an active readiness to give guiding suggestions at precisely those moments when they are appropriate and appreciated, and to point out the operating procedure which lies behind the efficient action, was in practice the chief single difference between the democratic and laissez-faire leaders. In laissez-faire such suggestions made up only 14 per cent of the leader's verbal behavior, as compared with 24 per cent in democracy. The absolute numbers of such remarks represent an even greater difference; ninety-one per meeting for the democratic leader as compared with thirty-two in laissez-faire.

In other words, democracy (as distinguished from laissez-faire) did not imply freedom alone—i.e., a relatively passive "regard" for the child's welfare, in the sense that the child's desires were not needlessly thwarted. The democratic leader took the viewpoint that if either individual welfare or group achievement is to be fully attained it is also necessary to have a very active respect for individual desires in the sense of constantly thinking about how they can best be realized. He was assuming that only by such full participation in the life of the group can the leader really lead. For instance, the following are examples in which a boy wanted guidance and did not get it. In some situations exactly the same behavior by the leader—throwing back the question the boy asked—would be a constructive device for stimulating self-guidance. In these situations, however, it seemed to be merely a result of insensitivity to the boy's legitimate needs for goal or means suggestions:

Reilly: "Where can we put this up?"
Mr. Rankin: "Where would you like to put it up?"

Leonard: "How do you cut it?"
Mr. Rankin: "What do you think? Cut it in the right shape . . ."

But, at the other extreme, the democratic leader had to avoid overcomplicated suggestions, such as the following, both of which are double-barreled and at least slightly confusing:

"Who wants to help who to get things finished up?"

"Have you been thinking about a G-man Club? Do you want a meeting now, fellows?"

Also, the effective use of a guiding suggestion seems to depend on timing. The democratic leader had to have a keen awareness of the shifting momentary needs and interests of the boys so that he could make his suggestions at just the moments when they fitted into those interests.

Here is an example of another typical mistake:

"Now that you have your table, don't you want stools to sit on?"

This was perhaps objectively a good suggestion, but the form of it was needlessly personal. The leader could have said, "Now that you have your table you might want something to sit on." The expression "don't you want" is a type of urging which may appear to the child as mild pressure, in case the suggestion is poorly timed and he does not actually follow it. In this case he did not follow it. Here is another illustration:

"Do you want to put a brace across here to make it hold?" A better wording might have been, "I suppose a brace across here would

make it hold better"; or better still, "This may not hold very well
. . . Do you suppose a brace here would help?" The leader did not
find in the boy any desire for "better holding" and he did nothing
to create such a desire before making his suggestion. The suggestion was not followed, and a mild impression of futile nagging was
created.

GIVING INFORMATION

Another major activity of the democratic leader was simply giving
information, or extending the knowledge of the members of his
group. This constituted 27 per cent of the democratic leaders' behavior, and 15 per cent of the autocratic leaders'. (In laissez-faire it
was 49 per cent, which is natural in view of the fact that the laissez-
faire leader's role was explicitly confined very largely to the giving
of technical information when asked for it.) Actually the total
amount of technical information given by the three types of leaders
was not significantly different, even though the proportion was so
much greater in laissez-faire.

Here are some typical examples of information giving:

Finn (holding up orangewood stick): "What's this for?"
Mr. Rankin: "That's an orangewood stick, and the flat end is for
smoothing down this way." (Demonstrates.) "This is more curved
here, and you can get a smoother tip of soap because it's narrower than
this."

There is a dispute between the two groups about the ages of the
knives. . . . Reilly, Sam, and Fred listen to Mr. Rowe talk about the
ages of the knives. They are all very interested.

(In laissez-faire) Finn (very plaintively): "Why can't we have a
crime?"
Mr. Davis: "I could have a crime for you next week if you wanted
me to."

One meaning of information giving, as compared with either orders
or guiding suggestions, is that there is almost no chance of its being
a form of social influence or pressure. The information is simply
there. The boy can take it or leave it, use it or not use it, depending
on his need at the moment.

On the other hand, it should not be assumed that all types of
social pressure are "bad" or undemocratic, even by our stricter defi-

nition of the term. A legitimate function of a democratic leader, related to the "teaching of group procedures," is to create new needs in individuals, or to *mobilize and make effective* those latent, inarticulate, half-conscious needs which are potentially most constructive in regard to functioning as an effective group or an effective member.

STIMULATING SELF-DIRECTION

Less frequent numerically, but probably far more important psychologically, is a group of leader behaviors which we have called "stimulating self-direction." This type of behavior was fairly frequent in democracy and almost nonexistent in autocracy; the percentages were, respectively, 16 and 1.2. Although this made up 13 per cent of the behavior of the laissez-faire leaders this only represented an average of thirty such acts per meeting, as compared with fifty-nine by democratic leaders. The meaning also tended to be quite different. In laissez-faire this type of action on the part of the adult tended to be a throwing back of responsibility on the individual member. In the democratic style it was more frequently a teaching of the total group to learn to depend on itself as a group. This type of behavior, because of its importance and the variety of its forms, deserves to be discussed and illustrated in some detail.

One way of stimulating democratic self-direction in setting new goals and choosing means is to inculcate the ideology of democratic procedure directly: group decision, majority vote, free discussion with an opportunity for every interested person to have his say, secret ballot when appropriate, delegation of special tasks to committees, minority acceptance of majority decisions, etc. For example:

Finn: "Guess I'll change the name of our club."
Bill: "No, it's still the Law and Order Patrol."
Mr. Rankin: "If the group wants to change the name they can—if a majority wants."

Bill: "Eddie should be a captain and Van should be a lieutenant-assistant."
Van: "Hey, that's lower than I am now, and I got a high score!"
Mr. Rankin: "In an army the general decides the promotions, but here, even if it is organized like an army, it seems to me the group ought to decide who should get the promotion."

Bill: "Now you stay out of it and we three will vote."

Mr. Rankin steps in to confer with Bill about taking a vote. He gives him a formal wording: "All in favor say aye, opposed, no," etc. (Bill is especially keen on formality and "having things regular.")

Finn votes for adjournment, and the motion passes. Bill starts to ignore the vote and keep on with the discussion.

Mr. Rankin: "All right, we don't have any meeting now if the majority votes to adjourn."

"I should think you'd need a committee to make up the story for the crime."

"The point of a secret ballot is so that no one will be embarrassed by what he puts down, since nobody will know how he voted." (A secret ballot is taken, and the boys seem to enjoy it very much.)

Reilly demands to know who is cleanup captain. Mr. Rowe suggests an election. Reilly says "I'll elect Leonard." (He means "nominate.") Fred says: "I'll nominate Sam." Sam protests, "It's my turn, and nobody's cheating me out."

Mr. Rowe reassures him: "You've been nominated, Sam. Are there any other nominations besides Leonard and Sam? Should we close our eyes and raise our hands? I won't vote unless it's a tie. All right, shut your eyes. Everybody in favor of Sam raise their right hand. Sam is elected, three to two."

Reilly is dissatisfied with the vote, so Mr. Rowe reminds him, "Majority wins." Reilly continues to be quite insistent that Leonard be elected, and he and Fred almost get into a fight. Mr. Rowe ignores the controversy, however, apparently taking it for granted, in a matter-of-fact way, that the issue is closed.

It will be noticed that in some of the above examples the role of the democratic adult leader is chiefly one of supporting or bringing to clear expression the feeling of the majority. He is a catalyst, releasing energies that already exist in the group. This was done formally by insisting on a majority vote when a dispute had arisen, and backing up the majority with his own prestige. It was also done informally by simply listening to and drawing out the less articulate or less vociferous members of the group. In the following incident, Mr. Rankin failed to do this with Lyman, the timid and withdrawn member of the Charlie Chan Club:

Lyman comes over and explains quietly to Mr. Rankin what he would like to do for a mask. He is interrupted by Reilly, who demands in a loud voice that his business be attended to. Mr. Rankin stops talking to Lyman and leaves him. When he returns his attention to Lyman, Lyman has withdrawn again.

A more democratic procedure was followed later by Mr. Rowe:

Mr. Rowe ignores the horseplay of the others and draws out the quietest member of the group. "Lyman, what were you thinking of?" Sam answers for him, "Not airplanes," and Lyman, apparently not having any idea as yet, fails to join in. (He is probably pleased, however, to have his opinion asked for, and later, under the same leader, becomes a very much more participating member of the group.)

It is also sometimes necessary to support a minority, especially if it is opposed by an even smaller minority. This occurred, for instance, when Finn and Hamil were refusing to accept the arbitrary leadership of Bill. The other two members did not take part in this little contest, so that it was actually a conflict of two against one.

Bill: "It's time for our meeting. The second half of our meeting will now come to order. Come on, boys."

Finn: "That's what you think." He and Hamil go just outside the burlap curtain surrounding the enclosure, but lift the curtain. It is cooler outside, because the moving-picture lights make the enclosure itself very warm.

Finn: "We'll just listen from out here."

Bill doesn't get the response he wants and pouts while he takes up his whittling again.

Mr. Rankin: "I shouldn't think a good chairman would whittle while the meeting was going on."

Bill: "Well, I can't get any of the guys to come."

Mr. Rankin goes over to the other two and holds up the curtain. Eddie and Van go too, so that four of the five boys are gathered at the edge of the enclosure.

Mr. Rankin: "The meeting is going on over here." (A satisfactory meeting is held, with Bill fully participating, as well as Hamil and Finn.)

A similar bringing out of latent opinion, this time on both sides, is represented by the following incident:

Van: "We ought to have an army and have military service." (Van repeats this suggestion several times and is pretty well ignored by the rest of the group.)

Van finally goes up to Mr. Rankin: "Hey, I said we want some military service."

Mr. Rankin: "What sort of military service? 'Squads right' and things like that?"

Van: "Bill, you come here and explain."

Bill: "This is what we mean. When we come to a person, salute. We ought to do it all the time, even at school."

Finn: "That's the worst resolution we could have. I disagree with it right away. It's so young acting it's nuts."

Mr. Rankin: "Why don't you bring it up at a meeting, Bill? The beginning of next meeting we could discuss it, and you get your arguments ready too, Finn."

The commonest form of stimulating self-direction, however, was simply to follow up a particular boy's ideas, encouraging him to elaborate them and think them through:

Mr. Rowe: "Let's all sit down and talk it over. Sam suggested glass painting. How does it go, Sam?"

Sam: "Get a picture under a piece of glass."

Mr. Rowe: "How would it be if I got a big piece of glass and a big painting? Does the paint come in tubes?"

Sam: "The stuff in bottles is better."

Mr. Rowe: "Would everybody like to do it?"

Reilly: "I'd like to do it."

Lyman: "I think I'd like to do it."

Van (in a doubtful tone): "I was thinking of a canoe (for soap carving)."

Mr. Rankin: "I think a canoe is probably the best idea. Can you see there (picture of canoe model) how almost straight it is for a distance in the middle?"

An illustration of failure to follow up a boy's ideas is the following:

Reilly proposes that they make book ends.

Mr. Rankin (not reacting at all to the book-end idea): "Have you been thinking about a G-man club? Do you want a meeting now, fellows?"

They discover the plaster of Paris, and are delighted. Reilly is full of suggestions, and talks to Mr. Rankin. He wants to "try out" the plaster of Paris. Sam comes around and tries to distract Mr. Rankin's attention from Reilly. Mr. Rankin replies to Reilly (not seizing and taking advantage of this strong new interest): "It all depends on whether you want to finish up the things you've started."

Here again, as in the case of guiding suggestions, it is necessary to stress the importance of timing. To try to stimulate self-direction at the wrong time, when the boys themselves are not ready for it, is worse than useless. Here is another illustration of a poorly timed effort to stimulate democratic discussion:

> They are not able to get into the tool chest, and suggest various methods for opening it without a key. Mr. Rankin suggests that they sit down and talk about plans. (The nonavailability of tools had been deliberately planned, in order to prevent the typical preoccupation with physical activity and lack of interest in discussion.) "There are two or three things I think you fellows may want to talk about. One thing we want to talk about is the name of the club."

This was both confusing and autocratic. To speak vaguely about "two or three things" was not appropriate for this immediate-minded group. It would have been better to wait until a single topic came up which the boys themselves were interested in discussing. And for the leader to assume the right to speak for the others—"One thing we want to talk about is a name for the club" —was essentially autocratic. Yet, even after failing to get any general or sustained response, the leader persisted in his untimely effort to force discussion:

> They vociferously argue. Leonard says, "Dick Tracy, or Junior G-men." Reilly is evidently irritated and keeps demanding that the box be opened up: "Open it up. Will you open this up?" Fred wants to know "Why is that thing locked?" Mr. Rankin tries to concentrate the group's attention on the question he has proposed: "How about putting the names of the club up here?" But Reilly and Leonard are now talking about something else in very loud voices. Reilly tries to get Leonard's brush; Leonard protests, "Oh, no you don't," and picks up the brush; then he repeats, "We want the box open."
>
> Mr. Rankin is still trying to promote discussion: "We are going to do two or three things. Somebody suggested Dick Tracy. How about Sherlock Holmes?" Leonard: "That's the one." Then no one pays any more attention to Mr. Rankin except Lyman. Fred joins Reilly and Leonard at the chest; the other two go over to the chest and leave Mr. Rankin entirely alone. He comes over to the chest and joins them. He keeps trying to plan, and says, "We have several things to plan." Reilly says, "Yeah, and several things to get out of the chest." Sam yells "Open up!" They all stand around and interrupt. Leonard flops on the chest and yells, "Open up!"

This is a clear case of mistaking the forms of the democratic role for its psychological meaning. Mr. Rankin was already greatly disturbed at the fact that his group had become anarchic, and he was blindly determined to "have a group discussion." But, in his anxiety, he failed to realize the implications of the group opposition which he clearly perceived, or to treat it as anything but an obstacle to be overcome by sheer dogged persistence. And, of course, as long as he was unready to use autocratic coercion, pitting himself against the unequivocal opposition of four members of the group was sure to be a losing battle, in which he lost most of whatever influence over the group he may have still had.

"Jovial" and "Confiding" Behavior

The last type of conversation that was measured and that significantly distinguished the democratic club atmospheres from the other two is one which, for want of a better term, has been characterized by the two terms "jovial" and "confiding." It represents the purely social aspect of the leader's behavior, and was far more characteristic of our democratic situation than of either autocracy or laissez-faire (7 per cent as compared with 0.7 per cent in autocracy and 1.7 per cent in laissez-faire). For example:

Fred talks and laughs with Mr. Rowe—far different from his behavior with Mr. Bohlen.

There is a very nice relationship between Mr. Rowe and the group.
. . . He seems to be having the most fun of all. . . .

(The acute conflict between Fred and Mr. Bohlen is still fresh in everyone's mind; and on this day Fred is absent. The following topic of conversation is therefore a natural one.)
Mr. Rowe: "Does Fred get into much trouble with the teacher?"
Sam says, "I'll say!" and Lyman adds, "He got sent out of the room two times. He always does something."

This is the clearest instance of a type of behavior which was not consciously planned, but which developed as a sort of by-product of the democratic leader's total relationship to his group, usually by the initiative of group members. It has nothing directly to do with freedom or lack of freedom, but it obviously does have something to do with the openness of communication which often develops as a result of the relationship created by the other types of leadership behavior which have been described above.

This completes our list of the types of conversation which were statistically analyzed and which clearly differentiated one or more of the three atmospheres. A number of incidental observations can be added, however, which were not statistically analyzed but which help to round out the picture:

DEMOCRATIC CRITICISM AND PRAISE

Although it did not occur frequently enough for statistical comparison the observers noted that the democratic leaders tended to use praise and criticism in a different way from the autocratic leaders (as reported on page 34–36). The democratic leaders recognized that "training in procedures" seemed to mean: (1) helping individuals to learn the criteria and methods for evaluating their own work without dependence on the adult, as well as (2) helping the group to learn the methods of mutual support and cooperative operation as a group (as described on pp. 40–45). This first type of training is exemplified in such incidents as:

Mr. Rankin: "That's good, Van, because if you leave as big a piece [of soap, during soap-carving period] as that you can try again [if the first try fails]."

Leader: "I think that's going to be pretty wobbly (piece of box furniture). Can you guess why I think so?"

Boy: "Maybe because there are so many bent nails and none that go through."

By this type of praise and criticism the democratic leaders attempted to extend their assigned function of "high teaching of group procedure for setting goals and means" to complementary teaching of criteria and methods for *evaluating* goals and means. This seemed to be a natural part of the same leadership role.

THE ENFORCEMENT OF LIMITS IN DEMOCRACY

One frequently asked question is, "Aren't there some necessary limits to a child's freedom, even in democracy? If so, what are they, and how can they be enforced without being 'autocratic'?"

Of course there are necessary limits. The physical safety of the boys themselves and reasonable safety for other people's property represent two limiting factors which (at least in our own culture) no responsible adult leader could be expected to ignore. Of course, too, there are occasions when action is required to enforce such limits. On the other hand, it should be emphasized that the question of where the ultimate limits should be set is not nearly as important in determining degrees of democracy as some people assume. For instance, it will be noticed that all of our previous discussion in this chapter is apart from the question of ultimate limits. A leader might be democratic by our criteria—giving few orders, being alert to the boys' own needs, stimulating self-direction, etc.— even though he was prepared to be very strict in prohibiting "bad" behavior, e.g., unsafe behavior in the particular physical environment of the group.

There are comparable limits made necessary by the larger social environment in which this little club group exists as a part. The leader must ask the group to confine their club activities to a given space because of the interdependence with the research group of observers who need to be able to see what goes on. The leader must enforce certain general legal or moral codes of behavior because he represents the larger supervisory adult society which is nurturing the growth and development of these young members.

But as long as there remained a considerable area of freedom within these safety or legality or morality limits the leader might be highly democratic or autocratic or laissez-faire within that area. In answer, then, to the question, "How can the limits be enforced without being autocratic?" there are three answers that are consistent with our definition of democracy: (1) "By using penalties that are not more drastic than they need to be to enforce the limit"; (2) "By giving explanation of reasons"; (3) "By seeking group acceptance of the occasionally necessary role of 'enforcer.' " Respect for the welfare of the particular child or other individuals or groups may require that the limit be enforced, but once this objective is obtained, any further severity of punishment shows sheer vindictiveness, and an undemocratic disregard for the needs and feelings of the individual on whom control is exerted. And, by the same token, if any legitimate devices other than punishment can bring about the same result, they are to be preferred.

In our experiments, the ultimate sanction available to the leaders was excluding a boy from club membership, and it was invoked only once, even as an explicit threat (by Mr. Bohlen, when Fred rebelled against his autocratic control. For a full description of the incident, see pp. 119–122). There is therefore little material available that might serve to illustrate democratic or undemocratic methods of enforcing ultimate limits. There is some material, however, on "devices other than punishment," which may have helped to forestall the need for punishment. From the records of the obstreperous Charlie Chan Club, after it was somewhat tamed and integrated by Mr. Rowe's skillful democratic leadership, the following items are of interest. They suggest the possible usefulness of representing the outer limit as a sort of impersonal necessity which even the leader himself must respect:

"O.K. I've got to pick up the knives now, fellows."

"Boys, that sign isn't ours."

Probably neither of these remarks would have been effective in the context of the same group's behavior under Rankin's laissez-faire leadership or Bohlen's autocratic leadership. Both were effective in the context of Rowe's democratic leadership, since he had already established himself in the eyes of the boys as a friend, a helper, and a non-meddler. But it is also worthwhile to notice that both refer to an impersonal necessity: "I've got to," not "I want to"; and "it isn't ours" rather than "you can't have it." In these instances Mr. Rowe was acting as the representative of society as a whole in invoking certain limits. He was not expressing a personal wish. He would therefore have misrepresented the actual situation, while also running the risk of impairing his identification with the group, if he had not taken the group's standpoint in looking upon these cultural norms as something impersonal and completely beyond his control.

Another illustration of his "we-minded" invocation of limits occurred when Fred and Reilly were playfully fighting with knives. Mr. Rowe quietly remarked: "I don't think we ought to do that, Fred. Do you?" and Fred stopped. The chief reason for his stopping was certainly his general rapport with Mr. Rowe, but an additional reason might have been the we-minded wording and tone of the remark. One hesitates to stress the mere fact that the leader used the pronoun "we" instead of "you," since the same word has been used so often by adults playing essentially the autocratic role and who (perhaps often without realizing it) have used it as a kind of insincere sugar-coating to their pills of autocracy. "Now we're all going to go in and wash our hands"; "we just don't do that sort of thing around here," etc. But if the spirit as well as the letter is one of identification with the group (as it was in this case) there is surely a gain from the standpoint of obviating any need for stronger sanctions.

EQUALITARIAN BEHAVIOR

It may be worthwhile also to cull a number of illustrations not falling under any one topic that has already been discussed, but illustrating again, in a variety of ways, some additional implications of "respect for members' own goals and means" which seem to flow from the leadership patterns that were defined for the leaders. There are, for instance, some egotistical uses of the pronoun "I," by autocratic leaders, which are clearly lacking in that sort of respect:

"I'm going to pick out the best one when you get done."

"Guess you'll have to put some more powder in that. I don't like it yet."

By contrast, the democratic leaders often showed equalitarian or even self-effacing behavior, and an absence of concern about their status and dignity. They took off their coats, they sat or squatted instead of standing, they worked just as the boys did and showed that they were enjoying the work just as the boys did. Other illustrations:

Mr. Rowe subordinates himself to the elected boy leader. "What should I do for cleanup, Sam?"

Mr. Rankin, on the first day of democracy in the Law and Order Patrol (after a period of laissez-faire) finds Bill in a position of temporarily revived leadership. He does not challenge this leadership, but helps Bill where he can do so without antagonizing the others.

Bill is administering a test which he has carefully made up, on crime-detection agencies in the community, safety rules, etc. Mr. Rankin asks: "Are you testing me too?" Bill: "No." Mr. Rankin (with a smile): "I'd probably get the worst grade."

"It belongs to all of us."

"You're doing that a lot more scientifically than I could."

.Observer writes: "Another characteristic of the democratic behavior of Rankin is his emotional expressions with the boys—'Oh,' 'Aha'— and his going thoughtfully into everything the children think they want to do."

On the other hand, the democratic leaders sometimes did not hesitate to accept delegated authority when it was unequivocally handed to them.

Mr. Rankin suggests a committee to make up the crime, but the group wants to leave it to him this next time. He agrees.

In other words, the democratic leader's lack of concern about his own dignity was not a blind or compulsive self-effacement; it was (or at least should have been) a sensitive awareness of and respect for the status needs (own social goals) of the boys in the group, as well as of the various other needs that they might have in this situation.

ROLE CHANGES BY THE SAME PERSON

In a later section of this book (Chapter 19) we will discuss the question of the extent to which a person can learn a new leadership role. At the moment our interest is in the question of whether the four leaders in this experiment actually changed their behavior to be consistent with the leadership policy they were supposed to be representing, or whether they primarily "kept on being like themselves" in each of the three clubs they led. The data clearly reveal that each leader was more like the others in the same role than he was like himself from one role to another. The interviews with each boy in which he compared his leaders also indicate that the boys were actually reacting to these behavioral differences rather than to other unchanging aspects of the leaders' personalities. There must have been some enduring characteristics which each individual leader took with him from one club to the other, and these characteristics probably exerted some influence on the perceptions and reactions of the club members, but these were evidently minor or irrelevant as far as the leaders' effect on the club life was concerned in the dimensions we have studied.

4

Glimpses of Group Life

THE major results of the experiments can be seen, in miniature, in the following excerpts from the record:

AN EXAMPLE OF THE SUBMISSIVE REACTION TO AUTOCRACY

Excerpts from Club Records

Interpretive Comments

The group comes in before the leader arrives. In his absence, they show little interest in their work. They kid the other group about being in the movies. The other group is the second club meeting in the adjacent club space. As mentioned previously, in all cases two clubs met simultaneously in adjoining clubrooms so that interaction between groups under different types of leadership could be studied.

Work is slack when the leader is out. *Work motivation is induced by the leader; not spontaneous.*

Ray says, "You ought to have Martha Raye and stick your head in." Ray looks into the box. The others sit around the mask they have been working on, paying no attention to it.

The leader, Mr. Rankin, enters the room, walking rapidly. He begins immediately to direct their work:

"The first thing we're going to do is to make footprints in the

No discussion or cooperative planning; only orders from above. The leader gives only a bare minimum of "time perspective." The boys get little sense of why he gives his specific orders. This is

plaster of Paris mold. Get your aprons on. . . . Vinnie, help Ben. . . . Now we need some plaster. That should be about two-thirds full. . . ."

The boys put on their aprons as directed and begin work.

Ben asks, "Me? Okay." He asks for approval of the detailed steps in his work: "Is that high enough, Mr. Rankin?"

Mr. R. answers: "It should be deeper."

They are all working steadily now under Mr. R.'s direction. Beaumont now seems to be the only one who is not really "in" the situation.

Mr. R. says, "Ray, you put your footprint in this while Beaumont keeps on stirring. And Vinnie, you put the sand up close around his foot; pack it down tight. Make a good print. . . . All right, take your foot out."

Ray asks, "How's this, Mr. Rankin? Do you think that will have to take a little bit more?"

Mr. R. answers, "A good deal more. Put some more plaster of Paris in."

Ray: "Now is she getting thicker?"

Mr. R.: "More yet. . . . That's right. That's plenty."

The same uneventful pattern of behavior continues until, after more than half an hour, the leader goes out of the room.

Within one minute after the leader goes out, all the boys have stopped working. Ray and Ben

probably a major factor in their lack of interest in the project as a whole.

The free, sociable, joking atmosphere disappears almost completely as hard work begins.

Efficiency is fairly high so long as the autocratic leader keeps everyone busy.

The boys are dependent upon the leader for detailed work directions. Having no time perspective or organized ideas in terms of which to evaluate their own work, they are forced to rely upon him.

The lack of spontaneous interest in the work shows itself again as soon as the leader goes out.

begin talking freely to each other; the others just sit.

After five minutes, wisecracks begin going back and forth between this group and the other group. Ray takes the lead; he yells, "Baby Reilly, playing in the sand. . . ."

Reilly, in the other group, throws over at this group a small plaster of Paris "marble." Ray shouts, "Give it to him," and throws it back. Ben backs him up, "Go ahead, give it to him now. . . . Stand back over there, you twirp." Observer writes, "Here goes the war."

The war relaxes, however, and becomes mainly verbal. Leonard, from the other group (which has been showing the aggressive reaction to autocracy), is making sallies into this group's territory. Ray says, "Hey, Leonard, what's your hurry? . . . Listen, you. Hey, rat—that backbone of yours looks like a snake." Ben backs him up again: "What'd you leave for? You cross-eyed rat!"

(Hostilities remain on this verbal level until the leader returns. The group then returns immediately to the same dull but industrious and efficient pattern of behavior which they showed before he went out.)

Are they "discharging tension" which was bottled up during their submission to an autocratic regime?

Under the autocrat, Ray's colorful personality was indistinguishable from that of the others. In a freer atmosphere, his individuality shows itself immediately.

An Example of the Aggressive Reaction to Autocracy

Excerpts from Records   *Interpretive Comments*

Immediately after coming in, the boys discover some slight damage done to their work by the "Monday gang." Sam is the loudest in voicing his resentment: "Look around and see if they got anything we could bust up. We'll get them for that this time."

Mr. Bohlen (the autocratic leader) heads off an attack on the "Monday gang's" day's work: "Today we've got to paint and letter the sign." Sam interrupts, "I'm doing the painting." Mr. B. continues, "Before we start there's something we have to do. That's to make work aprons." Sam interrupts again, "Where's the apron that was in here?" Mr. B. goes on, "You each make an apron and paint your name on it. Start before you mix any of the other paint." Leonard demands, "I get some of this burlap." Sam warns the others, "Don't make the red paint, Reilly. . . . And don't mess with my red paint, guys."

Fred, Leonard, and Sam get under way. Reilly protests and says he'll make up the paint first. Mr. B. says, "No, the apron first."

By the eighth minute the group has quieted down and is hard at work. Observer writes,

"This is a picture of individual industry I've not seen presented by this group before. Some of the horsiness has gone out of them since their arrival, but I'm afraid it's not permanent."

In the fourteenth minute the other group come in and are

Although most of the restrictions come from their autocratic leader, most of the boys' aggression and competitive self-assertion is directed against scapegoats: the "Monday gang," the other club which meets on the same day, or other members of the same club.

grected by derisive remarks. Leonard says, "I thought I heard those dopes coming up." Reilly says, "Here come the skunks. I thought I smelled something." Sam says, "Give us a gas mask. Here comes the other gang."

Mr. Bohlen asks who left the scissors on the floor. Fred says Lyman worked with them last. Lyman says he gave them to Leonard. Leonard denies it, "No, you didn't." Lyman flushes with anger but says nothing except, "I did, too." Observer writes, "I've never seen an outfit any busier in pointing out each others' faults."

With continued restrictions (which are not accepted with resignation, as in the submissive reaction), the boys become tense and irritable.

Fred is definitely sullen, and responds to Mr. B. (the autocratic leader) by muttering under his breath. . . . He is getting madder and madder and is kicking things about. He kicks the stool under the sign. . . . Everybody is yelling at once and getting rather cross, but Fred is the most objectionable. . . .

Direct rebellious aggression against the autocrat is partly suppressed, and the footstool becomes an inanimate scapegoat.

AN EXAMPLE OF LAISSEZ-FAIRE

Excerpts from Records

Interpretive Comments

The boys come in and immediately cluster around a blueprint on the table. Their adult leader, Mr. Davis, stands apart from the group, leaning against a post. The group pays no attention to him.

Van says, "Come on, let's make plans, boys." Bill (who was elected "captain" at the last meeting) answers, "We're going to draw something. I don't know just what we'll do. . . . We want to draw a ship, see? Let's draw plans of a gun or a building or something."

Finn mocks Bill: "You don't seem to know much." Bill replies, "Well, what do you suggest?" Finn only makes a wisecrack and starts out on some little wood project of his own.

Eddie (in sympathy with Bill) urges, "We gotta have some plans to work on."

Bill goes on, "Let's make a map or something. Any suggestions? . . . This is the crooks' hideout and we've got to plan ways to get in. . . . We have to cover it from these sides now. There are electrical wires on the bushes." All of them are intent on the plans except Finn, who is very restless. He lies down on the table.

(The discussion continues on a very constructive level for about twelve minutes.)

Finn feels out of it. He makes a smarty gesture with his stool, saying, "Here's my idea." Bill hasn't given him any recognition.

Suddenly the table on which they have been leaning breaks down. Finn is utterly delighted. The others seem dismayed, but start out, somewhat haphazardly, to fix the table.

(After three minutes the prospect of fixing the table seems hopeless, and the group disinte-

The boys are all in an "unstructured field," and all of them except Finn have a need to structure their field more clearly.

The group is making a real effort to get together on something constructive and for the time being they are successful.

Finn, who feels left out, has been feeling more and more hostile to the group.

grates almost completely. They
do not really get together again
during this meeting, nor, for
that matter, throughout the remaining five meetings of laissez-
faire leadership. Of course the
adult leader does nothing to promote reorganization.)

Finn is now very smarty, but
gets no response. Eddie paints
dots on Bill's pants. Finn says,
"Oh, gee, I guess I'll make this
thing polkadottie."

Eddie shows his restlessness by
throwing darts. They begin to
talk about generals, just as they
did last time when things became anarchic.

They are now at the high
point of disorganization so far
today. Bill has suggested "doing
something" but there is no plan
yet.

Eddie is whittling, Van painting, Hamil hammering, Bill playing shotgun with a board. Finn
tries to grab it from him.

Eddie and Finn start a play
fight for the wooden gun, which
lasts about half a minute.

After half an hour of restlessness, boredom, and rising tension, the play becomes more active.

There is a noise from behind
the burlap—yipping like a dog.
Finn and Hamil are making and
painting guns. . . .

Machine-gun game behind
burlap. Much burring of guns.
Finn points gun at Dave (in
other club) and says, "We're go-

There is nothing to do except
horseplay.

Three major factors which
make for aggressive behavior are
now present: (a) absence of a
respected adult; (b) idleness;
and (c) frustration, leading to a
high level of psychological tension.

Finn, who is not at all adult-
value-centered, is now in his element.

ing to have a war. . . . We want a war."

Much noise of guns. Most of the other club (with democratic leadership) pay no attention. Eddie yells, "They retreat!" Bill is sitting pensively on a stool and looking at the other club as if envious of their cohesion and efficiency. Eddie yells, "Give 'em the first degree." . . .

But Bill, who in some ways is highly adult-value-centered and hates confusion, is miserable.

An Example of Democracy
(Same group as in example of laissez faire)

Excerpts from Records	*Interpretive Comments*
Van and Finn come in together. Van finds a bar of soap and says, "Look, here's the soap for the soap carving we decided on."	"We" decided—not "I" and not "our leader."
Bill and Eddie come in, and Bill says enthusiastically, "That's a good kind of soap!"	Interest in work is keen, even before leader enters.
Finn asks the leader, "What's this for?" The leader, Mr. Rankin, answers, "That's an orange-wood stick, and the flat end is for smoothing down this way." Finn: "Well, what about this flat end? Oh, I'll bet that's to make grooves."	Finn is thinking for himself and thoroughly interested. Note the contrast between this and his behavior in laissez-faire.
Bill holds up his piece with a laugh, "Look, Mr. Rankin, I might make a bed out of this." Finn admires it, "Well, nice going, Bill." . . . Bill later returns the compliment, "Oh, that's good, Finn. That's a good idea. Mine's too weak."	Pleasure in successful work project promotes friendliness; friendliness results in mutual praise; and praise, in turn, promotes pleasure in work.
Eddie, Bill, and Finn are busy	Status can be gained by good

on their projects, but Van is still casting around for the kind of boat he wants to carve; he is looking at pictures in the book. Mr. R. looks with him. Mr. R. exclaims, "Oh, boy, look at this model of a racing shell!" Van says doubtfully, "I was thinking of a canoe." Mr. R. agrees, "I think a canoe is probably the best idea. . . . Can you see there how almost straight it is for a long distance in the middle?"

Mr. R. remarks that if they're going to have the crime they planned last time, it's about time to begin. Van says, "I'd like to finish my carving." Mr. R. asks the group, "Shall we finish this work and have the crime next time? How many think so?" Bill, "That's okay with me." The others also agree.

Van: "Well, I guess I'm not even voted against."
Mr. R.: "Yes, it's unanimous."
Finn: "What does that mean?"
Van: "It means not voted against. (Turning to Mr. R.) Doesn't it?"
Mr. R. nods.
Bill: "We ought to learn those rules about voting and have things regular."

Van (who is probably the most insecure member of the group and also the most childlike) holds up his motorboat for everyone to see, but no one seems to notice him. He takes it to the pail of water and pushes it

work; there is no need to get it by aggressive horseplay.

The leader tries to follow up the boys' own ideas, and, by giving necessary information, helps to make them more effective.

Vote shows high interest in present project.

Leader attempts to develop both the skills and the vocabulary of democracy.

In this atmosphere, each boy feels more free to be himself, and individuality of behavior is consequently more marked than in the apathetic reaction to autocracy.
The leader tries to respect in-

around the surface making a motor noise. Still no one looks at him, until Mr. R. turns and comes over to join him and comments on the "good motor." Van seems satisfied and settles down to quiet work again immediately.

After a full hour, Bill says to the group, "Let's get ready to go home." He begins to pick up.

Mr. R. (picking up a broom), "We don't have much cleaning up today."

Finn (picking up a large chunk of soap from the floor): "Here's something we might want."

Mr. R. sweeps and Van holds a paper for him to sweep into.

dividual differences and gives interested attention to those who seem to need it most.

In laissez-faire, no one cleaned up except Bill. Now everyone seems to join in naturally. Group goals are accepted and taken over by each individual.

5

Major Differences in Boys' Behavior

In this chapter the results of the experiments are presented more fully and systematically, in terms of the chief statistical differences between the boys' behavior under autocratic, democratic, and laissez-faire types of leadership. These differences can be grouped under six major generalizations:

1. Laissez-faire Was Not the Same as Democracy

It was less organized, less efficient, and definitely less satisfying to the boys themselves.

Since there is a general tendency to attribute to democracy certain results which are actually results of laissez-faire, it is necessary to make this distinction very clearly before going on to any further thinking about differences between democracy and autocracy. The boys' behavior in laissez-faire differed from their behavior in democracy in the following ways:

Less work done, and poorer work. In democracy, the time periods during which there was a general absorption in constructive activity, or high psychological involvement in the work situation, represented 50 per cent of the total time; in laissez-faire, 33 per cent. In democracy, the time periods of general out-and-out loafing consisted of 0.2 per cent of the total time; in laissez-faire, 5 per cent. And in quality of work accomplished, the difference was considerably greater than these figures indicate. The lack of active guiding suggestions in laissez-faire often resulted in disorganization and in failures and setbacks in work, which were discouraging and exasperating. Some outright aggression can be directly attributed to such work failures, as well as much loss of interest in the job that was being done. For instance:

Eddie and Bill have mixed the plaster of Paris before getting the sand and making a print. Mr. Davis doesn't step in to tell them it will soon get hard. Van tries the plaster of Paris and finds it quite stiff. Eddie, Bill, and Van finish a handprint and go to pour the plaster of Paris, but find it has hardened in the can. Bill pounds at it. Eddie stamps in the sand with his shoe, spoiling the print they had prepared. Finn and Hamil finish some new guns. Everybody is now milling around idly except Bill, who keeps on trying to get the hard plaster of Paris out of the can. Horseplay is about to begin.

Sam and Leonard's desk collapses because a leg is too short. They disagree as to what is the trouble.

Fred has made a bad mess of his part and is busy trying to clean it up with turpentine.

They have written "No. 1" in one place and "No. 2" in another place. They are rather disturbed but decide to paint it out next time.

Fred breaks his cast; is discouraged; goes on and tears up the whole thing. (Later in the same hour, he was the leader in destroying the work of the "Monday gang.")

Fred watches, sitting on a stool he made, from which a leg falls off. He breaks up the rest of it.

More play. Play-minded conversation with other boys was more than 2.5 times as frequent in laissez-faire (33 per hour as compared with 13 in democracy). Pure silliness was included in this category. For instance:

Leonard (hearing the term "orangewood sticks"): "Orangewood sticks—pick up sticks."

Ray: "Hooray, hooray—I—O—W—A!"

Hamil: "Finn's red; he's got red on his hair." (This was a joke of some sort; Finn has red hair.)

(Organized play) Bill: "This is the crooks' hideout, and we've got to plan ways to get in. . . . We have to cover it from these sides now. There are electric wires on the bushes."

(Disorganized play) Bill: "Is there anything you can add to this book of laws?" Eddie (who is ordinarily very work-minded, but is finally fed up with the impractical character of Bill's suggestion): "What's the matter, Bill? I think I'll go to sleep." Eddie then tries to climb one of the posts, goes around behind the burlap, pushes a hand through slowly and catches Van by the shoulder, and laughs loudly (for him). He sits on a bench and sways back and forth until it suddenly breaks. Eddie and Van grab up the broken bench and pretend to use it as a two-man saw to saw the table in two.

More expressions of discontent. The frequency of such expressions to other club members, during the meetings themselves, was almost four times as great in laissez-faire as in democracy (3.1 per hour as compared with 0.8; significant at the 1 per cent level). For example:

Van: "How about us doing something? There's nothing to do. We got to have a meeting."
Finn (very critically): "Yeh, how about us doing something?"

Finn: "Well, that ain't doing nothing."
Bill: "Well, it's because we haven't got no cooperation."

"So far we haven't gotten anywhere."

Stranger asks, "Do you have a good time?"
Finn: "Sure we have a good time."
Hamil: "Don't say 'we.' " (Implying that he doesn't have a good time.)

Expressed preference for democratic leaders. There were ten boys who had both a laissez-faire and a democratic leader. All of them preferred their democratic leader. Typical comments:

"Mr. Rankin (democracy) has good ideas and goes right to the point of everything. Mr. Davis (laissez-faire) gave us no suggestions like Mr. Rankin did, and didn't help us out at all, though he was very nice to us; . . . but he let us figure things out too much."
"Mr. Bohlen (democracy) was the best. He's done a lot for us. We accomplished more than we did the other two times."
"Mr. Bohlen (democracy) is a swell guy. If you don't like things you can decide what to do, he told us. He suggested things we could make."
"Mr. Davis (laissez-faire) let us go ahead and fight, and that isn't good. He just didn't give us much to do."
"Mr. Davis (laissez-faire) didn't do much, he just sat and watched; there wasn't much I didn't like about him, but he didn't help us much."
"Mr. Rankin (democracy) had interesting things to do . . . Mr. Davis (laissez-faire) was too easy. He didn't know anything about the

club; he didn't know about its ways. He didn't understand us boys at all."

"Mr. Rowe (democracy) is about the best one. He asks us what we want to do, and if two or three want one thing we do that next week. Mr. Rankin (laissez-faire) . . . wasn't quite bossy enough."

"Mr. Bohlen (democracy) was a good joking fellow . . ." (This group actually had had no experience under a laissez-faire leader, but their other democratic leader had been somewhat more "laissez-fairish" than Mr. Bohlen.)

2. DEMOCRACY CAN BE EFFICIENT

Since arguments for autocracy often take the form of claiming that democracy is not efficient enough to accomplish a certain end (such as winning a war, reducing production costs, or educating a child in necessary basic skills), it is of interest to consider the degree of efficiency of the democratic groups in our experiments. Did these groups achieve the ends the boys themselves wanted to achieve?

On the whole they did. The question is not a simple one, since the boys did not want work achievement to the exclusion of other goals. (And in this respect, of course, the situation was also not comparable with the many situations in which society demands that a certain end be accomplished by methods that are inherently distasteful.) The clubs in the experiments were recreational clubs. They were "to have fun," and the boys came to them expecting to have fun through sociability, and probably through occasional good-natured horseplay, as well as through carpentry, painting, and organized crime games. A truly democratic respect for the boys' own legitimate goals would perhaps necessitate evaluating "efficiency" as much in terms of the achievement of these social goals as in terms of the achievement of work goals. And certainly from this combined standpoint democracy was decidedly more "efficient" than either autocracy or laissez-faire, since it achieved simultaneously both work goals and social goals, while autocracy, in the main, achieved only work goals, and laissez-faire achieved (if anything) only social goals. But even from the narrow standpoint of work goals alone, the evidence suggests that in the experimental situation the democratic groups were about as efficient as the autocratic ones.

This conclusion is based mainly upon over-all impressionistic judgments by the observers. It is also based partly on a balancing

of certain factors of efficiency which appeared to be more prominent in autocracy and others which appeared to be more prominent
in democracy. On the one hand, there was a large quantity of work
done in autocracy—or at least, in those autocratic groups in which
the reaction to autocracy was a submissive one. In such groups the
time-periods of general absorption in work constituted 74 per cent
of the total time, as compared with 50 per cent in democracy, and
52 per cent in the one instance (in the second experiment) of an
aggressive group reaction to autocracy. On the other hand, the
amount of genuine interest in work was unquestionably higher in
democracy. This was shown by a somewhat larger amount of "work-
minded" conversation in democracy (63 such remarks per hour, as
compared with 53 in the aggressive reaction to autocracy and 52
in the submissive reaction). Some illustrations of work-minded remarks:

"Let's see, who's got the saw?"
"I'm going to get a chisel to chisel that out with."
"How come some of these pieces are bigger than others?"
"Because they belong to the end of the wing out here."
"I guess all these pieces go together."
"Well, this is supposed to stand up straight."

More significantly, the difference in amount of genuine, spontaneous work interest was shown by the difference in the boys' behavior when the adult leader left the room. Typically, the boys in
democracy kept right on working whether their leader was present
or not, while in autocracy, when the leader left, the boys stopped
working, as if glad to be relieved of a task that they "had" to do. In
democracy there was a very slight drop in proportion of general
work involvement during the leader-out periods—from 50 per cent
to 46 per cent. On the other hand, in the one group which reacted
aggressively to autocratic leadership, the drop in work involvement
was from 52 to 16 per cent, and in the three groups reacting submissively it was from 74 per cent to 29 per cent.

There was, finally, an impression on the part of the experimenters that both work and play showed a higher level of *originality* or
creative thinking in the democracies than under either of the other
types of leadership. There was a larger amount of creative thinking
about the work in progress than in autocracy, and it was more sustained and practical than in laissez-faire. This showed up in such
comparisons as the painting of murals in the different clubs.

3. AUTOCRACY CAN CREATE MUCH HOSTILITY AND AGGRESSION, INCLUDING AGGRESSION AGAINST SCAPEGOATS

The word "can" is important here, because this reaction did not always occur. It occurred to a very marked degree in Experiment I, and to some degree in one of the four groups that took part in Experiment II; but the other three groups in Experiment II showed, instead, a "submissive" reaction in which there was significantly *less* overt aggression than in democracy. In this other reaction the boys became extremely "good"—unnaturally good, one might almost say. The radical difference between these two reactions (at least outwardly) presents a challenging psychological problem, which will be considered in some detail in Chapters 9 and 10. Why is the reaction sometimes aggressive and sometimes submissive? And are the two reactions fundamentally as different as they appear to be on the surface? For the present we will postpone these questions, and simply review the evidence that an aggressive reaction sometimes occurs—*in spite of* the aggression-inhibiting influence which under other circumstances is unquestionably exerted by an autocratic adult.

The clearest evidence comes from Experiment I. For example:

Dominating ascendance occurred 392 times in the autocratic group and only 81 times in the democratic group. The category "ascendance" showed no significant difference between the groups (63 per cent of all child-to-child behavior in autocracy, and almost as much—57 per cent—in democracy). But the reason for this apparent similarity was that the term "ascendance" was so broad as to be somewhat meaningless psychologically. When three kinds of ascendance were distinguished, "dominating," "objective," and "friendly" ascendance, it was found that dominating ascendance was highly characteristic of the autocratic group, while objective and friendly ascendance were characteristic of the democratic group. Some illustrations of dominating ascendance:

"Shut up."

Two children look in, and Sarah and Jack repulse them with comments of "not wanted."

"You put them away; you dumped them."

"Give me some of that paint." (Remarks of this sort are classified

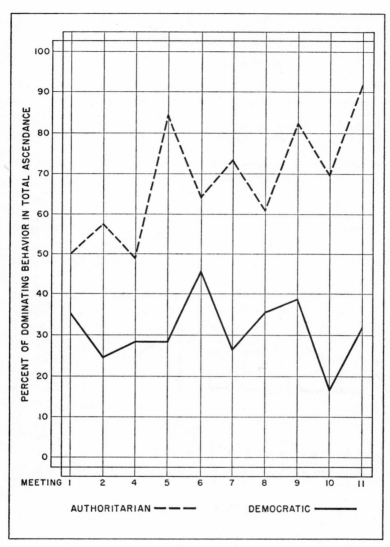

FIGURE 2. "Dominating Ascendance" in a group that behaved
aggressively in autocracy.

as dominating or objective, depending upon context and upon tone of voice. In this case it was classed as dominating.)

> "Get a pan of water, Jack."
> "Why don't you get it yourself?"

Friendly ascendance, on the other hand, occurred 24 times in the autocratic group and 34 times in the democratic group:

> Sarah: "I know how to color it."
> Jack: "Sure, you color it, Sarah."

And objective ascendance occurred 167 times in the autocratic group and 230 times in the democratic group:

> "Let's do coloring."
> "Carry the bottles over there."
> "You've got to get all the cracks filled in."
> "Better fill in your side there."

The percentage of dominating behavior in the total of all ascendant behavior is shown in Figure 2.

It will be noticed that the proportion of dominating behavior in the autocratic group tended to increase from meeting to meeting while in the democratic group it remained relatively constant. It may also be noticed that the difference between the groups was consistent; the proportion of dominating behavior in the democratic group never reached the level represented by the lowest point in the line representing the autocratic group.

Definite hostility occurred 186 times in the autocratic group and only 6 times in the democratic group. It represented 18 per cent of all the recorded social interactions in the autocratic group, and 0.6 per cent of all interactions in the democratic group. (This category is included in the larger category of dominating ascendance.) Some illustrations:

> "You guys haven't got nothing done yet."
> "Hey, you, don't throw water on my hair."
> "Look out, Tom, quit throwing things."
> "Don't start crabbing. I wouldn't talk too much yourself."
> "Oh, God, Tom, don't you know anything?"

Aggressive demands for attention occurred 39 times in the autocratic group and 3 times in the democratic group. For example:

> Joe (in a loud voice): "I guess this is a mighty fine job I'm doing!"

Tom: "I'm a lot smarter than you are. Boy-oh-boy, can I ever brag!"
Harry: "I'll say you can."

Joe: "Sure, I've got three radios; I ought to know."
All the others: "You have not!"
Joe: "Oh yes I have."

Destruction of own property was conspicuous at the end of the meetings of the autocratic group, and did not occur at all in the democratic group.

Peculiar actions begin after the leader (in the autocratic group) announces that there will be no more meetings. The leader asks Harry and Jack to put more paper on the floor to work on. They put it down and then run and jump on it time and again in a wild manner. The masks are divided out as had been decided by the voting, and Jack immediately begins to throw his around violently, pretending to jump on it. He throws it down again and again, laughing. Ray wants to know if it won't break, then starts to throw his down too. Later Jack and Harry chase each other around the room wildly with streamers of toweling.

Scapegoat behavior was conspicuous in the autocratic group, and scarcely occurred at all in the democratic group. "Scapegoat behavior" is here defined as the concentration or polarization of group aggression against a single "innocent" object—i.e., a person or group which does not actually threaten or frustrate the group to an extent comparable with the aggression that occurs. Presumably in this case the autocratic leader was the source of most of the frustration in the autocratic group, yet only a small part of the resulting aggression was directed against him; most of it was directed by the club members against each other. It could therefore be called "displaced aggression" (a deceptively simple term, covering psychological processes that may be far from simple; see Chapter 11). When this displaced aggression is concentrated against a single person, as occurred twice during the course of the meetings of the autocratic group in Experiment I, it can be called scapegoat behavior. Figure 3 shows the dramatic emergence of two successive scapegoats in the autocratic group, and the absence of any comparable developments in the democratic group.

The first scapegoat to emerge was Tom; during the fifth and sixth meetings he received much more dominating behavior than any other group member. After the sixth meeting he left the group.

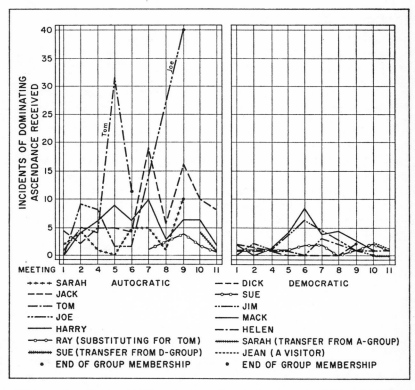

FIGURE 3.   Concentration of aggression on two scapegoats in autocracy.

(It would be fortunate for some other scapegoats if they could escape from the situation as easily as Tom did.) During the ninth meeting a similar development occurred, and the group's aggression was largely concentrated against Joe. An even higher peak of scapegoat behavior was reached, and Joe in his turn left the group.

The above facts and a number of others are summarized in Figure 4, which gives an over-all picture of the children's behavior toward each other in Experiment I.

This table brings out the facts which have already been discussed with regard to the predominance of dominating ascendance in the autocratic group, as well as hostility and aggressive demands for attention. In addition, it brings out the fact that in autocracy there was a markedly larger amount of unfriendly behavior, resistant be-

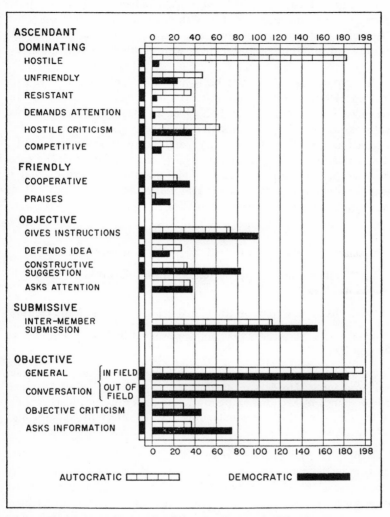

FIGURE 4. Analysis of children's behavior, Experiment I.

havior, hostile criticism, and competitive behavior, while in democracy there was more praise, more "submission," and more objective behavior, including especially "out-of-field" conversation and asking for information; and also there were more constructive suggestions.

In Experiment II, as has been indicated, only one of the four groups of boys showed the same type of aggressive reaction to autocracy. The Charlie Chan Club had an average of 45 aggressive actions per meeting, as compared with 37 in the democratic club periods and 38 in laissez-faire (not significant at 1 per cent level). The category of "aggression" was fairly comparable with the category of "dominating ascendance" in Experiment I, except that it did not include aggressive demands for attention. Some illustrations of aggression in the Charlie Chan Club:

Leonard: "Get out of here! You can't have the hammer."

Leonard: "If they get this desk dirty, I'll swat them one."

Reilly (to the outgroup): "Come on over and I'll have you a fight . . . I'm going to kill him."

Fred: "If anyone steps on this, I'm going to bust you in the mouth."

Lyman (the pacifist): "Boy, you sure spilled it. You shouldn't have broken it."

Fred is told he must ask before going behind the burlap, and is quite sullen about it. He does go behind it. . . . Fred is definitely sullen, and responds to Mr. Bohlen by muttering under his breath. (For a detailed record of this one outstanding case of direct rebellion against autocracy, see pp. 119–122).

It may be that one reason for the relatively moderate character of this aggressive reaction, as far as boy-to-boy aggression is concerned, was that in this group boy-to-boy aggression was not the only kind that was available. The adult leader himself received a considerable amount of direct and indirect aggression, as the above instance of Fred's behavior suggests. By no means all of the aggression was "displaced" in this group; much of it found expression in thoughts or actions that were hostile to the autocrat himself. Also, two outgroups were readily available as targets of aggression, and both were utilized—the Secret Agents, who met at the same time in the other half of the enclosed work space, and the "Monday gang" who met in the same spot on Monday instead of Thursday. Their work materials were by no means immune from attack when the Charlie Chan Club appeared on the scene. The possible importance of the outgroup as a target of aggression is suggested also by the fact that, in Experiment II as a whole, the proportion of aggression in all behavior toward outgroups was 42 per cent in groups under autocratic leadership and 30 per cent in groups under democratic leadership.

4. AUTOCRACY CAN CREATE DISCONTENT THAT DOES NOT APPEAR ON THE SURFACE

Less dramatic but more fundamental than the question of aggression is the question of total need satisfaction. Under which major type of leadership is there likely to be more satisfaction of the boys' own needs, and why?

The answer is far from simple. As has been indicated in Chapter 2, there is no reason to think that democracy is necessarily superior from the standpoint of immediate personal satisfaction. It is a well-established fact that autocracy is often satisfying to some of the needs—the regressive needs, perhaps—of the ruled as well as the rulers. (For a fuller discussion of this see Chapter 9.) There can be satisfactions in passivity, satisfactions in not having to think, satisfactions in identifying (on a fantasy level) with a strong, dominating leader-image. There is such a thing as "escape from freedom." On the other hand, it is also obvious, and needs no proof, that autocracy is frustrating insofar as it imposes barriers to the satisfaction of individual needs. The real problem, then, is to pin down and describe objectively the specific factors that determine whether, in a given case, the regressive need satisfactions or the frustrations will predominate. Some of the evidence bearing on this point has already been presented. The aggression shown in some of the autocratic groups points to probable frustration—if the frustration-aggression hypothesis has any weight, even as a first approximation. Also, the lack of spontaneous work interest in autocracy is a relevant fact. If the boys stopped work when the autocrat left the room, it was an indication that they had not been particularly enjoying it when he was in the room. It meant that the work had become merely a task, rather than something to be done with spontaneous zest and enjoyment. What now needs to be made clear is that much of the discontent which existed was not immediately obvious.

The deceptiveness of autocracy in this respect is a fact that needs more emphasis than it has usually received. For example, out of our six autocratic setups (one in Experiment I and five in Experiment II), five were in some degree deceptive, insofar as the discontent which existed did not show itself to any appreciable extent in protests to the autocrat himself.

In Experiment I there were many indirect indications of discontent in the autocratic group, including the scapegoating which has already been described, but literally none of it was visibly directed to the adult leader himself. If he had had a psychological need not to see the indirect indications, he could have fooled himself into thinking that things were going rather well. And in Experiment II, with its five instances of autocracy (two for the Dick Tracy Club and one for each of the others), only one brought forth an appreciable amount of overt protest. Fred's sullenly mischievous defiance (see pp. 119–122) and an incipient "sit-down strike" led by Reilly were the two outstanding instances of overt protest, and they both occurred in the Charlie Chan Club under the autocratic leadership of Mr. Bohlen.

The evidence that latent discontent did exist in at least some of the other five autocratic situations can be summarized as follows:

Four boys actually dropped out, and all of them did so during these autocratic club periods in which overt rebellion did not occur. Two of these were the two scapegoats, Tom and Joe, in Experiment I. A third was the hypersensitive child, Beaumont, who was definitely antagonized by the impersonal dictatorship of Mr. Rankin. The fourth, Steve, although he did drop out from the same club during the same Rankin regime, is probably not actually a case in point; the reasons for his dropping out seemed to be rather different and involved relations outside the group meetings. It would be fairer, then, to say simply that three boys dropped out for reasons related to a given type of club leadership, and that these three defections occurred during autocratic club periods in which discontent with the leadership did not directly manifest itself. And, since such periods constituted only five out of a total of fourteen club periods, it is not likely that chance alone accounted for the difference.

Of twenty boys who made direct comparisons between their au-

tocratic and democratic leaders, nineteen preferred the democratic leader. These comparisons were made in private interviews with a third person who was not identified in any way with the leader who was being explicitly or implicitly criticized. It was also noticeable that most of the criticisms that did occur were mild and qualified. Nevertheless, when forced to make a choice, their vote was almost unanimous. For instance:

"Mr. Bohlen (democracy) is a swell guy. If you don't like things you can decide what to do, he told us . . . We all should do what the majority wants, but we don't always. . . . The boys didn't like Mr. Rankin (autocracy). He'd make us—well, the other leaders let us—but we had to do what he said. With the other fellows we could do things they suggested or not, but not with Mr. Rankin."

"Mr. Bohlen (democracy) was a good joking fellow. . . . He takes part in the cleanup. When I was elected cleanup leader he said, 'Well, what shall I do, Ben?' . . . Mr. Rankin (autocracy) was too strict. I didn't have much fun. He wouldn't let us go out without permission."

"Mr. Rowe (democracy) is about the best one. He asks us what we want to do, and if two or three want one thing we do that next week . . . Mr. Bohlen (autocrat) lets us do a lot of things, but he wanted us to—well, he was too bossy. Maybe it wasn't exactly him, but it wasn't as much fun as with Mr. Rowe."

"I liked Mr. Rowe (democracy) best and Mr. Bohlen (autocracy) least. With Mr. Rowe we made wood carvings, and he let us go behind the burlap when we wanted to. Mr. Bohlen was too strict, especially about going behind the burlap."

"Mr. Rankin (democracy) thinks of things just like we do and was just one of us. He never did try to be the boss . . . Mr. Rowe (autocrat) was all right mostly; he was sort of dictator-like, and we had to do what he said pretty nearly."

The twentieth boy was Eddie, the son of a National Guard officer. His comment was:

"Mr. Rowe (autocrat) was the strictest, and I like that a lot. Mr. Davis and Mr. Rankin let us go ahead and fight, and that isn't good. . . . A club leader ought to keep us from loafing."

It should not be assumed that Eddie was a docile, over-regimented robot. He was ordinarily quiet and "good," but by no means lacking in independence (see pp. 192–197). His father was evidently strict in enforcing his commands, but he was also a companion to his boys, and there is no reason to think that he gave too many commands or that he was autocratic in any way except firmness of enforcement. In Eddie's mind, therefore, "strictness" had apparently become identified with this father whom he greatly admired for reasons other than strictness as such.

Discontent in autocracy was occasionally expressed even during the meetings themselves. In Experiment II, the average number of discontented remarks to other boys was 4.4 per meeting in autocracy (aggressive reaction), 2.1 in autocracy (submissive reaction), 3.1 in laissez-faire, and only 0.8 in democracy. The difference between democracy and the submissive reaction to autocracy is significant at the 1 per cent level.

Similar, but not as significant statistically, is the difference in the number of expressions of discontent directly to the adult leader. In autocracy (aggressive reaction) these averaged 11.1 per meeting; in autocracy (submissive reaction) the average was 2.0; it was 1.5 in laissez-faire and again only 0.8 in democracy. Some illustrations:

"Will you open this up?"
"Why can't we make what we want?"

In Experiment I the only comparable fact is that an apparently purposeful ignoring of what the leader said was especially characteristic of the autocratic group. Such ignoring was the response to 26 per cent of the leader's approaches in the autocratic group, and it was the response to 15 per cent of his approaches in the democratic group.

"Release" behavior on the day of transition to a freer atmosphere suggested the presence of previous frustration. As the following graphs indicate, there were three occasions when a group which had shown the submissive reaction to autocracy came out of this somewhat repressive atmosphere into the freer atmosphere of democracy or laissez-faire. In two of these cases, the first day of freedom was marked by an especially large amount of aggressive behavior (much of it playful in character).

The first explanation that suggests itself is that on these days the boys were "blowing off steam"; discontent in autocracy had led to bottled-up tension, and when the lid was off the tension discharged itself in a more or less explosive way. Actually the explanation is probably somewhat more complex than this. (For a fuller discussion see Chapter 11.) On the first day of permissive leadership, the boys apparently still had the status needs and self-assertive impulses

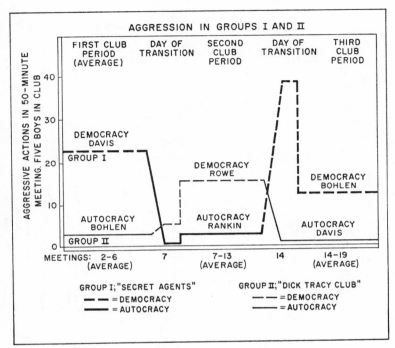

FIGURE 5.   Changing levels of aggression in two clubs. (Note spurt of aggression on first day of a freer atmosphere.)

which were frustrated by autocracy, but they no longer felt any great need to inhibit these impulses. They were in the same general situation, so that they were reminded of their former frustration, and yet their new freedom contrasted with the old restraint in such a way as to make itself prominent in the psychological field —as if each boy said to himself, "Aha! Now I can do what I've been wanting to do in this club!" On later days the thrill of new-found freedom apparently wore off, and, in addition, the spontaneous interest in work which tended to develop in democracy was stronger on later days than it was at first.

If anything of this sort entered into the observed reaction, it can be considered as tending to support the generalization that autocracy is often deceptive. The "good" and industrious behavior in the submissive reaction to autocracy does not tell the whole story. And, just as autocracy is likely to appear "better" than it actually is, so,

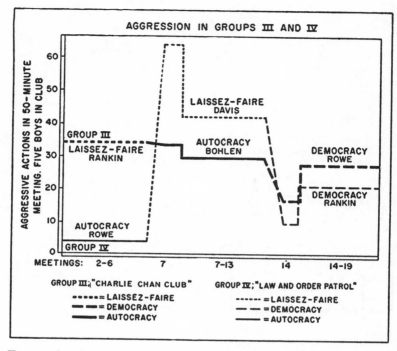

FIGURE 6.   Changing levels of aggression in two other clubs. (Again note spurt of aggression on first day of a freer atmosphere.)

by the same token, democracy is likely at first to appear "worse" than it is. Experiments in the direction of greater freedom, in any group that has been in a repressive atmosphere, may at first lead to a disappointingly large amount of disorder, but this does not necessarily mean that the disorder will be permanent.

5. THERE WAS MORE DEPENDENCE AND LESS INDIVIDUALITY IN AUTOCRACY

The evidence:

In autocracy, more of the boys' behavior was classified as "submissive" or "dependent." In Experiment I, the number of "submissive" actions toward the adult leader was 256 in autocracy and 134 in democracy. In Experiment II, the number of "dependent" remarks to the leader by each boy averaged 14 in the aggressive reaction to autocracy, 16 in the submissive reaction, 4 in laissez-faire, and 6 in democracy. Some illustrations:

"Is this O.K.?"
Bill starts to hold up his hand to ask for advice.
"Mr. Rowe, shall I paint the bottom of this or not?"

Conversation in autocracy was less varied—more confined to the immediate club situation. In Experiment II, the amount of "out-of-field" conversation was significantly less in the submissive reaction to autocracy than in any of the other three group atmospheres. The figures: democracy 14 per child per meeting, laissez-faire 13, aggressive reaction to autocracy 12, and submissive reaction—5. The difference between the last figure and any of the other three is significant at the 1 per cent level. Some illustrations of what was called "out-of-field" conversation:

Van: "Remember last night, Eddie?"
Eddie: "Yeah, did you have any bad dreams?"
Bill: "Did you see Hollywood Hotel?"
Hamil: "I did."
Bill: "That was awful good."
Finn: "I saw it too."
Hamil: "Wasn't Louella Parsons good? And Mabel Todd was good. What was she in?"

Bill: "Some day I'm going to get a job at the glass works."
Van: "I wish I could get a job."
Bill: "You should get out and get a job in the newspaper and then work yourself up. That's what I did." (He sells papers on the corner.) "And maybe some day you'll be able to get a good job."

Big conversation about pussy willows; then about places where the boys had traveled.

Leonard: "I saw your girl's picture in the paper, in the Press-Citizen. She's fat, boy."
Reilly: "She's not fat, boy. You probably didn't see her."
Leonard: "She is fat. She's not slender."

No figures are available for Experiment I, but the impression of the experimenter (Lippitt) is that the same difference held good there also.

In the submissive reaction to autocracy there was an absolute (though not a relative) reduction in individual differences in the various behavior categories. The essential fact here is that the total volume of conversation was significantly lowered in the submissive reaction to autocracy, even though the adult did not tell the boys to "keep still" or directly discourage sociability in any way. The mean total amount of recorded child-to-child conversation was 298 interactions per hour in laissez-faire, 220 in democracy, 200 in the aggressive reaction to autocracy, and, in the submissive reaction to autocracy, only 126. The difference between this and the figure for democracy is significant at the 1 per cent level. In other words, there was a sort of general subduedness in the atmosphere; the animal spirits of the boys were damped down and they kept rather soberly at work. With this reduction in total amount, the range of individual differences in amount of "aggressiveness," and "demands for attention," was correspondingly reduced. This absolute reduction in individual differences may or may not have any psychological significance, apart from the general reduction of volume with which it coincided.

The observers' impression was that in autocracy there was a loss of apparent individuality. This impression emerged unexpectedly in Experiment I when some of the observers reported that it was harder for them to remember the names of the children in the autocratic group. The individual children stood out less, and it was therefore harder to recall their names. Similar impressions were reported in Experiment II, at least in the case of the submissive reactions to autocracy. The reader of the excerpts given in this book may notice the same thing. The sharply differentiated personalities of Bill and Finn, for instance, do not appear as especially different during the autocratic period, but they come out in bold relief—and in dramatic conflict—during laissez-faire and democracy.

6. There Was More Group-Mindedness and More Friendliness in Democracy

The evidence:

The pronoun "I" was less frequent. One highly objective approach to the problem of group-mindedness is simply to count the number of times the members of a group use the pronoun *I* (or *me*, or *mine*) in comparison with the number of times they use the pronoun *we* (or *us*, or *ours*). Which is more frequent, I-centered remarks such as "I want this," or we-centered remarks such as "We need that"? In Experiment I, this appeared to be a very promising index. In the autocratic group the proportion of singular pronouns in the total of all first-person pronouns was 82 per cent, and in the democratic group only 64 per cent. In Experiment II, however, although there was some difference in the same direction, it was not statistically significant.

Spontaneous subgroups were larger. In Experiment I, a count was made of the frequency of subgroups representing the highest amount of unity possible in a five-person group (5 and 4-1) and the lowest possible amount of unity (2-1-1-1 and 1-1-1-1-1). The high-unity structures occurred 14 times in the autocratic group and 41 times in the democratic group, while the low-unity structures occurred 41 times in the autocratic group and 19 times in the democratic group. This difference is in spite of, rather than because of, the direct influence of the leader; he exerted his influence in the autocratic group much more often in the direction of higher group unity than in the opposite direction. But in autocracy his direct influence was more than balanced by a strong spontaneous tendency to group fragmentation or disintegration. (In Experiment II, this type of data was not obtained.)

"Group-minded" remarks were much more frequent. The "we/I ratio" is atomistic insofar as it deals with words out of context. The word *I*, for instance, may be used in the sentence, "I think we'd better pour in the water now." Here it does not indicate egotism or individualistic competition; in its context it is clearly subordinate to a wholly group-minded idea. More significant than the we/I ratio, therefore, is the number of remarks which—as whole sentences, seen in their context—were classified as "group-minded." This was done only in Experiment II. The results showed that the highest percentage of group-minded remarks was in laissez-faire—which is paradoxical, in view of the small amount of effective group cooperation in laissez-faire. But an analysis of the actual remarks showed that many of them expressed not the existence of group unity but a *desire* for it:

"Hey, how about us having a meeting?"
"Well, we have to do something."
"Now if we just had a club. . . ."

On the other hand, the contrast between democracy and both forms of autocracy seems to show a genuine difference in effective group-mindedness. The figures are: democracy 18, aggressive reaction to autocracy 7, submissive reaction to autocracy 4. The difference between democracy and each of the others is significant at the 1 per cent level. Some illustrations:

Finn: "I wish that guy (the hostile stranger) would stop telling us stuff and tearing down our work. We won't be able to finish it."

Eddie: "We're going to vote about it."

Finn: "We can't leave it here. It's our last day. We're all in charge of this airplane from now on."

Leonard: "I'll take it home and hang it up."
Reilly: "You won't if this club doesn't say so."

"Friendly" remarks were slightly more frequent. In Experiment I, as we have already noted, "friendly ascendance" occurred 24 times per meeting in the autocratic group to 34 times in the democratic group. Similarly, "submissive" behavior of one child to another (which might better have been called "agreeable" or "cooperative" behavior in many cases) occurred 120 times in autocracy and 188 times in democracy. The category of "friendly" behavior was not used in the analysis.

In Experiment II, the category of "friendly" was used, and a slight difference was found in favor of democracy as compared with either form of autocracy, but it was not statistically significant. The figures were: democracy 26, submissive reaction to autocracy 17. The difference between democracy and the submissive reaction was significant at only the 5 per cent level, and the difference between democracy and the other two atmospheres does not even reach the 5 per cent level of significance. It should also be noted that the *proportion* of friendliness in the total of all conversation was actually larger in the submissive reaction to autocracy than it was in democracy.

How can we account for this surprisingly large amount of mutual friendliness in the submissive reaction to autocracy? It seems likely that the unfriendliness which would naturally result from frustration is here counterbalanced by one or both of two factors: the general atmosphere of moral goodness which the presence of the leader seems to have inculcated (the boys were "on their good behavior"), and perhaps also a drawing together of the group because of the feeling that "we're all in the same boat." The common experience of being subjected to the same frustrating experience may have created a feeling of comradeship similar to that which has often been described as existing in army groups subjected to a common danger and a common discipline. In our experiments this did not result in any responsible type of group cooperativeness ("group-minded" remarks) but it does seem to have resulted in a certain amount of individual friendliness ("friendly" remarks). Many joking and half-joking remarks are included. For instance:

Finn: "Well, so long, I'm going to get my hair cut."
Van: "Look at Finn, he's going to get his head cut off."

"Now, my fine feathered friend, does this suit you O.K.?"

(Friendliness to individual in outgroup). Finn is over near the box, and Rudy (in the other group) holds up the work he is doing in a friendly manner for Finn to see.
Finn: "What is it?"
Rudy: "It's a tin can thing."

Mutual praise was more frequent. In Experiment I there were three instances of child-to-child praise per meeting in the autocratic group, to 16 in the democratic group. In Experiment II praise was not counted as a separate category, but was included in the category of "friendliness." Some instances of its occurrence, under democratic leadership:

Finn: "Well, nice going, Bill—such an idea. You could take a bit more out of that one." (Bill is Finn's archenemy but Finn is also changeable, and he is now in the best of spirits.)
Bill (reciprocating, a minute or two later): "Oh, that's good, Finn. That's a good idea. Mine's too weak."

Bill: "Oh, Van, that's coming good."

Bill (to Mr. Rankin): "Eddie really did a swell job on that, didn't he? I couldn't do as good as that."

Friendly playfulness was more frequent. In a number of "play-minded" remarks the average meeting figures for Experiment II were: laissez-faire 33, democracy 13, submissive reaction to autocracy 8, and aggressive reaction to autocracy 3. The difference between democracy and the submissive reaction is significant at the 5 per cent level. (Illustrations of "play-mindedness" have already been given on pp. 62–63, in differentiating laissez-faire from democracy.)

There was more readiness to share group property. This was shown most conspicuously in Experiment I. At the end of the meeting series, each of the two groups was asked to vote, with individual secret ballot, on the question "What would you like to have done with the masks?" In the autocratic group (in which each child had already identified with one mask) three out of four gave wholly "individualistic" answers: "Give us our masks," "Give us our mask(s)," and "Let me have mine." In the democratic group, not one of the five regular members gave a completely individualistic answer. The five answers were: "Give the pirate to Mr. Lippitt and the rest to those that had the ideas," "Give the pirate to Mr. Lippitt and divide the others," "Give them to the ones that had the ideas," "Give Diana to Miss Doe," and, "Give Diana to Miss Doe, keep the pirate for our puppet show, and then give it to Mr. Lippitt." There are no comparable data for Experiment II.

SUMMARY

A bird's eye view of the more important results of Experiment II is given in Figures 7 and 8, which represent, respectively, the boys' behavior toward their leader and toward each other. The chief differences to be noted in Figure 7 are: (1) the large number of leader-dependent actions in both reactions to autocracy; (2) the large extent of critical discontent and of aggressive behavior in the aggressive reaction to autocracy; (3) the frequency of "friendly, confiding" conversation and of group-minded suggestions in democracy; and (4) the contrast between democracy and laissez-faire in work-minded conversation.

The behavior of the boys toward each other is summarized in similar fashion in Figure 8. Here the following differences should be noticed: (1) the large difference between the two reactions to autocracy in amount of aggressive behavior, and the intermediate position of democracy and laissez-faire in this respect; (2) the generally subdued atmosphere in the submissive reaction to autocracy, as shown by the small absolute totals of aggressive behavior, attention demands, group-minded suggestions, out-of-club-field conversation, and play-minded remarks; (3) the small proportion of group-minded suggestions in both reactions to autocracy; and (4) the small amount of play-minded conversation in both reactions to autocracy, and the very large amount in laissez-faire.

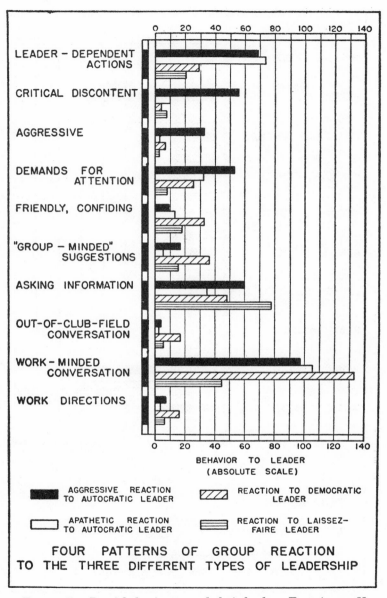

FIGURE 7. Boys' behavior toward their leaders, Experiment II.

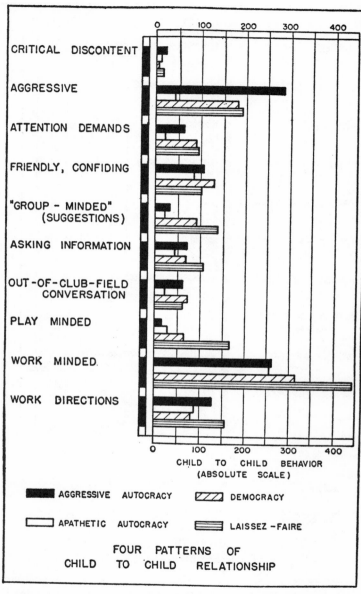

CHILD TO CHILD BEHAVIOR
(ABSOLUTE SCALE)

AGGRESSIVE AUTOCRACY   DEMOCRACY

APATHETIC AUTOCRACY   LAISSEZ-FAIRE

FOUR PATTERNS OF
CHILD TO CHILD RELATIONSHIP

FIGURE 8. Boys' behavior toward each other, Experiment II.

Summarizing, then, we can say that the statistical results and other qualitative types of evidence tend to support the following descriptive generalizations:

1. *Laissez-faire was not the same as democracy.*
   a) There was less work done in it, and poorer work.
   b) It was more characterized by play.
   c) More discontent was expressed during the meetings.
   d) In interviews the boys expressed preference for their democratic leader.

2. *Democracy can be efficient.*
   a) The quantity of work done in autocracy was somewhat greater.
   b) On the other hand, work motivation was stronger in democracy as shown for instance when the leader left the room.
   c) Originality was greater in democracy.

3. *Autocracy can create much hostility and aggression, including aggression against scapegoats.*
   a) In Experiment I, the autocratic group showed more dominating ascendance.
   b) Much more hostility (in a ratio of 30 to 1).
   c) More demands for attention.
   d) More destruction of own property.
   e) More scapegoat behavior.
   f) In Experiment II, one of the four clubs showed a similar reaction.

4. *Autocracy can create discontent that does not appear on the surface.*
   a) Four boys dropped out, and all of them did so during autocratic club periods in which overt rebellion did not occur.
   b) Nineteen out of twenty boys preferred their democratic leader.
   c) There was more discontent expressed in autocracy—even when the general reaction was submissive—than in democracy.
   d) "Release" behavior on the day of transition to a freer atmosphere suggested the presence of previous frustration.

5. *There was more dependence and less individuality in autocracy.*
   a) There was more "submissive" or "dependent" behavior.
   b) Conversation was less varied—more confined to the immediate situation.

c) In the submissive reaction to autocracy there was an absolute (though not a relative) reduction in statistical measures of individual differences.

d) The observers' impression was that in autocracy there was some loss of individuality.

6. *There was more group-mindedness, and also more friendliness, in democracy.*

a) In Experiment I, the pronoun "I" was relatively less frequent in the democratic group.

b) Spontaneous subgroups were larger.

c) In Experiment II, group-minded remarks were much more frequent in democracy.

d) Friendly remarks were slightly more frequent.

e) In Experiment I, mutual praise was more frequent in the democratic group.

f) In Experiment II, friendly playfulness was more frequent in democracy.

g) In Experiment I, the democratic group showed more readiness to share group property.

6

The Law and Order Patrol

It is time to put some meat on the bare bones of the statistics just presented. This chapter first introduces the five boys who made up the Law and Order Patrol, and then shows them in action, quoting at length from the records of the club meetings.

Eddie, Finn, Hamil, Van, Bill[1]

Eddie, the quiet favorite—A "boy's boy" who ranked first in his schoolroom in popularity according to the sociometric questionnaire (see p. 17), Eddie was also an "adult's boy" in that he was thoroughly liked and approved of by his teachers, parents, and adult club leaders. Quiet and well-behaved when the situation called for obedience and hard work, he was also physically sturdy and quite capable of roughhouse horseplay when the situation had disintegrated, under laissez-faire leadership, and the possibility of cooperative work seemed to have evaporated. Though not a leader (perhaps partly because of his apparent lack of hostile, aggressive, or even competitive attitudes), he was nevertheless thoroughly liked by the other boys; and the qualities that made him the favorite of the boys were probably similar to the qualities which made him liked by adults: emotional stability, unobtrusive self-confidence, readiness for any sort of constructive group activity, and the absence of hostility or competitiveness already mentioned.

Examples of Eddie's club behavior:

"We gotta have some plans to work on."

(Has just been elected "dictator.") Eddie goes right to work quietly and makes no use of his position. He is entirely work-centered and an-

[1] Names have all been changed to prevent identification.

89

swers quietly the two or three work-minded questions that are asked of him.

Finn, the impulsive redhead—A freckle-faced, redheaded youngster, whose outgoing exuberance won him the immediate liking of all the adults who participated in the experiment as leaders or observers. Impulsive and immediate-minded, with a constant desire for action in place of what he called "talk, talk, talk," he was a thorn in the flesh of Bill, the moralistic "would-be president"; and the conflict between them was a major theme in the club life of the Law and Order Patrol. Finn was in his element in the disorderly freedom of laissez-faire; democracy sometimes irked him, simply because discussion took up so much time.

Examples of his behavior:

(When the table breaks, on which all of the others are working): "Ha ha, everything is busted! Everything is busted, and I'm going to start busting things."

Bill (trying to get the group together for discussion): "Come on now."

Finn: "Blah!"

Bill: "Well, suppose you be quiet then."

Finn: (pompously imitating Bill): "The meeting will come to order. I want a meeting."

Hamil, the colorless—There is almost nothing to say about Hamil, since he had less apparent individuality than anyone else in the group of ten boys which we are here considering. Like Van, he took his color from his immediate social environment; but unlike Van (who stood out as somewhat immature and poorly adjusted), Hamil seemed to be more or less "average" even in maturity and adjustment. Even physically, there was nothing except his curly hair that seemed to distinguish him from the others.

Examples of his behavior:

Bill: "Come on and help me and we'll make something." Hamil complies willingly, seemingly glad to get to work.

Bill continues his catechizing of the group on civic matters, naming of crime-detection agencies, safety rules, etc. Hamil loses interest first and breaks away to begin planing a piece of wood.

Van, the childish. Van was a thin-faced boy who looked as if he had adenoids, and who acted as if he were one or two years younger than most of the others in his club. Like Hamil (the colorless), he lived in the immediate present, and took his color from his immediate social environment, with no obvious needs or standards that would characterize him as a unique individual. Essentially a follower, he oscillated between a respectful acceptance of Bill's moral ideology and a childishly irresponsible type of horseplay somewhat like that of Finn.

Examples of his behavior:

Van: "Well, we got quite a bit done today."
Bill: "Not very much."
Van: "Well, the other day we didn't get anything done. Today we got our signatures down . . . and some things."

Van yells: "You guys be Germans and I'll be Americans." He repeats this twice, but gets no response.

Bill, the would-be president—Bespectacled and earnest, though not a student, Bill had grandiose ideas of making something important of the club in which he found himself. Under his leadership it was to "clean up the city," like the real G-men after which it was named. His ambitions, however, were as impractical as they were grandiose. After achieving a transitory leadership of the group, based apparently upon their need for the definite "psychological structure" which he offered them (under laissez-faire adult leadership), his leadership evaporated as quickly as it had arisen.

Examples of his behavior:

(To Hamil and Finn, who are whittling, and paying little attention to him): "Come on, fellows, cut it out. Put them aside so you won't be monkeying with them."
(To whole group): "Now, these are our laws. I'll pass them around so you can read them." (Reads the first one): "At school, prevent all fights and scraps between the children."

SUMMARY OF REACTIONS TO THE THREE GROUP ATMOSPHERES

We have already had two "glimpses" of the behavior of this group, under laissez-faire and democratic leadership (pp. 55–60), and the reader may now want to reread these, with special attention to the different roles of the five boys who have just been described, and their different reactions to the two types of leadership. In general the group was not a difficult one to handle. Its first experience was autocracy, to which it reacted submissively. This submissive re-action could perhaps have been predicted from the fact that the group was composed of two very conscientious, "adult-value-cen-tered" boys (Eddie and Bill), two characterless boys (Hamil and Van) who took their cue in this instance from Eddie and Bill, and only one boy (Finn) who was not at all adult-value-centered. Even Finn conformed, readily enough, to the very strong atmosphere of obedient work-mindedness. Next, under laissez-faire leadership, the group showed at first a good deal of responsiveness to Bill's efforts to provide effective organization and definite structure; it was only his marked lack of realism and organizing skill (including his com-plete lack of ability to handle Finn) which frustrated the general desire for organization and led to complete group disintegration. Finally, under democratic adult leadership, the desire for organiza-tion was satisfied without repressing individuality, and the group became fairly productive and harmonious—except for the fact that the conflict between Bill and Finn, which had been gathering strength throughout the laissez-faire period, did not actually come to a head until the democratic period.

Excerpts from an Autocratic Meeting (Submissive Reaction)

(Note the predominance of the autocrat, Mr. Rowe, in the con-versation record; his firm but not unfriendly manner; the depend-ence of the children upon him for work directions; and the general absence of differentiation as between the children. Their separate individualities had little opportunity to show themselves under the autocratic leadership and the uniformly work-minded reaction of the group to it. This excerpt can be a short one, since the atmos-phere did not change appreciably during the whole period of auto-cratic leadership.)

Observers' Record	Interpretive Comments
Mr. Rowe: "Eddie is going to be 1-X, we'll let Finn be 2-X, Hamil 3-X, Van 4-X, and Bill is 5-X."	
Hamil: "Wouldn't it be bet-ter to have them arranged ac-cording to slips of paper, and then—"	

Mr. Rowe: "We're going to have it this way now."

Mr. Rowe: "Yours is all done, isn't it, Eddie, you can paint with him."

Disregard for boy's idea.

Bill: "Shall we start painting now?"

Bill asks for guidance.

Mr. R.: "Yes, you can start painting now."

Mr. R.: "That's enough; you'll have to get a stick, Bill."

Mr. R.: "Cut some string and make aprons out of those. Here, cut this down here: the scissors are right there."

Detailed work directions.

Mr. R.: "Use paper towels for that."

Bill: "Use paper towels?"

Mr. R.: "You'll have to give that two coats."

Van: "I know it."

No interest in boy's previous knowledge.

Mr. Rowe is standing with hands in his pockets.

Leader does not identify himself with group by working with them.

Mr. Rowe: "Bill, I'll put you in charge of the table for awhile." Eddie raises his eyebrows, but paints diligently on the table. Bill says to Eddie: "That's going to show through . . . No, get down there in the other corner . . . Let's do it with a straight stroke now. Sort of do it like this, Eddie."

Bill, given the role of deputy leader, takes on Mr. Rowe's manner of authoritative but work-minded superiority. An ideology of supervisory status has been created.

Mr. R.: "All right, put your brush away and each of you cut off a piece of brown paper over there."

Bill: "Where?"

Mr. R.: "There."

Bill: "About how big?"

Mr. R.: "About like this. The scissors are right there."

Leader does not give time perspective, or reasons for his commands.

EXCERPTS FROM THE FIRST LAISSEZ-FAIRE MEETING

Observers' Record

Interpretive Comments

Mr. Davis is there ahead of the boys, and greets them with a smile when they come in rather noisily.

Someone asks, "Can we make a sign for the club today?" Mr. Davis answers, "You can do whatever you'd like to do."

Mr. D. defines the new ideology very simply.

Van: "O.K., we will, then."

Bill (to Mr. Davis): "Boy, what a cell there (on the burlap hangings, painted by the other club)! I'd hate to be behind those bars."

Bill gladly makes friends with the potentially powerful adult.

Finn, Eddie and Bill gather around the "Secret Agents" sign of the other club, while Van is already getting paint ready.

Bill, to Mr. Davis: "Let's make some plans."

Need for structure is manifest almost at once, especially in Bill.

Hamil, to Mr. D.: "I don't know what to do." (He is wandering around aimlessly.)

Bill (to Finn): "Let's have 'law' on one side and 'order' on the other."

Bill and Eddie start painting as Hamil still wanders around, and then begins to get a brush and paint ready like the others.

Van to Bill, but looking at Mr. Davis: "Let's give up 'Sherlock Holmes' (the name given to the club by the autocrat during the previous series of autocratic meetings) and have a Law and Order Patrol, huh?"

They want to change the name given to them by the autocrat. A gesture of belated rebellion?

Mr. D.: "Anything is O.K. with me."

Finn (to Mr. D.): "What kind of Law and Order? How do you spell it?" Mr. D. spells it out, as requested.

Bill to Hamil: "Hey, suppose you get busy."

Hamil reaches over and rubs Van's head playfully but rather hard with his knuckles.

Van: "Boy, that hurt, even if it didn't have no force to it."

Finn (to Hamil): "Hey, do you want somebody to pull your hair?"

Hamil: "Aw, quit arguing."

Hamil has an accident, letting some paint run down over the city jail picture.

Finn: "Aha, look what somebody did!"

Van: "I bet you two bucks that was Hamil."

Hamil: "Oh, I didn't do all that."

Bill: "Yeh, you didn't do all that."

Finn: "That's the end of the city jail; we gotta tear it down. It's ruined."

Eddie laughs.

Hamil threatens Eddie and Bill with his brush full of paint.

Bill (to Finn): "Let's not put any more paint on that picture. You'll ruin it."

Finn: "Aw, nuts to Hamil."

Hamil goes and brings in a piece of beaverboard with Bill, but Mr. Davis has to tell them that it doesn't belong to the club. Hamil puts the board back.

Everyone is wandering around at loose ends.

Mr. D. gives information, but only when asked.

Verbal and physical horseplay are developing.

A rather small precipitating factor disintegrates the group as a working and socially cohesive unit.

Bill, who is very adult-value-centered, is becoming more and more dissatisfied with the disorder. He protests against "ruining" property.

Van sits on the bench rather forcefully.

Finn (who made the bench himself): "Hey, git off, that might break."

Bill: "We don't want to ruin anything."

Bill protests again against ruining property.

Hamil and Eddie sit on the bench with Van, with much laughing, and it breaks.

Finn hits Van over the head: "I'll kick you off. You're cracked."

Bill: "Why don't we start on something? Something that we can get interested in?"

Bill (to Mr. D.): "Let's get started on something that we can get interested in."

Mr. D.: "What would you like to do?"

Finn: "Aw, we're interested. He's a heap big nut." (i.e., Bill is)

Actually, Finn is probably the only one in the group who is not feeling bored, restless, and eager for something definite to do. They are in a mood to be fairly receptive to Bill's ideas, when he begins to take some initiative.

Bill (to Mr. D.): "Well, I wish we had some paper."

Mr. D.: "Well, I guess there's some paper over there."

Finn and Hamil are making passes at one another.

Van has finished nailing up the sign he made and calls attention to it. Nobody makes any response. Van is disgusted and sits listlessly on a box.

Bill: "Let's do something."

Mr. D.: "Well, what are you interested in doing, Bill?"

Bill: "I want to do some secret detective work and keep in touch with the newspapers, and want ads, and all that. I listen to the Gang Busters—the inside facts of crooks and what they have done, and then they give some clues at the end that they read. I usually take them down, if they're anywhere near Iowa."

Finn: "We'll take them down anyway. I listen every day."

No one is very involved in Bill's ideas yet except himself.

Bill, Van, and Eddie are sitting doing nothing, and Finn and Hamil are fooling around wrestling.

Finn (to the outgroup, in a friendly voice): "Hey, want a job? Come over here and knock this guy (Hamil) crazy."

Hamil (to the outgroup): "No, come over here and try to knock senses into him (Finn)."

Bill (to Hamil, in impatient voice): "I'm trying to figure out a real club here."

Filled with his one idea, Bill has little conception of how to be tactful at the same time.

Van holds his hand over Finn's eyes and Finn struggles to turn around and wrestle with him.

Bill (in irritated voice): "Here, boys, I thought we were supposed to make this club a better one."

Van (still wrestling): "Yes, we ought to practice special grips."

Van: "Let's nominate a president. Let's vote for a leader."

Bill: "We've already got a leader" (looking at Mr. Davis).

Since the surrounding culture is politically a democracy, democratic ideas crop up even in this laissez-faire group.

Van: "I mean one of the boys."

Eddie: "Yah, let's vote for a leader."

Bill: "Let him (Mr. Davis) elect us."

An attempt by Bill to get deputy leadership by apple polish-

Finn: "No, we'll all vote among ourselves and I'll tell you the names."

Eddie: "We'll close our eyes and put up our hands."

Van (to Mr. D.): "You tell us the names, and we'll hold up our hands if we want them, and we can only vote once, and we'll keep our eyes shut."

Finn: "Yah, we can only vote once."

Hamil (to Mr. D.): "Why don't you have anybody vote for you too if they want to?"

Mr. D. declines to be considered a candidate.

Mr. D.: "Go ahead, name somebody."

Bill: "Wait—you name each one in the group, and then we'll keep our eyes shut and put our hands up for the one we want, and you tell us which one gets it."

Mr. D.: "O.K., how many vote for Van?" (None.) "How many vote for Hamil?" (None.) "How many vote for Finn?" (None.) "How many vote for Bill?" (Three—Van, Finn, and Eddie.) "How many vote for Eddie?" (One—Bill.)

"All right, hands down. Bill got it." The group in general seems pleased about the results.

Hamil: "I didn't vote."

Finn: "Why didn't you? Did you want to vote for yourself?"

Hamil: "O.K., then Eddie gets my vote, so that's two for Eddie."

Bill: "First, let's pick up our things."

ing? Or real need for adult guidance?

Even the idea of a secret ballot (eyes closed) seems to be more or less familiar and accepted.

Hamil seems to have a real need for adult guidance, but the laissez-faire leader refuses this role. Hamil may also be antagonistic to Bill (see below).

The election of Bill is interesting, since his sociometric status in school was considerably below Eddie's. This probably reflects the boys' need for structure, which no adult is providing, and Bill's strong initiative in trying to provide it.

Hamil is probably antagonistic to Bill, or he would not stay off the bandwagon so publicly.

Van: "Come on, we must do what he says."

All but Hamil hurry to follow out orders and pick things up quickly.

Bill: "Now, if we can get some good clean paper we can make plans for something."

Finn: "Oh come on, we've gotta vote for second."

Bill to Mr. Davis (ignoring Finn): "Hey listen, how long have we got to play yet?"

Mr. D.: "Well, about five or ten minutes."

Van: "He (Bill) can name us (for other officers)."

Finn (in disgusted tone): "Aw, why don't we have a majority?"

Though Finn is sometimes bored by too much talk, he enjoys the self-government aspect of democracy.

Bill stands in back of the table, separated from the rest of the group, and begins to name the other officers, ignoring the fact that there is any controversy over the method of choosing them.

Bill: "Eddie can be captain. I'm inspector general. You (Van) can be colonel-lieutenant, and sergeant for you (Finn), and the rest of you can be just lieutenants." (Hamil has been omitted from the specific naming, either on purpose or by mistake.)

This ignoring of Finn's democratic impulse by Bill is apparently the beginning of the long feud between them, which comes to a head several meetings later.

Finn: "Aw, why don't we have a couple of privates? Anyhow, I'm second lieutenant."

Finn to Hamil: "You're just a plain leevie—that's what we call lieutenants at home."

Finn raises his own rank; partly joking defiance of Bill?

Hamil sits alone and looks as though he is about ready to cry. There have been some comments

A disadvantage in any thoroughgoing status hierarchy—someone feels lowest. And, because their

tossed around about lieutenants being the lowest rank, and he isn't even sure he is that. He feels completely isolated.

Finn's restlessness also looks like dissatisfaction with the fact that he was named to the next-lowest rank of sergeant.

Bill: "Now we'll make our plans."

Hamil to Finn (trying to sound boastful): "I'm special on the job."

Finn and Hamil make some comments to the other club.

Bill (to Finn and Hamil, pounding the table): "Order! Come on, turn around and listen."

Hamil: "Well, what am I?" (i.e., what rank)

Bill (ignoring the question): "Now if you'll wait we'll plan to get together at certain times for special arrangements, and we want to cut all laws and reports out of the newspapers. And all crimes that have just been solved, and we'll get some kind of cigar box to keep our belongings in so that the other kids won't get them."

Van: "I can bring a cigar box."

Finn: "I could bring lots of paper. My brother gives me lots of it."

Hamil is showing more cheerfulness on his face, but not the enthusiastic participation of the others.

newfound organization has not yet led to real work-mindedness, the boys are still very status-minded.

Definite suggestions find an enthusiastic reception.

Note: The first meeting under laissez-faire, which has just been presented, was followed by the one reported as a "glimpse" on pp.

55–58). It will be noted that Bill's hold on the group continued through the first several minutes of the next meeting, but that after the table broke down the forces of group disruption were too much for him. The later meetings under laissez-faire leadership presented the same picture—Bill trying unsuccessfully to bring some order out of the chaos, with some help from Eddie and much hindrance from Finn.

The typical behavior of the group under the subsequent democratic adult leadership is well represented by the glimpse already given (pp. 58–60). In addition, we present here an excerpt from the fourth democratic meeting, not because it is especially typical of democracy (though the consecutiveness of the discussion should be noticed), but because it brings out certain aspects of ideology, and carries to its climax the little drama between Bill and Finn.

Excerpts from a Democratic Meeting

Observers' Record   *Interpretive Comments*

At the previous meeting, Van and Bill had proposed "having an army," with salutes, etc., and Finn had opposed the idea. Discussion of it was postponed to this meeting, and postponed again during the first part of this meeting, which consisted of a "crime." Finn and Van played the coveted role of criminal, while Eddie was the corpse, and Bill and Hamil were the detectives. The detectives failed to solve the mystery, and, according to the record, Finn was "quite verbal in his triumph." The boys are at last ready to discuss "having an army."

Mr. Rankin: "Well, let's have our regular meeting. Let's see that every point of view is represented. Who wants to talk in favor of the army idea?"

Bill (to the group; there is quite a bit of shouting still): "Well listen, if we all have different salutes we won't get any place. We ought to have one salute to use, and when we meet each other act decent, and be kind, and all that sort of stuff. If we did that we could have fun—much more fun, won't we?"

Bill is still promoting an authoritarian and moralistic ideology, and probably feels that he now has some support from Mr. Rankin.

"Won't we"—not "wouldn't we." A verbal *fait accompli* illustrating Bill's tendency to grandiose thinking, on the level of unreality.

Mr. Rankin: "Does anybody second the idea that we have an army?"

Hamil: "I second it."

Van: "Well, I'm in favor of it."

Eddie: "I'm in favor of it, or something like an army, but not come up and salute, and stuff like that."

Mr. Rankin (to the group): "Do you know what a regular army is like?"

Word needs definition. Leader offers realistic information. (Note: The year is 1938; the boys have had very little knowledge of army life.)

Finn: "I don't."

Hamil: "I do. They have drills and—(he is interrupted by much loud and somewhat irrelevant conversation).

Mr. Rankin: "We ought to listen to what Hamil has to say, and take our turns." (The volume goes down considerably.)

Hamil: "My father was in the army, and it's no roses either."

Van: "Well, they don't have a special step. They just walk around in step."

Unlike the laissez-faire leader, this one actively tries to promote the skills and attitudes of democracy.

Bill (to Mr. R.): "Here's a good salute" (demonstrates).

Finn (to Bill): "Don't interrupt a guy when he's talking."

Mr. R.: "One thing about an army is that one person has almost all the say."

Van: "Not in the United States Army."

Mr. R.: "Yes, it's just ·the same in our army."

Finn: "Well, we don't want a regular army."

Van: "We don't want to have it just like any particular army. We want it so they can go up high [i.e., plenty of promotions]. We would obey orders, but we would all have something to do with it."

Bill: "Van's got something there."

Van: "Sure, if we have any good ideas we could give them to the officer. We want somebody that will let other people vote."

Finn: "We'll vote again for the highest officer."

Van: "We want to vote again for a different officer."

Mr. Rankin: "Well, we could vote again, but after that the officer appoints all the other officers. That's the way it is in the army."

Finn: "I think it's O.K. if we don't salute too much, and I say we need a new high officer. Bill is too goofy."

Hamil: "Well, I'm not so much in favor of it (the army). If we have one officer we all go down to private and the privates in the army have all the work to do."

Bill is obviously pouting at the idea of a new head officer and at the criticisms he is receiving. He turns rather aggressively on Hamil and Finn: "You don't have such good ideas. If you'd

Not a bad definition of democracy itself: "We would obey orders, but we'd all have something to do with it." Is this a criticism of Bill?

Finn and Van are both playing leader roles unusual for them. Is it because of their recent triumph in the crime game?

listen once in a while you'd get some good ones."

Bill: "I think we should all stay in the same rank."

Finn: "Listen to him; he knows he won't get back (to his present high rank). He won't get my vote."

Hamil: "Bill is all crazy in the head."

Bill: "Well, go ahead and have an election then."

Eddie (coming to Bill's rescue): "Well, if you guys would listen to him he'd have some good ideas for you."

Mr. Rankin: "Well, it looks like the majority would like a new election."

Bill has started crying openly, but doesn't get a great deal of sympathy.

Finn (derisively): "Hey, anybody got a handkerchief? Bill wants to wipe his eyes."

Bill (recovering with remarkable speed): "Well, I still think we ought to keep our ranks until we are really started with an army, and then if we still want officers we could have an election."

Van: "We might vote to reelect."

Finn: "We've already voted to decide on a new commander-in-chief, and I nominate Eddie."

Hamil: "I second Eddie."

Van: "I'll nominate myself."

Mr. Rankin: "Do you want a secret ballot?"

Hamil: "Yah, a secret ballot." (Mr. R. begins to prepare paper.)

Hamil (the colorless) and Van (the childish) are both now taking their cue from Finn instead of Bill. Bill has completely proved his ineptness, and under the democratic adult leadership they no longer look to Bill as a possible giver of structure.

Bill struggles with no little skill to maintain the *status quo*.

Van is probably not joking; his need for status is childishly undisguised.

Bill: "Listen, Van, come here. I want to say something." (Bill takes Van out of the room.)

Hamil: "I knew something like that would happen."

Finn: "Those two hadn't ought to vote."

Bill and Van return almost immediately.

Bill: "I nominate Van."

Van: "I nominate Bill."

Mr. R. pauses to point out that Eddie is the only candidate whose nomination has been seconded.

Bill (tries another flash to save the day): "I'll make another nomination—Mr. Rankin."

Mr. R.: "No, I can't be it. The club is for you fellows."

Finn to Bill: "Nobody's seconded your nomination, and you can't second yourself."

Bill (tries still another tack, turning to Mr. Rankin): "I think you should do the nominating." Again Mr. R. has to turn down Bill's face-saving idea, but Eddie comes through with a second for the nomination of Bill.

Finn puts through a vote that the candidates can't vote; he seems to feel that Bill might vote for himself and save the day. Finn and Hamil vote for Eddie, and Van for Bill, and that settles it.

Bill immediately buttonholes Eddie and gets him to decide on the new officers. When Finn sees this going on he remarks, "I'll bet I'm last."

His prophecy was correct. Eddie's appointments were:

Bill has sensed Van's need for status, and realized that he is the most buyable member of the opposition.

Eddie, being very adult-value-centered, feels that Bill is a kin-

Bill—general
Van—colonel
Hamil—lieutenant
Finn—sergeant

Hamil (to Mr. R.): "I knew there was dirty work around here."

Finn (to Mr. R.): "I heard Bill speak to Eddie."

Bill: "He can do that. He can ask advice from a lot of people, but he can use his own judgment too."

Mr. Rankin: "His duty is to use his own judgment. Nobody should be telling him what to do."

Eddie seems inspired by this: "If I think any of you need promoting you get it, and if I don't think you do, you stay there."

Bill: "That's it. Now you're talking, Eddie."

Van (to Finn, with a smirk): "That's right. He can do it too."

Bill (authoritatively): "Well, next week is the salutes, and that's your job, Eddie."

Finn (with a sneer): "Yah, think up a good goofy salute." (Exit)

dred spirit. He also shares Bill's disapproval of the unabashed aggression recently shown by Finn (and Hamil to a lesser extent).

"Being last" apparently does not bother Finn, who has never especially aspired to status. He has had his triumph over Bill, and that is what matters.

7

The Charlie Chan Club

THE boys in this club were:

Reilly, the popular hell-raiser—Blond, slick-haired, and good-looking, Reilly was fairly bursting with aggressive good spirits and animal vitality. According to the sociometric questionnaire, he was the best liked boy in the fifth grade of the McKinley School. In many ways, though, his personality was at the opposite pole from that of Eddie, who was the best liked boy in the fifth grade of the Jackson School. Where Eddie was conscientious, quiet, unassuming, and genuinely friendly, Reilly was exuberant, self-advertising, and apparently successful in getting a rather gullible public to accept him at his own evaluation. Though not as clownishly smart-aleck as Leonard, nor as sullenly rebellious as Fred, Reilly's competitive self-assertion and shrewdness in handling adults made him very much of a problem for the adult leaders who were unfortunate enough not to win his liking or respect.

Examples of his behavior:

Reilly: "No, you guys are going to use green."
Leonard: "Who said we weren't going to use blue? We can use it if you can."
Reilly: "We'll just sock you in the mouth, then."
Leonard: "Oh yeah?"

Reilly interrupts and contradicts Mr. Rankin (who is playing a laissez-faire role) although Mr. R. isn't even talking to him. . . . Reilly pompously explains to Mr. R. that his and Sam's models are in the rafters. Reilly is very condescending to Mr. R., talking to him as a peer and sometimes even as he would boss about a younger boy.

Fred, the rebellious hell-raiser—Loose-jointed and unkempt, Fred was more definitely a disciplinary problem than any other of the

107

ten boys we are describing here. When his happy-go-lucky horseplay was restricted by an autocratic leader, he changed from a happy-go-lucky fun seeker to a sullen and defiant rebel. During one whole meeting the chief preoccupation of the leader was how to control Fred, and Fred's chief preoccupation was to see how far he could go without causing the leader to use the ultimate sanction—exclusion from the club.

Examples of his behavior:

Fred (joking): "I have a rocking chair instead of a stool. Look, I have a rocking chair instead of a stool."

Fred yells for nails. Mr. Rowe shows him where they are and says there are plenty. He mutters under his breath, "Yeah, two or three," and threatens to "bend them all over" instead of pounding them in as ordered. He is getting in an ugly mood.

Leonard, the smart-aleck hell-raiser—Small, freckled, and irrepressible, Leonard was as little interested in constructive work and as much interested in aggressive horseplay as Reilly or Fred. Unlike the horseplay of Reilly or Fred, however, his clowning was so silly, so purely attention-seeking, and occasionally so mischievous that it did not endear him to the other boys. On the contrary, he was the least liked boy in the Charlie Chan Club, and the other boys sometimes expressed real irritation with him for disrupting their work. This disapproval, instead of deterring him from continuing with the clownish behavior which brought it down upon him, seems to have increased it—since (we may infer) he continued to act on the largely mistaken assumption that his type of horseplay was *the* way to get the group approval which he did not have. In his unrealistic "psychological environment," his smart-aleck type of horseplay was the "distinguished path" to group acceptance.

Examples of his behavior:

Leonard and Fred notice that the outgroup is building a house and raising walls, and they are disturbed. Leonard sings out in a loud voice, "The bedbugs made a home run; the pitcher was asleep," and adds, "We probably got some of their paint brushes." Sam says, "Oh we do not, you dumb Leonard." Some one on the other side is counting, and Leonard chimes in with "Ten."

Leonard has given up any pretense of being busy and is just tearing around raising the roof. Leonard is flipping water off the end of his brush. Then Fred begins to chase Leonard, and Leonard yells, "Watch him, Sam. I'm throwing water on him and he's chasing me."

Sam, the work-minded normal—One had to respect Sam. In the peculiarly constituted Charlie Chan Club, with its three "hell-raisers" and one "unboyish misfit," he played the role of sturdy independence. He combined a good deal of constructive work with a full participation in the aggressive horseplay of the majority whenever—in his own good time—he decided to take part in it. Usually quiet, he could shout with the best of them when he felt like it. He was not a leader, though, nor was he especially well liked—possibly because his healthy self-sufficiency did not give others the feeling that he especially needed their friendship or depended on their approval.

Examples of his behavior:

Sam seems a purposive, determined, rather self-sufficient boy. . . . He is not as loud as he was at the first meeting, and has done a lot of work.

Only Sam is still working; he asks Mr. Rankin if his clay is stirred up enough, and says again, "Look out, you guys."

Lyman, the unboyish misfit—Tall, but physically inadequate, Lyman was usually dressed in an ill-fitting, musty-looking suit, while the other boys wore shirts or sweaters. While they were shouting and "horsing around" he was often awkwardly sitting or standing on the fringe of the group, in placid bewildered immobility. The outstanding scholar and pacifist in the group, he was also socially the most peripheral, and quite possibly the worst adjusted of any of the twenty boys in the second experiment.

Yet, curiously enough, he never became a scapegoat. The reason, possibly, may have been that he was physically so unformidable, and socially so completely innocuous from the standpoint of threatening anyone else's status or frustrating anyone else's activities. The others tolerated him—and ignored him. For them it was almost as if he did not exist.

Examples of his behavior:

Seems to be most inadequate and dependent—can't find anything to do by himself . . . Still just watching . . . Watching, and would like to join, but doesn't quite know how.

Argument between group members (except Lyman) on who is going to paint. Lyman pays no attention.

SUMMARY OF REACTIONS TO THE THREE TYPES OF LEADERSHIP

It was the Charlie Chan Club which first forced upon the authors of this book the concept of laissez-faire as something different from democracy. At the beginning of the second experiment it was placed under Mr. Rankin's supposedly democratic leadership, but by the end of the third meeting the atmosphere had become so anarchic, and the leader so generally ignored, that it was clearly as different from a well-integrated democracy as a well-integrated democracy was different from autocracy. Accordingly a virtue was made of necessity, and from that point on, Mr. Rankin deliberately restricted his attempts to participate in the group life, and consciously conformed to the definition of laissez-faire leader behavior which was set up at that time. The anarchy, of course, continued.

There were probably two reasons for the initial breakdown of integration: Mr. Rankin's lack of group-work experience, and the mischance which led to the inclusion of Reilly, Fred, and Leonard all in the same group. It is probable that they were naturally the three worst "hell-raisers" in the whole experiment; but, whether or not they would have acted the same way if separated, putting them together certainly made an explosive combination.

Next, under autocratic leadership, the group showed the aggressive reaction rather than the submissive one which was shown by three clubs in this second experiment. Their aggression was directed partly against scapegoats—outgroups, and each other—but also partly against the autocrat himself.

Fred's active rebellion was very difficult to handle, and Reilly led a sort of "sit-down strike" which at first threatened to end the group itself.

Finally, under the experienced democratic leadership of Mr. Rowe, the group settled down and became fairly well integrated and productive.

A LAISSEZ-FAIRE MEETING

Observers' Records   *Interpretive Comments*

Reilly comes in, takes off his coat and hat and sits down nonchalantly to take off his galoshes. Fred, Leonard, and Sam follow:

Leonard is whistling. There is a great deal of loud talk and hilarity. They open the chest of work materials.

Mr. Rankin comes in with Lyman. (As always, the adult leader has brought the boys in a car from their school. The other four boys have run ahead into the clubroom, but Lyman has lagged behind with Mr. Rankin.) Lyman walks around and takes off his coat. He is not greeted by the boys, and makes no comment.

Leonard and Fred have a squabble in a friendly way. Leonard is whistling all the time loudly through his hands. General confusion. Leonard is trying to climb the beams.

General disorganization. Fred goes and gets a long board. Reilly goes over to him and they discuss their problem. Mr. Rankin explains to Sam how to make a mask which he has asked about.

Mr. Rankin is still talking to Sam, but when Fred comes up, Sam ignores Mr. R. and talks to Fred. Lyman is standing watching Sam.

Leonard: "Is this yours, Sam?"

Sam: "Yes, but you can break it up."

Leonard: "I want to rip Walker's and Schmidt's." (Walker and Schmidt are in the Monday club—the group from the same schoolroom which meets here on Monday instead of Thursday.)

All the boys' voices are very loud. Leonard and Sam aggressively defend what they consider their rights against Lyman and

Lyman probably has two reasons for lagging: lack of physical energy, and lack of psychological closeness to the group.

Characteristic confusion.

Disregard for adult leader.

Lack of pride in own work.

Persisting hostility to the Monday club—with no provocation, as far as could be discovered.

This aggressiveness (aggressiveness is a better word here than "aggression") does not seem to be a result of frustration. All the

Reilly. Reilly goes out and gets another saw, knocking the tool chest around in the process. This is as obstreperous as this group has yet been. (It is the sixth laissez-faire meeting.) They are like little bickering animals.

The rest of the outgroup comes in. Loud greetings are exchanged. Leonard shouts, "Hello! How do you do! They hide their water, the snakes."

Lewin enters and talks with the two leaders, Davis and Rankin. All three leave the room.

Sam: "They are painting guns over there" (pointing to the outgroup).

The group is now all lined up on this side, watching the outgroup and looking up into the rafters. Fred tries to climb up and isn't as successful as he had hoped. Reilly says, "Get down, I'll go up." Fred then goes up another rafter.

Mr. Rankin returns and gives the boys the glad news: "I just heard some news. We are going to have the opportunity to make a large picture, of a fireboat on the river. It's for the kindergarten room over at the preschool. We can paint it. It's drawn already."

It's their first clear opportunity for cooperative work. Reilly and Fred dash madly out, apparently to get the poster. Sam keeps on with his work; Lyman just sits. Leonard urges Sam to get a paintbrush before they are all gone.

Mr. Rankin, Fred, and Reilly

boys are in good spirits except Lyman and he is not overtly aggressive. It is rather a case of highly competitive, self-assertive individualism with few inhibitions, and with a premium on joking hostility as a hallmark of real group membership. It is, however, a fertile soil for genuine aggression, since mutual jostling can lead to anger, and the absence of cooperative achievement leads to idleness, restlessness, and increasing frustration.

Sam is probably jealous of the democratic group's work efficiency.

With the leader out, the potency of the work situation declines still further. Now even Sam is idle. The whole group is in an "unstructured field," and casting about for something to do.

This is one of the planned experimental situations (which also included the leader's leaving the room, and, later, criticism by a hostile stranger).

Since the new task seems to offer simultaneously a new experience and a clearly structured field, the initial reaction of the group is an eager one—at least on the part of those boys (Reilly, Fred, and Leonard) who have been most restless. The prospect of real cooperation may be an-

return with the poster. They leave Mr. R. to adjust it, which is more than one person can do, while they all dash around and try to grab a brush. Leonard says to Sam: "Get a brush. We are going to paint it, you dope." Sam answers, "I know it," and bestirs himself now to get a brush. Reilly comes to Mr. R.'s assistance.

Everything in the room seems to fall on the floor. Everybody yells. Leonard and Reilly accuse the other group of having taken the paints. Leonard says, "You robber. Give us that back. They got it."

It's a bit difficult to get the group to divide the paints with the outgroup. Leonard says, "Do you really want this paint?"

Mr. Rankin leaves the room for a minute. Bedlam breaks loose. Everyone quarrels about just what part they are going to paint. Every boy for himself. Sam says, "Who drew it? They can't draw." They are now all gathered in front of the poster, making derogatory remarks about the drawing.

Sam suggests that one of them make everything red and one of them everything blue. This is their first effort at organization and division of labor. Fred boos him.

They are all busy painting, even Lyman. They are quiet and intent, until Leonard yells out to the outgroup, in an extra loud

other factor, but in these particular boys it is probably a minor one.

The slightest cue from the environment is enough to touch off verbally hostile behavior. The outgroup, the Monday club, each boy as a competitor of each other boy, and even the imagined person who drew the picture, evoke loud, good-natured criticism.

(It is interesting that neither Lyman nor the adult leader does evoke such criticism. They are usually ignored and occasionally dominated, but not criticized. This may be because neither of them offers enough of a challenge to be interesting.)

There is resistance even to *seeing* the objective desirability of a division of labor. The psychological environment, set in a competitive pattern, is relatively uninfluenced by the "real," objective environment. Or, to put it differently, the potency of the work situation is so low (except for Sam) that not even the most

voice, "You guys must be dumb. Thought it was a rock garden." There is good-natured bickering within the group too. Fred says, "That's what you think," and Leonard retorts, "You couldn't think."

Becker (the "hostile stranger" whose role is to criticize the group, as one of the planned experimental situations) comes in with a ladder looking like a janitor. He is obviously going to repair the lights. Leonard says, "Got some new lights. We won't stand for this. Never. Maybe it will be lighter when he gets a new one in." (Becker has taken out the bulb and it has gotten rather dark.) They all stop work and watch and comment. When the light comes back on they all continue. When Becker is on the stepladder Sam says, "Ride 'im, cowboy!" and when the light goes on, Leonard says, "Thank you, Mister."

Becker: "Is this a regular club meeting? . . . What are you doing that for?"

Sam: "Painting for the preschool."

Becker (looking at it very critically): "That's a pretty sloppy job. Look at the lines there. That's a pretty crooked line."

Most of them ignored Becker at first; now they all agree with his criticism.

Fred: "I can't help that. Don't blame me."

Sam (good naturedly): "You drew it, didn't you?"

rudimentary sort of creative thinking occurs with reference to it. To Fred, booing Sam is much more interesting than listening to him.

Since work efficiency is not a primary basis of this group's competitiveness, they do not much resent criticism on that score. But when Becker's criticism begins to appear as "being mean," so that their social status begins

Becker (continuing the attack): "Look at this."

Leonard (taking up the cudgels): "I don't think he can see straight."

Becker: "I wouldn't want that on my wall."

Leonard: "It isn't your wall."

Sam: "We didn't ask your advice."

They all talk at once.

Leonard: "You're talking politics and we're talking unitics."

Becker leaves, amid a shower of comments.

Sam: "I wonder if old lady so-and-so could do a better job than this."

Leonard: "Look what somebody did."

Now they are all making fun of the drawing.

Mr. Rankin returns.

Leonard: "Tell that guy he can't see straight."

Fred: "Who was that guy that came in here? Tell him he's blind."

Mr. Rankin: "What did he do?"

Leonard: "He can't see straight."

They repeat all of Becker's comments, with additions of their own.

Fred: "He's been blind for fifty years."

Becker comes into the outgroup's part of the room, and they all yell over to him.

Leonard: "Hey you. You can't see out of one eye and you're blind in the other."

to be involved in not taking it meekly, they are ready to give blow for blow.

Injured self-esteem continues to rankle, although the stranger is no longer physically present. All inferiority is projected onto the stranger himself—though on a half-joking "level of unreality" which is recognized as such.

They are all still painting, although getting a bit rougher and talking more and painting less. Mr. R. begins to paint too.

Reilly is yelling at Fred, who just laughs. Leonard comes back to the poster and yells and comments: "Get to work, boys. Sam, we got to get to work." Then he gets a bench from the outgroup's side, and says to the outgroup, "Is this your bench over here? Maybe we had better keep it. Look at the swell bench I made."

Leonard has given up any pretense of being busy and is just tearing around raising the roof. Reilly, Fred, and Lyman are still painting. Sam and Leonard have lost interest completely, the difference being that Sam has gone to a more attractive task and Leonard has quit doing anything.

Reilly quits painting: Fred is the only one still working on the mural. Leonard is flipping water off the end of his brush. Then Fred begins to chase Leonard, and Leonard yells, "Watch him, Sammies, I'm throwing water on him and he's chasing me."

Mr. Rankin tells Reilly that it is a good job of painting. Reilly says it's lousy, and asks Mr. R. if he doesn't think that what he (Reilly) did is bad. Complete confusion and disorganization. Steve, in the outgroup, is chasing Leonard with his paintbrush. Sam says, "Are you guys nuts or something?" Leonard is conducting a tease-and-run-fight. He yells, "We can capture him."

Interest in group project never fully revives after this powerful distraction.

Leonard, the smart-aleck, is the first to show overt physical aggression against the outgroup. There was apparently no provocation at all from the outgroup. Leonard's mischievous aggression is very diffuse, determined almost entirely by his own mood, and the choice of outgroup or ingroup objects seems almost accidental.

Reilly, who seemed really interested in his work, for once, is also [amazingly] now ready to criticize his own work.

Full-dress "war" is preceded by much individual skirmishing. Since there has not yet been any such "war," it may not yet exist as a real possibility in the boys' psychological environment. Later

Reilly joins in the sport. It's getting to be a conflict between the two groups. This group has all lined up. Leonard is chasing Steve, while Reilly chases Fred around the poster. Leonard sees a man standing on the edge and yells, "Let's go get him. Are you the guy that took the light out?"

Fred and Leonard begin to throw water at the other group. Steve threatens to stop them, and Leonard retorts, "Do you think you're big enough?" Then he shouts, "Come on, Reilly. There's going to be a war." Almost at the same time (it is not clear from the records whether Leonard or Reilly was first to use the word), Reilly yells, "Let's make war!" Leonard and Fred run wildly about; and Reilly joins in. Sam seems to be unperturbed by the commotion.

Reilly, Fred and Leonard are running wild. Sam joins in verbally.

Lyman is not participating. He talks with Mr. Rankin. Then he says to the others, "You kids quit this."

Steve makes a sally into this group's territory. Leonard drives him out and then boasts to one of his own group, "He went out of here sixty miles an hour."

Reilly devises a fancy method of wetting a rope and manages to sling a lot of water. Sam retorts to a challenge from the other side: "Why don't you? You've been going to for three minutes." Five more minutes

"wars" began much more suddenly.

After an interlude, back to the "war" with gusto.

This is the moment when the all-out war starts, if it can be said to start at any one time.

Reilly fully joins in at the prospect of a full-dress war. If it is really going to be a group affair he has to be the leader of it.

Lyman, the pacifist, shows adult - value - centeredness especially in his attitude toward aggression. (In the previous meeting he said, "Don't you think you've done enough destroying for one day?")

Sam is apparently participating now. He is not averse to horseplay, but simply wanted to finish the work he had started.

and they'll have the rest of this place torn up. Reilly says, "I'll get him."

They've gone further each time in general lawlessness. This is undoubtedly the limit. So far the picture is uninjured. The other group is attacking; Sam says, "Here come those guys." Leonard shouts, "Here's a new man. Get him. We're just washing you off." Mr. Rankin begins to clean up.

Mr. R. has decided that things are going a little too far and is beginning to exert mild pressure to stop. But Leonard, Fred, and Reilly are having entirely too good a time to stop now. Mr. R. says, "It's ten minutes to five," and Fred, willfully misunderstanding, says, "He means that is too early." Leonard says jokingly, "Let's quit fighting," but keeps right on doing it. Mr. R. says, "Time to quit, fellows"; but they are still running around, Leonard with a piece of burlap dripping water.

The place has begun to smell like a barn in the spring. The outgroup begins to leave . . .

Fred begins to throw clay, although told by Mr. Rankin that it is pretty sloppy. When Mr. R. gives him the can to put his clay back, he takes more out, looking mischievously up into Mr. R.'s face and grinning. Leonard says, "Here's my ammunition."

Lyman begins to put on his galoshes. He has not taken any part at all in the process, and has

"They've gone further each time" — increasingly reassuring themselves about Mr. Rankin's noninterference, probably, and also tasting more and more of the thrill of combat.

Disregard for leader; he has never earned the respect of the group.

Even now the spirit of the "war" is hilarious rather than angry or grim. No one has been hurt, and no one really wants to hurt.

Though he seems to like Mr. Rankin, Fred has absolutely no respect for his suggestions.

Lyman's pacifism must be partly adult-value-centeredness and partly physical fear.

ducked even when no one was throwing at him.

Reilly gets in one last crack. Mr. R. passes out towels. Fred insists on having more clay. Mr. R. is firm, this time, about not giving him any. . . . The outgroup leaves.

The group begins to put on their wraps. Fred tries to get out with the hammer. They all dash out to continue the fight on the outside.

Mr. R. finally prevails, though continuing until the end to use relatively mild, laissez-faire methods. But war might have started again if the outgroup had not left almost immediately.

Excerpts From an Autocratic Meeting (Aggressive Reaction)

(See also the "glimpse" of the same aggressive reaction of the same group on pp. 53–55; and note the radical contrast between the aggressive reaction to autocracy, as represented either by that record or by this one, and the submissive or apathetic reaction of other groups, as represented by the records on pp. 51 and 92. Unlike the other three groups in this second experiment, this group did not become outwardly obedient and excessively "good" under autocratic leadership. On the contrary, it showed nearly as much disorderly horseplay and much more real hostility than it had showed under laissez-faire leadership.)

The following excerpts from the fifth autocratic meeting are chosen in order to bring out the character of the most extreme disciplinary problem that any leader faced during any of the club meetings: Mr. Bohlen's effort to control Fred, on the day when Fred was most rebellious.

Observers' Records

Reilly and Leonard are chosen by Mr. Bohlen to commit the crime. Fred is sore, and says he'll do one too. . . . He is definitely resentful, and begins to push the stool roughly around the room with his feet.

Interpretive Comments

Note the radical difference in quality between this sullen resentment and the hilarious horseplay shown by most of this group, including Fred, under laissez-faire leadership. This is real hostility, though its forms of ex-

When Mr. Bohlen explains about the crime they all listen intently; Fred becomes interested in spite of himself. They are all quiet, but then Fred complains and is sullen, pounding on the floor with the hammer. . . .

When Mr. Bohlen reads the directions for the detectives they all listen, but Fred has many objections: "What if they don't, though?" and "Why don't you let us do it?"

Fred keeps up a running fire of smart-aleck remarks: "I'll hit them in the heads," "they are dumb dopes," etc. He tries to leave the group, but Mr. B. calls him back. Fred is provoked.

Mr. Bohlen says they must finish the curtain first. Fred says he won't; he is sullen and starts to paint. He tries to goad Lyman into doing it and tells Mr. B. that Lyman said he'd finish the painting. Lyman, showing some spunk, says "You're a big liar."

Lyman says he will do a part if Fred will do a part. Fred refuses; he is nasty, and is being extremely uncooperative. Lyman is being extremely decent and cooperative about helping Fred. Fred needs his face slapped.

Fred tries to get out of the room to hunt up Reilly and Leonard. He is shoving boards all over the place, and I don't think it would take much to make him get actively obstreperous. . . .

He knocks down the boundary around the tool chest.

Mr. Bohlen tells him to fix

pression are often similar to those of joking self-assertion.

Note the forms it has taken so far: stool pushing, floor pounding, interruptions, verbal expression of physical aggression, smart-aleck criticisms, mild active disobedience, and strong passive disobedience.

Autocracy has been much better for Lyman than laissez-faire was; he now has more self-confidence and is more a member of the group.

Should the observer have permitted herself to write that Fred "needs his face slapped"? (This question involves some interesting points with regard to what constitutes valid observation.)

The list of manifestations of

the broom up and quit walking around. He groans. Then Mr. B. says, "One thing that's going to happen to you if you don't obey the rules is that you're going to be out of the club altogether." Fred says, "If I quit, Sam will too. Won't you, Sam?" But Sam isn't so sure; he says, "I don't know"—and leaves Fred holding the sack. Mr. Bohlen follows up his advantage with a positive threat: "You won't quit. You'll get kicked out."

The threat apparently works, after a fashion. Fred stops talking about quitting, but still walks around with the broom and finally throws it over the curtain at Sam. Sam says, "Missed me by a mile." At Sam's request he then goes behind the curtain, but refuses to do any work when he gets there. Mr. Bohlen says quite positively, "You come around and do something constructive, or else you're out."

Fred stalls for a minute or two, painting a star.

Then Mr. Bohlen calls for a decision: "What have you decided to do?" Fred comes sullenly around the curtain and gets the ruler, supposedly to start work. However, he opens up the ruler and tries to start a duel with Lyman.

He is being extremely objectionable, although he has not succeeded in disrupting the rest of the group, as Sam and Lyman are still working.

. . . (Reilly and Leonard return after committing their

Fred's hostility now includes also non-cooperation with other club members, another attempt to escape, board shoving, knocking down the boundary, groaning, and attempt to get social support for complete rejection of the whole club situation.

Add, now, broom throwing and more extreme passive disobedience.

What is it that all of these expressions of hostility have in common? Could it be defined as an attempt (real or symbolic) to hurt or belittle someone else?

With his pride involved, and not quite sure that he does want to stay in the club, Fred is willing to remain poised on the ragged edge of Mr. Bohlen's patience. He is really angry—*and it is an exciting game.*

crime, and the business of crime detection, by free association, begins.)

Fred feels better now that he is being important (reading the sentences in the crime detection game).

He thinks he has caught Reilly, and is very pleased with himself.

(For the rest of the meeting —30 more minutes—Fred is somewhat smart-aleck and disinclined to do any work, but not actively disruptive as he had been.)

The conflict ends in a sort of draw, with Fred's pride half-saved, and with a transformation of the total situation which makes further decision unnecessary.

EXCERPTS FROM DEMOCRATIC MEETINGS

A meeting of the same group after it had become somewhat settled down and fairly well integrated, under the influence of a democratic leader, presents a dramatic contrast to the excerpts which have just been given. We present first, however, an excerpt from the very first meeting under democratic leadership, as an example of the difficulties involved in democratizing a particularly difficult group, and some of the techniques used. Excerpts are then given from the third democratic meeting, which showed a much higher degree of integration.

Observers' Records

After coming in, the group walks around rather aimlessly in the absence of the leader. The outgroup comes in and they all start yelling together. Leonard is being very silly: "Oh, eek! Scram, the G-men! April fool! This is April Fool's Day. Ray, you know you got a hole in your pants? You guys are dumb."

Mr. Rowe comes in. Leonard says, "We want carving today," but instead of taking this pro-

Interpretive Comments

Before the new leader comes, the group shows its lack of work interest—a thing which it did not develop either in laissez-faire or in autocracy.

Time perspective is given immediately.

nouncement at its face value, Mr. Rowe says, "One of you asked me how long this thing would last yet. We should decide what we are going to do in the six weeks that are left." His manner is quiet, but definite.

They all talk. Sam is hammering all the time.

Mr. Rowe goes on: "There's a piece of paper, Reilly. You be secretary and keep track of what we say."

Fred has the first suggestion, "I want to carve."

Mr. Rowe follows it up: "You mean carving airplanes?"

Reilly is writing, busy and important.

Leonard makes fun of the airplane idea: "Make airplanes for Girl Scouts!"

Reilly defends it: "My brother made one. He had carving on it."

Leonard protests, "You're no Girl Scout."

Mr. Rowe calmly ignores this horseplay, and draws out the quietest member of the group, "Lyman, what were you thinking of?"

Sam answers for him: "Not airplanes," and Lyman, apparently not having any idea as yet, fails to join in.

The group as a whole, however, is reacting with a great deal of interest to Mr. Rowe as a leader. Fred is quiet, and not the least bit sullen acting. The group has gotten more and more attentive and quieter as Mr. R. has gone on with his suggestions.

"We should decide" — not "Shall we decide?" It is necessary at first to structure the situation rather definitely and give it a strong push in the direction of democracy.

Not "Who wants to be secretary?" nor even "Let's elect a secretary" but a deliberate choice of the natural leader and loudest talker in the group.

Not "What do you want to carve?" but a definite structuring suggestion.

Though he does not have an idea, Lyman is probably pleased to have been automatically included in the group.

This definiteness of structuring is not "an element of autocracy," nor a halfway point between laissez-faire and autocracy. To clarify alternatives—which the boys can still take or leave—is not coercion. Though some use of authority is often necessary in inte-

Now he suggests, "We could do soap carving. I can get the things we need. Orangewood sticks."

Reilly says: "I was going to mention that. I know. This is going to be personally ours. You could make the same out of soap as out of wood."

Leonard is still in a joking mood: when he hears "orangewood sticks," he says "Pick up sticks"; but then shows his beginning interest with the suggestion, "I could get some of them."

Reilly suggests, "We could make plaster of Paris ash trays. We made some." Leonard is practical: "If you know how to do it." Then he relapses into his old silliness; "Reilly, you got platter Paris."

Reilly has another suggestion, when Mr. Rowe asks for more. He says, "Let's make some spears and bows and arrows." Fred is practical now: "Well, I don't know." Reilly explains, "You could use willow. We could use cheap wood."

Sam suggests, "We could make a footstool."

Leonard has actually paid attention; he follows up Reilly's suggestion: "You can buy arrows to make."

Mr. Rowe now tries to arrive at a final decision: "Shall we decide what we want to do today?"

The decision is hard to get, however, since the boys start to talk about a picnic. Sam says, "Let's have a picnic tomorrow." Reilly asks, "How about Satur-

grating a difficult group, this is not a use of authority.

One clear suggestion by the leader is enough; the boys carry on from there.

There are enough ideas now, and the discussion is threatening to last too long for the patience of these hyperactive boys.

Mr. R. feels this need, and tries to bring the discussion to a focus. Note again: helping the boys to clarify *their* own ideas is not "an element of autocracy."

day?" Leonard suggests, "Let's go Monday."

Mr. Rowe quietly brings them back to the question in hand: "Well, what are we going to do today?"

Leonard says, "Well, carve. That's what we want to do."

(Mr. Rowe senses the approval of the group for this proposal, and doesn't take time for a formal vote, but goes on immediately to the more specific question.) Mr. R.: "What would you like to make today?"

I have never seen the group so quiet and cooperative for so long a period of time. Those who are not attentive are at least quiet.

When there are no immediate answers to his question about what they would like to make today, Mr. Rowe rises and gets knives with brightly colored handles, one for each group member. They all run after him, and eagerly divide up the knives.

Lyman does not follow the group and does not get a knife. Fred points out this omission loudly and the cry is passed on by Sam, so that Lyman is provided for. This is the first sign of interest in anyone but themselves I've almost ever seen in the group.

Reilly refuses to give a member of the outgroup a piece of paper. This group has always put up great resistance to any invasion of what it considers its property rights.

Bringing discussion back to the main topic is one of the essential functions of a democratic, as distinguished from a laissez-faire, discussion leader.

"Roberts' Rules of Order" were made to facilitate democracy—not vice versa.

Leader senses group's need and substitutes action for talking.

New cooperative atmosphere. Possible reasons: a respected leader has set an example of interest in each boy's individual needs; developing work interest reduces the potency of individualistic competition (while at the same time opening up noncompetitive paths to status—which is, perhaps, another way of saying the same thing).

But in another context (relation to outgroup) the old possessiveness continues.

There is a big conversation about pussy willows; then about places where the boys had traveled.

The volume of personal conversation has greatly increased, and they are talking about things that are outside of the club at the same time that they are working. They are not as tied up in the situation as they have been.

The outgroup try to make this group mad by throwing something, and all they get in return is a jeer; Sam says, "Just wait till you guys get out of here. I pity you."

Out - of - field conversation. Hitherto, apparently, the high potency of individualistic competition has inhibited both thinking about each others' needs and thinking about more remote topics.

Last week this would have been a welcome pretext for counter-aggression. Now the need for aggression is much less, and, in addition, the potency of the work situation is very high.

Someone in the outgroup throws something at this group. It lights on Fred, but this time they fail to get a rejoinder.

The clock rings too long. No comment from group; even Fred doesn't notice.

From the third meeting under democratic leadership:

(Note: An additional reason for the exceptional cooperativeness and work-mindedness of this meeting was that two of the three "hell-raisers," Fred and Leonard, were absent. The resulting change of atmosphere had an interesting effect on both Reilly and Lyman. Reilly, having no "hell-raising" audience to play up to, changed his tune and became much less self-assertive. The realism which he shows here, in seeing and adapting to a change in the objective situation, is perhaps a major reason for his popularity in the school situation. As for Lyman, the combination of democracy with the absence of two of the boys who had frightened him most has an extremely good effect on him. His frightened withdrawal from the group largely disappears, and he becomes a friendly, self-confident, full-fledged group member.)

They are all exceedingly friendly.

The group is still working and talking together. They are all equal; no one is ascendant. (Even with Reilly in the group!)

Mr. Rowe is working too. There is a very nice relationship between Mr. R. and the group; there is no conflict, and he seems to be able to work right on, yet keep control.

Lyman goes to the water and floats his model, calling Reilly to see. Reilly actually comes over. Sam follows, and for a moment they are all around the bucket.

Reilly has never worked so intently on a project before, or been so friendly. He is not even making a special effort to attract the leader's attention, which is new for him. (He is carving a gun out of soap.) He is making rapid progress in his work also; at the end of twenty-two minutes he says, "Look at my gun. It is pretty good for my first thing."

The outgroup is running around, but this group hasn't even noticed.

From the looks of the group this time the cause of most of the racket seems to have been Leonard and Fred with Reilly, and even Reilly by himself isn't bad.

After his gun is made, however, he becomes much more active and restless.

Mr. Rowe seems to be having the most fun of all.

Mr. Rowe asks, "Does Fred get into much trouble with the teacher?" Sam says, "I'll say!"

Chameleon-like, Reilly senses the different atmosphere and conforms to it. His type of boy is not in the majority today.

The high interest value and non-frustrating character of this soap carving may be another factor in the change. And, as his remark shows, he is still seeking egoistic goals. His path, but not his goal, has radically changed.

The combination Leonard-Fred-Reilly has a Gestalt character; the whole is more than the sum of its parts. More specifically, each stimulates the others to greater competitiveness and aggressiveness.

Compare this with Fred's reaction to Mr. Bohlen, pp. 119–122.

and Lyman adds: "He got sent out of the room two times. He always does something."

Lyman is talking more than he ever has before in all the rest of the time together. He talks quite a bit about the school situation —marks, etc., as usual.

(At the end of the following meeting, the observer wrote, "The change that has taken place in Lyman in the last two meetings has been quite phenomenal. He has been actively participating in the group life, and has contributed more in the way of conversation than in all the other meetings put together. He has enjoyed his occupation and has not spent any time standing around and gazing out into space the way he used to. The group have responded to him and have directed questions and kidding to him where formerly they just plain ignored him.)

Autocracy was better for Lyman than laissez-faire, because it was more orderly and gave him something definite to do. But democracy was much better still, because it was at least as orderly as autocracy (to which his group reacted aggressively) and because in the friendly, cooperative atmosphere he becomes a more genuine group member.

8

Why Laissez-Faire Was Disliked

PERSONS who assume that children are little untamed animals, that they never want to do anything but play, and that the more freedom they have the better they like it, may find surprising the fact that in these experiments the boys showed a strong preference for democracy with its controls as compared with laissez-faire. In laissez-faire they had more nearly complete freedom (outwardly, at least) than in democracy; yet they liked democracy much better. Why? The probable answers are more complex than might at first be supposed, and they are of interest partly because they have a bearing on certain "progressive" theories of child rearing and education.

LESS SENSE OF ACCOMPLISHMENT

Perhaps the chief single reason was that the lack of any adult initiative in helping them to accomplish their own goals made their efforts relatively bungling, disorganized, and ineffectual, so that they did not often have a sense of solid accomplishment. These are some of the examples that have already been noted:

Eddie, Bill, and Van finish a handprint and go to pour the plaster of Paris, but find it has hardened in the can. Bill pounds at it. Eddie stamps in the sand with his shoe, spoiling the print they had prepared.
They have written No. 1 in one place and No. 2 in another place. Are rather disturbed but decide to paint it out next time. (They never did.)

Fred breaks his cast; is discouraged; goes on and tears up the whole thing.

Many of the boys' own expressions also suggest that the lack of a sense of accomplishment was important:

"So far we haven't gotten anywhere."
"Mr. Davis didn't help us out at all."
"We'd start something and we'd finish it" (in democracy).
"We did get a lot of things done" (in democracy).

It should be added that continuous progress toward a goal can be satisfying, even apart from the satisfaction of completion:

"Mr. Rowe kept us hard at work, and that was real nice" (in autocracy).

Less Clearness of Cognitive Structure

Clearness of cognitive structure means, roughly speaking, the clearness of a person's picture of his environment and of his own relation to it, including goals and action possibilities available to him at the moment. In the laissez-faire groups the lack of clear cognitive structure was apparently a factor in at least five different ways:

1. *Lack of clear goals.* Having a goal—almost any goal—was apparently preferable to having none:

Lyman (in laissez-faire) seems to be most inadequate and dependent—can't find anything to do by himself. . . . He is still just watching. . . . Watching, and would like to join but doesn't quite know how.

Lyman (in laissez-faire) runs out of something to do and wanders aimlessly.

Bill (talking to stranger while laissez-faire leader is out): "Rowe (as autocratic leader) was keen. This guy just lets us do what we want."

Hamil: "Yeah, Mr. Rowe kept us busy doing something. This guy just lets us do what we want, and I don't like it."

"He (democratic leader) has good ideas."

"He (laissez-faire leader) doesn't give us any ideas."

But having a goal is not enough; it is also desirable that the goal be clear enough so that the discovery of paths to it is not too hard. Bill's meteoric rise to leadership was largely due to his confidence in his own ability to show the group what they could do, but his ideas turned out in practice to be so vague and grandiose that he quickly lost his position of leadership:

Bill: "All right, come on and listen, we've got something. Come on, Hamil. I'd like you to listen too, Mr. Davis. Come on over, Finn."

Finn continues his lazy whittling: "I'm listening. I'm all ears."

Bill: "What do you say we make up laws and give them to each other to work out and see the truth about them. We can go to the library or something and find out the truth about them. I think it's a good idea."

Van, Finn, and Hamil do not respond verbally at all. Finn shrugs his shoulders, and all three keep on with their separate small woodworking tasks.

Bill looks very exasperated. "Well, whatever you say, we still will do it." (They never did.)

2. *Lack of clear paths to goals.* After they knew what they wanted to do or to make, the boys wanted to know how to do it or make it:

"He (democratic leader) explained things more."

"He (laissez-faire leader) let us figure things out too much."

3. *Lack of clear limits.* As has been suggested (p. 47) it is necessary to distinguish between the size of the space-of-free-movement and the clearness with which its boundaries are drawn. Democracy ordinarily means a space-of-free-movement that is much larger than in autocracy, but the outer limit of that space may be as clear and as rigorously enforced as in autocracy. What now needs to be added is that the children themselves may feel more secure and at home if they know just where the outer boundary is. During the water fight in the Charlie Chan Club, for instance (pp. 116-9), some of the boys probably felt uncertain as to whether they were coming to the ragged edge of Mr. Rankin's patience. But, being a laissez-faire leader, he remained passive and allowed the uncertainty to continue.

4. *Lack of clear role expectations.* In the above incident Mr. Rankin was probably not acting like any adult the boys had ever seen before, and they may have been puzzled by his behavior. The puzzlement was apparently not very frustrating in this case, because they had tried him out gradually, going a little farther each time and finding that he seemed to be sublimely indifferent to their aggressive activities. It is probably fair to say, however, that there is

unpleasant ambiguity whenever an adult behaves very differently from the way a child has seen other adults behave in similar circumstances, and that there is an especially unpleasant ambiguity whenever an adult vacillates between lenience and unpredictable severity.

5. *Lack of clear time perspective.* The democratic leaders made a special effort to develop time perspective (Lewin, 1948, pp. 103–124) through group discussion and planning—a realistic mapping out of future activities, including both goals and steps to those goals, set in a realistic time framework. Such time perspective was lacking in both autocracy and laissez-faire. It was lacking in autocracy because the leader kept the time perspective in his own hands, telling the children step by step what they were to do next without giving them an insight into the plan as a whole. And it was lacking in laissez-faire because, although some of the boys (e.g., Bill) had enough ideas about distant goals, there was little realistic appraisal of the goals in group discussion or effective thinking out of practical intermediate steps. The kind of shared planning that establishes and clarifies time perspective is a democratic art. For instance, the following illustration shows how one democratic leader helped his group to do it:

Mr. Rankin: "Do you want to have another crime next week, or what?"

Finn: "Let's have another crime next week."

Van: "I'm a G-man next time. We ought to have the same G-man."

Mr. R.: "Let's decide first whether we have a crime or something else. There are lots of other things we can do." (He goes on to list about a half dozen other possible group projects.)

Finn makes a motion that they have a crime next time, and everyone votes in favor.

Mr. R.: "Now the question is, who wants to be the G-men?" (All speak.)

In this case, Van's announcement, "I'm going to be a G-man next time," threatened to disrupt the process of group decision as to what would be done; it was a premature effort to fill in the details of the plan before its main outline had been blocked out. By firmly bringing the discussion back to the question of choosing a major goal, Mr. Rankin helped the group to become clear and certain as to what its major goal would actually be.

It should be added that the strength of the need for clearness of psychological structure seemed to vary greatly from boy to boy. It was strongest in the good boys, the industrious boys, the adult-value-centered boys (see chaps. 12–14), such as Eddie and Lyman, and weakest in the harum-scarum troublemakers such as Reilly and Fred. This is probably a major reason why the good boys usually preferred autocracy to laissez-faire, while the troublemakers preferred laissez-faire to autocracy.

Less Adult Support for the Boys' Own Moral Standards

Those who assume that eleven-year-old boys have little or no moral sense are probably thinking of boys like Reilly and Fred, and not of boys like Eddie and Lyman. Among these more conscientious boys it appeared to be a real satisfaction to have an adult who saw to it that things were not only clear, orderly, and productive but also morally right:

"He (autocratic leader) has to be as strict as he is."
"I think he (laissez-faire leader) ought to make some rules."
"He (autocratic leader) never gave us time to fight, and that's the right way to do."
"I'd rather do what I want, just so we don't get into any fights."
"He knows how to make the children behave."

The above quotations are actually open to two interpretations: that these boys disapproved of fighting as morally wrong, and that they disapproved on the basis of order and productivity considered as satisfactions rather than as moral values. Probably both factors entered in, in the minds of those boys (Lyman, Bill, Eddie) who valued order and productivity most. The existence of a moral element in their attitude was perhaps most clearly indicated by Beaumont, who had been something of a troublemaker and who later said, somewhat ruefully, "They ought to keep the kids in order up there—and that means me, too."

Less Friendship with the Adult

The typical passivity of the laissez-faire leader made him scarcely more of a friend than the autocratic leader was. There were therefore some comments such as these:

"Mr. Davis (laissez-faire) . . . didn't know anything about the club; he didn't know about its ways. He didn't understand us boys at all."

Similar comments were made about autocratic leaders:

"He'd stand around and tell us what to do, but he wouldn't say much else."

But democratic leaders drew comments such as these:

"He thinks of things just like we do and was just one of us."
"He seems to want to do things with us."
"He was a good joking fellow."

LESS SENSE OF GROUP UNITY

The integration of group activity and the diffuse sense of friendliness promoted directly and indirectly by the democratic leaders apparently produced in the individual boy a feeling of being nearer to the other boys as well as to the adult. It was only in laissez-faire groups that comments such as these occurred:

"Couldn't we all work together on one thing at a time? I mean we don't help each other enough. . . . Sure, I think Mr. Davis is all right, but we do too many things instead of being together."

The above samples are enough to illustrate that a well-integrated democracy is as different from laissez-faire as it is from autocracy. The inveterate human tendency to think in terms of only two opposed categories—heroes and villains, angels and devils, progressives and reactionaries, Americans and foreigners, Communists and non-Communists, democrats and autocrats—is as inappropriate here as it is anywhere else. If there must be some kind of oversimplification as a first approximation to the very great complexity of reality, it should in this case be at least in terms of three basic categories instead of two—a trichotomy instead of a dichotomy.

It should also be noticed that democracy as represented in the experiments cannot be accurately thought of as a golden mean between the two extremes of autocracy and laissez-faire. It has many characteristics of its own which are not those of a mean. To think of a mean or midpoint means to think in terms of only one dimension when, as a bare minimum, two dimensions are necessary for even a first approximation to the facts. The following two-dimensional diagram (Figure 9) is still an oversimplification, but it is at least better than any one-dimensional representation:

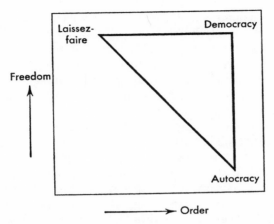

FIGURE 9. The three "climates" represented in terms of two dimensions: freedom and order.

Here the three type concepts are thought of not as three points on a single line but as the points of a triangle. In the dimension of freedom, the vertical dimension, democracy is here pictured as equal to laissez-faire (which is an oversimplification), while in the horizontal dimension which is here called "order"—and which can be defined as including productivity, firm enforcement of outer limits, clearness of psychological structure, and degree of organized cooperation—it is pictured as equal to autocracy (again an oversimplification). According to the diagram laissez-faire is low in order but high in freedom; autocracy is low in freedom but high in order; democracy is high in both. Democracy is not the midpoint of the line between laissez-faire and autocracy. It is not a half-measure of order and a half-measure of freedom, because order and freedom are not opposites. As far as two dimensions can serve to define it, democracy is a full measure of *both* order and freedom.

To keep this from being quite such an oversimplification it should be added immediately that there is a third dimension consisting of friendly, creative intercommunication within the group, and that in this dimension democracy as represented in the experiments was high while both of the others were low.

No diagram, however, in any number of dimensions, can do justice to the qualitative uniqueness of democracy. It involves order, freedom, and friendly interaction, but it is more than the sum of all three added together. It is a different pattern, a fresh synthesis. This helps to explain why it is that some groups, both large and small, can swing from anarchy to tyranny or from tyranny to anarchy, from thesis to antithesis and perhaps back again, without finding on their path the democratic synthesis that they vaguely seek. To those who are preoccupied with questions of domination and submission, and who therefore cannot clearly conceive of any alternatives except freedom or slavery or some midpoint of half freedom and half slavery, democracy is incomprehensible.

Some of the ways in which this bears on the task of the parent or teacher seem fairly clear. It suggests, for instance, that the emphasis on being permissive, which is often assumed to be the "progressive" point of view, needs to be tempered by a good deal of wisdom from a broader perspective. Actually, recent years have seen a renewed recognition of children's need for limits among parents, psychologists, and educators. Those adults who implicitly assume that by being very permissive they are being particularly democratic would do well to ask themselves whether they may be actually creating a kind of anarchy, and if so, what this is doing to their children's fundamental sense of security.

The experimental evidence suggests, too, that the whole question of permissiveness vs. restriction or lenience vs. punishment has been given undue emphasis in much current discussion of adult–child relationships. To state it in terms of only two alternatives is a gross oversimplification, and to regard it as *the* major problem in child rearing is to give it an altogether disproportionate importance. To focus only on this issue is to cast the adult primarily in the role of a potential policeman, to give too much weight to the question of whether he should be active or passive in his role as policeman, and to pay too little attention to the many things which an adult can be other than a policeman. It means overlooking all of the more positive aspects of democratic leadership which, in the experiments, represented the major differences between democracy and laissez-faire.

POLITICAL COMMENTARY

Political history shows many instances in which anarchy has been felt to be intolerable, and a pendulum swing from anarchy to tyranny has occurred. Such a swing occurred often in the Greek city-states. It occurred in Russia when a time of troubles in the seventeenth century led many Russians to prefer even the dark despotism of the Romanoffs to a continuation of civil war. It occurred in Russia again when widespread impatience with the Kerensky government's "weakness" helped Lenin to establish the dictatorship of the Bolsheviks. It added great impetus to Hitler's plea that he could save Germany from the weakness of the Weimar regime, and to Mussolini's claim in 1922 that without him Italy would slip into anarchy. The mood in which the Law and Order Patrol turned to Bill during laissez-faire and made him commander-in-chief (though without actually accepting his authority when he tried to exercise it) was only a faint and feeble analogue of the imperative urge to escape from anarchy which has often existed in the political world.

Such facts raise a question: can the danger of dictatorship be combated more realistically by adding to, or by subtracting from, the strength of the more or less democratic governments in the non-Communist world? There are some who view every increase in the power or scope or unity of government as inherently a step toward dictatorship. The facts mentioned above suggest that another danger is at least equally great: the danger that if a democratic government fails to cope effectively with great evils such as war, defeat in war, or depression, it will be regarded as weak, as verging on anarchy, and a strong man will be brought in to "bring order out of chaos." Both the experimental and historical facts suggest that the royal road to dictatorship is not a strengthening of democratic government but a weakening of democratic government, a slipping into anarchy which sets up the psychologically inevitable urge to escape from anarchy into tyranny. (For discussion of how democracy can be safely strengthened, see Chapter 19, "What Can be Done about the Inefficiencies of Democracy?")

9

Autocracy without Frustration

UP TO now in this book attention has been focused mainly on the dissatisfaction resulting from autocracy. Such an emphasis has its place, but may lead to superficial conclusions. There can be no fundamental understanding of the tenacity of autocratic institutions, or of the problem of keeping democracy strong where it now exists, unless attention is also given to the psychological sources of an autocrat's strength.

Autocracy has three lines of psychological defense. An autocrat is not likely to stay in power unless he succeeds in at least one of three tasks:

1. *Promoting real satisfaction* in the minds of his subjects. Willing or even glad acceptance of chains is the most effective guarantee that they will never be broken.

2. *Immobilizing discontent.* Even when frustration and discontent exist, there are ways of hemming them in, psychologically, and keeping them from resulting in impulses to aggression.

3. *Diverting aggression to scapegoats* inside or outside the group. Even when discontent exists and leads to aggressive impulses, these impulses may be displaced from their natural object, the autocrat, and turned against others. The autocrat, who normally works simultaneously on all three lines of defense, is in great danger of losing power only if this last line is breached and scapegoating gives way to rebellion.

Since the experiments have a bearing on each of these three "lines of defense," this chapter will be devoted to the first of them, and the next two chapters to the second and third.

Under a deceptively smooth surface, as we have seen, autocracy may conceal explosive tensions. On the other hand, the fact that the surface is smooth does not prove that what is underneath is explosive. It may be as smooth as the surface. In the experiments, five factors apparently promoted willing acceptance of autocracy. Two of them can be called narcotic or frustration-reducing factors: the impression of inevitability, and vagueness of the democratic alternative. Three others can be called gratifying or positive satisfaction-producing factors: the satisfactions of order and productivity (if, and only if, the alternative is seen as anarchy rather than democracy), the satisfactions of dependence, and the satisfactions of identifying with a leader who is effective and who "sets high standards."

1. A Narcotic, Frustration-reducing Factor: the Impression of Inevitability

When an unpleasant thing is perceived as completely inevitable, it does not necessarily become thereby less unpleasant, but there often develops a numbing or narcotizing process that goes by the name of "resignation" and that leads to a more or less successful pushing of the unpleasant thing out of one's mind while concentrating on something else.

Actually, of course, this is a normal and often a highly adaptive process; a human being could scarcely live without it. If the frustration is a mild or obviously temporary one, as it was in the autocratically led experimental groups, cheerful resignation is perhaps the most adaptive of all responses, and it would be unfair to apply to the boys who showed this reaction any such pathological-sounding word as "narcotic." As they saw it, the strictness of Mr. Rankin or Mr. Rowe was a not-so-pleasant aspect of a situation that on the whole was definitely pleasant, and since apparently nothing could be done about his strictness, they made the best of it and turned their attention to the pleasanter aspects, especially to the work itself. It was as if they said to themselves, "Mr. Rowe is too strict, but I can't do anything about it, and I'm having fun making this stool anyway." On the other hand, it is easy to see how in a more pervasive autocracy this numbing of the nerves of frustration can be fatal from the standpoint of a democratic value system. It can paralyze, at their source, the impulses that might otherwise lead to organized action against the autocrat.

Perception of autocracy as inevitable is largely a matter of perceiving the autocrat himself as firm and consistent. Any vacillation, any hesitation or change in a previous autocratic pattern, may bring about perception of him as vulnerable and of the total situation as subject to change. This was illustrated especially by the reaction of the Charlie Chan Club to Mr. Bohlen. He was the only leader in any group who had to face any sort of organized rebellion. It took the form of a sit-down strike led by Reilly (p. 110). The somewhat indecisive conflict between him and Fred (pp. 119–22) also shows how possible it was for the whole club to begin to see him as vulnerable and challengeable. On the other hand, Mr. Rankin, though probably more disliked, preserved a façade of vigorous autocracy in which the boys apparently never saw any chink, and their reaction was therefore consistently submissive. They did nothing more rebellious than to "talk about him on the way home."

POLITICAL COMMENTARY

History offers many illustrations of the danger in which a ruling group stands if it is weak or vacillating:

The French Revolution was preceded by many years during which France had been ruled by kings—Louis XV and Louis XVI—who appeared weak or silly. The French Revolution as a whole was carried through mainly by a self-confident middle class which felt its own strength in relation to the weak kings and the decadent, no longer functional aristocracy.

In 1775 British rule in the far-off Thirteen Colonies was loose enough to permit a great deal of unhampered agitation and preparation for war.

The first of the two Russian revolutions in 1917 was made possible by the weakness of Czar Nicholas II, by a twice-repeated demonstration of the government's weakness in warfare, and by refusal of the government's troops to fire on unarmed masses in the streets.

The riots in East Germany in 1953 were precipitated not by new acts of oppression by the Communist autocracy but by new acts of lenience, after the death of Stalin, and by a remarkable lack of firmness on the part of the Communist authorities when the first overt disturbances occurred.

Similarly, the mass character of the Hungarian uprising of 1956 was made possible by the lenience of the authorities in handling the uprising during its earliest stages.

By way of contrast, there are many instances in which a vigorous autocrat—Ivan the Terrible, Peter the Great, Stalin, Hitler—has never had to face a serious mass rebellion. It is perhaps legitimate to generalize that weakness or vacillation in the ruler or the ruling group is usually a more important factor than the amount of discontent in determining whether rebellion will or will not occur.

2. A Narcotic, Frustration-reducing Factor: Vagueness of the Democratic Alternative

The Charlie Chan Club, which reacted rebelliously to the restrictions imposed by its autocratic leader, Mr. Bohlen, had in mind a very clear alternative. His regime followed the super-lenient laissez-faire regime of Mr. Rankin, which three of the boys (Reilly, Fred and Leonard) had definitely enjoyed. As they watched Mr. Bohlen bearing down on them they perceived him against the background of Mr. Rankin's very different behavior, and they perceived their own newly restricted activity against the background of the freedom they had so recently enjoyed. True, the alternative they envisaged was not a true democracy but laissez-faire. Nevertheless, their behavior seems to illustrate a principle of rather general applicability: there is not likely to be a vigorous effort to change any situation unless the possibility of some more attractive situation is clearly conceived.

The rebellious behavior of the Charlie Chan Club contrasted sharply with that of two other clubs, the Dick Tracy Club and the Law and Order Patrol, who were especially contented and showed the "abnormal goodness" of the submissive reaction to autocracy. One reason for their contentment, probably, was that autocracy was their first club experience. To them the total club experience was certainly more pleasant than unpleasant, and they probably saw the behavior of the autocrat as an integral, inseparable part of this on-the-whole-pleasant situation. They knew nothing better. It was as if they thought: "Mr. Rowe is pretty strict, but I guess that's just the way a club leader is, and I like the club."

The clearest illustration of the mechanism, however, is provided by the Sherlock Holmes Club under the autocratic rule of Mr. Rankin. It showed the submissive reaction to autocracy, but was by no means wholly contented ("We talked a lot about him on the way home, and nobody liked Mr. Rankin"), and the discontent seemed clearly related to an immediately previous experience of democracy. The difference between Mr. Davis's democracy and Mr. Rankin's autocracy was too conspicuous to be ignored. Mr. Rankin's actions could not possibly be perceived as simply "the way a club leader is." They were thrown into sharp relief by being perceived against the background of Mr. Davis's democratic behavior, which at the same time proved that democratic leadership was a *possible* role for a club leader to play.

POLITICAL COMMENTARY

As of 1960, there is a striking contrast between the acute conscious anti-Soviet feeling in Poland, Hungary and other European satellites of the USSR and the more philosophical, resigned, or even seemingly contented attitude of at least the urban population in the USSR itself. While this is partly explainable in terms of nationalist sentiment in countries subjected to foreign Soviet rule, it may also be related to the comparative recency of the imposition of Communist dictatorship in the satellites. In the USSR a new generation has grown up that has never known anything but Communist dictatorship. Any alternative is vague and, in many individuals, psychologically almost nonexistent.

3. THE SATISFACTIONS OF ORDER AND PRODUCTIVITY, WHEN ANARCHY IS SEEN AS THE ALTERNATIVE

Since productivity or group effectiveness is not possible without some degree of order, and the chief value of order is that it makes productivity possible, these will be treated here as a single factor, although, as we have seen (p. 129), order or clearness of psychological structure is also a directly satisfying experience. The combination is, surely, a tremendously strong motivating force whenever a group sees its very life endangered by anarchic disintegration. If at such a time tyranny seems to be the only alternative, the swing from anarchy to tyranny may acquire an imperative urgency.

Whatever else might be said about them, the autocratic groups in the experiments were orderly and productive. The things done in the meetings—mask making, woodwork, crime-detection games, soap carving, painting—were inherently satisfying. The fact that nearly all of the children kept on coming voluntarily to the club meetings even under autocracy is itself convincing evidence that they were not too unhappy. There was enough satisfaction in the order and productivity of the meetings to balance, and more than balance, the frustration of submitting to "strictness." To be sure, there was definitely more satisfaction in democracy, but this was made possible only by the fact that democracy was comparable with autocracy in order and productivity, and offered, in addition, individual freedom and full group participation. If democracy had not been comparable to autocracy in order and productivity, it seems quite unlikely that it would have been definitely preferred.

Two conclusions, then, seem justified: (1) The absolute level of satisfaction in an autocratic group may be kept fairly high if an activity that is perceived as worthwhile is progressing well. (2) If in the group's experience (or in what it has learned from other sources) the only alternative to this group effectiveness seems to be the futility of anarchy—i.e., if the democratic alternative is vague and the anarchic alternative is vivid—the full force of the desire for order and productivity may be mobilized to sustain or to embrace autocracy.

POLITICAL COMMENTARY

Hitler and Stalin both knew that, important as "bread and circuses" may be, they are not enough. There is also a thrill in any great cooperative activity such as eliminating unemployment, winning a war, or "overtaking and passing" the United States. If this thrill is associated with autocracy rather than democracy, so much the worse for democracy.

As for the swing from anarchy to tyranny, some of the many historical examples of it have already been mentioned (p. 137). Hitler, Mussolini and Lenin are only three of the many who have capitalized upon the urgency of the need for order and productivity, when autocracy has appeared to be the only way to achieve them.

One implication seems clear: those who want to preserve democracy where it now exists can do so most effectively if they combine it with the greatest possible amount of order and productivity, so that a situation may never arise in which autocratic order appears to be the only escape from chaos.

4. The Satisfactions of Dependence

One of the commonplaces of present-day psychology and psychiatry is the importance of the regressive, childlike need to depend on others and let them make decisions. This conception is, on the whole, supported by the experiments, since the entire picture of frustration in laissez-faire implies a need both for psychological structure and for the kind of fatherly or big-brotherly relationship that only an active leader—whether autocratic or democratic—can provide.

POLITICAL COMMENTARY

It is probably as futile to deplore the need for a father figure as it is to deplore the needs for order and productivity. The urge to lay all the burdens of political decision making on a Roosevelt or an Eisenhower can be strong and widespread even in a democracy. As long as essential freedoms are maintained it is perhaps a strength of democracy, rather than a weakness, that it can find within itself ways of satisfying this need.

The danger, of course, is that respect will become worship and dependence a blind, slavish absence of thought. An awareness of these distinctions is obviously needed, and also an eternal unreadiness to endow any merely human individual with godlike attributes.

5. The Satisfaction of Identifying with a Leader Who Is Effective and "Sets High Standards"

A somewhat obscure but probably extremely important psychological mechanism is the tendency of followers to identify with their leader and gain vicarious satisfaction from his strength, from his effectiveness (even when it is directed against themselves), and perhaps most of all from his association with standards which are seen as "higher," in some sense, than those that the unaided individual would set for himself.

Two groups, the Dick Tracy Club and the Law and Order Patrol, showed during autocracy remarkably little discontent in any way. A major reason for this probably was the fact that, in the judgment of observers, the autocratic leaders of these two groups (Mr. Bohlen and Mr. Rowe) gave an impression of being particularly absorbed in "doing a good job" and in getting the boys to do likewise. Probably, then, the boys often saw their strictness as a result of this dedication to the work. Since most of the boys in these two groups were relatively conscientious and interested in their work, they probably saw the leader as a man with high standards, demanding that they do their best in the service of an inherently worthy goal. The perceived similarity of his motivation to their own probably made identification with him easy, and in addition, by supplying an acceptable reason for his strictness, it probably kept them from perceiving it as a deliberate and arbitrary assertion of his superior power position. It was as if they said to themselves: "He isn't being mean; he just wants this table to be good and solid."

On the other hand, Mr. Rankin's autocratic leadership of the Sherlock Holmes Club was more arbitrary and capricious. It gave some of the observers, and probably some of the boys, the impression that he was enjoying domination for its own sake. It is understandable, then, that this was the period during which Beaumont dropped out of the club. As one of the boys put it:

"We talked a lot about him on the way home, and nobody liked Mr. Rankin. I don't mean I don't like him personally, but not the way he leads us."

POLITICAL COMMENTARY

For those of us who assume not only that Hitler was essentially evil but also that he "appealed to the worst in human nature," it may be difficult to believe that he also appealed to the best in human nature. But there is reason to believe that, in a certain sense, he did.

"What impressed me most about Hitler was the courage with which the war-time corporal attacked all evil."

"I do not know how to describe the emotions that swept over me as I heard this man. His words were like a scourge. When he spoke of the disgrace of Germany, I felt ready to spring on any enemy. His appeal to German manhood was like a call to arms, the gospel he preached a sacred truth. He seemed another Luther." (Abel 1938, pp. 152–153.)

Heavily alloyed with ego-inflation and unreasoning hostility— surely two of the most dangerous elements in "human nature"— there is also in these quotations an unmistakable appeal to idealism. Hitler was calling these people to action and to sacrifice in a cause which they believed to be far larger than their individual selves. As for Lenin, the ideal for which he asked the Russians to sacrifice was much broader than the narrow nationalism of Hitler. One of the most repulsive features of political autocracy is this tendency to clothe itself in the robes of self-sacrificial idealism.

Along with the primitive allure of uncensored group egotism and aggression it normally offers the more subtle intoxication of *feeling morally right* (White, 1949).

One of the most interesting consequences of this factor in the experiments was that the boys who felt most at home in autocracy were as a rule the good, hard-working, adult-value-centered boys, such as Lyman, Bill, and Eddie. If the form of autocracy in the experiments had been evil in any obvious way this could hardly have been the case, but these boys tended to enjoy its order and productivity definitely more than the disorder and futility of laissez-faire, while the harum-scarum troublemakers like Reilly and Fred, not caring so much about order and productivity, preferred the anarchic freedom of laissez-faire. Both groups—with one exception—preferred democracy to autocracy. The exception was Eddie —one of the most conscientious boys in the entire experiment, and the only one who actually preferred autocracy to democracy.

To Summarize

In large groups as well as small ones, the psychological balance sheet of autocracy is likely to add up to a positive or satisfying total:

If frustration is reduced by resignation to the inevitable—that is, if the autocrat seems firm and unchallengeable.

If lack of any taste of freedom makes the alternatives to autocracy seem vague and only half real.

If order and productivity seem attainable only under autocracy, because the disorder and unproductiveness of anarchy are vivid while the order and productivity of democracy are vague. (It follows that actual experience with an orderly and productive form of democracy is one form of insurance against a ready acceptance of tyranny.)

If democracy has not adequately satisfied the need for dependence and for a father or big-brother figure.

If the autocratic leader stirs the imagination of his followers and gives them a vicarious satisfaction in identification with his power, and a sense of being better persons through acceptance of his high work standards or "high ideals." (The more conscientious a person is, the more likely he is to be moved by this last and most insidious appeal of autocracy.)

10

Autocracy with Frustration but without Aggression

The Immobilizing of Discontent

The idea that frustrated, discontented human beings are often irritable is a matter of everyday observation. No one doubts that unhappiness often tends to breed anger—either realistic anger against those who have caused the unhappiness, or unrealistic anger against innocent scapegoats. What is not so clear is the nature of the psychological connection between the frustration and the anger (i.e., the impulse to aggression). Why does frustration breed aggression—when it does so? And why, for example in Mr. Rankin's autocratic group, does it often fail to produce aggression or any discernible impulse to aggression? The problem of the psychological sources of anger and hostility is more complex and puzzling than it is sometimes assumed to be, and yet it cannot be avoided at this point. To understand the way in which aggression varied in the autocratic, democratic and laissez-faire groups it is necessary first to consider this broader and more fundamental problem.

A relatively systematic coming to grips with it must be postponed until scapegoating is discussed in the next chapter. It is necessary to say here, however, that a number of the experimental facts do not seem adequately covered by the very simple theory of those psychologists who make the connection between frustration and aggression their most basic assumption. These psychologists suggest that frustration always leads to at least an impulse or "instigation" to aggression—that unhappy people are in some sense always angry, though the expression of their anger in action may be inhibited by fear or by moral scruples. (Dollard, Doob, Miller, Mowrer and Sears, 1939.) The experimental findings suggest, instead, that this connection is not inevitable, that there is an intermediate step between frustration and aggression, and that the emotional tension which often arises in autocracy can be in a sense hemmed in or immobilized before it ever becomes translated into a definite impulse of aggression, even against scapegoats. Under certain circumstances, which we can begin to try to define, an unhappy person can remain dumbly, docilely—or wisely, realistically—lacking in anger.

The facts suggest that discontent can be immobilized in at least four ways: by hero worship, by continuous activity, by resignation, and by vagueness of the idea of aggression.

IMMOBILIZATION BY HERO WORSHIP

When an autocrat causes frustration on the part of those he controls, the most natural object—and usually the only realistic object—of their anger is the autocrat himself. But anger against him is unlikely to develop if the opposite attitude of hero worship is already established.

In the experiments it seems likely that a predisposition to a kind of hero worship was the rule rather than the exception. The readiness of many preadolescent boys to like and admire benevolent young men has often been observed, for example in the reaction of campers to camp counselors. In the democratic groups there were many signs of an eager reaching out for the friendship of the young adults who played the role of democratic leaders, and in autocracy the same tendency may well have led to a readiness to ignore or minimize or excuse autocratic behavior on the leader's part that otherwise might have been personally resented. It is significant that, in groups in which the reaction to autocracy was submissive, the boys' disapproval of their leader, when asked about him in the interview, was usually remarkably mild. A typical response was "Mr. Rowe was all right mostly; . . . he helped us work but he was kind of bossy."

It should be remembered that all of the leaders, regardless of the role they played, were probably regarded by the boys as the generous givers of work materials, as well as givers of the privilege of belonging to the club in the first place. They obviously had superior knowledge about interesting things to do, and in all three of the leader roles, even that of the laissez-faire leader, they were givers of knowledge as well as of material things. If in addition the leader appeared to be effectively coping with the club situation and maintaining high work standards (see above, pp. 144–5), it is understandable that in some cases the tendency to hero worship might be rather strong.

POLITICAL COMMENTARY

On the last page of George Orwell's Nineteen Eight-Four, the central character, Winston, is utterly defeated and numbly unhappy. He is not angry. In fact, in the final, most pitiful line of the book, he discovers that he "loves" Big Brother.

Whether Orwell's picture of love as a response to torture is psychologically realistic must remain open to doubt. What is not open to doubt, however, is the importance of hero worship in sustaining modern dictatorships. Perhaps it can be best described as a perversion of religion. At any rate, the readiness of human beings for worship, manifested in their nearly universal acceptance of some kind of religion, is manifested also in their recurrent readiness to endow a merely human being with godlike attributes, thereby narcotizing their capacity for realistic anger.

The curious reverence of the Japanese for their Emperor, even though he was largely a figurehead and a front for a military clique that plunged Japan into a disastrous war, is well known. The strangely intense feeling of millions of Germans for Hitler is also well known, and postwar research has shown how important it was in sustaining the fighting morale of the Nazis, down to the final days of utter Nazi defeat.

Less familiar, and even more difficult to believe, but well established by much recent evidence, is the fact that many millions of Russians had a similar feeling toward Stalin. At least after World War II, when he could be plausibly regarded as the savior of his country, a great many of his subjects did look upon him as something of a god. To us in the West, accustomed to picturing him as stolid, morbidly suspicious, and implacable in destroying every potential political enemy, this particular type of hero worship necessarily seems incongruous if not unbelievable. To Khrushchev too it may have seemed in February 1956 that the Stalin image must be repulsive to most of his countrymen and that he could gain politically by dissociating himself from it in the public mind. The recent evidence indicates that he was wrong. He underestimated the Russian people's need for worship. Millions of them hated Stalin intensely, but many other millions had swallowed eagerly the Stalin myth that was fed to them continually by every technique of education and mass propaganda. On balance, Khrushchev apparently lost ground politically when he attempted to deprive them of their hero.

For example, these are the words in which some of them expressed their feeling (USIA, 1958):

"Until the letter of the Central Committee became known, I loved Stalin almost as my own father. I cried when he passed away. Only now do I realize what harm he had done."

"I believe in Stalin as some people believe in God. Therefore I cannot accept the idea that he had committed crimes."

"Stalin was a great man who led the country to victory."

"The majority of the Soviet people still love Stalin and consequently criticize the present government because of its attitude toward the deceased leader."

"The teacher said that the government had enough evidence regarding the mistakes and crimes committed by Stalin, and should be believed. Many students openly disagreed and defended Stalin."

In other words, the political as well as the experimental evidence seems to indicate that hero worship may operate powerfully to sustain autocracy on two different psychological levels. On the deepest level, as was suggested in the previous chapter, it may give direct satisfaction to dependent needs and to the need to identify with one who is seen as both powerful and righteous. At the same time, on an intermediate psychological level, the existence of a strong positive feeling inhibits the development of negative feeling *toward the autocrat.* Even if frustration exists, the emotional tension that results from it remains diffuse and may never be transformed into a focused impulse of aggression.

IMMOBILIZATION BY CONTINUOUS ACTIVITY

No matter how frustrated and discontented a person may be, if he is kept busy enough he has little time or attention to give to anger.

Psychologically this is perhaps a special case of a generalization that will be made later in this chapter: that aggression is not likely to occur if the idea of aggression remains vague. It is a familiar fact that the "salient" parts of the psychological field—the parts on which attention is focused—tend to be clear, while the non-salient parts, on which attention is not focused, tend to be vague and blurred. If a person's focus of attention is kept steadily on any particular activity, then, any aggressive or hostile ideas that might otherwise enter his mind may remain in the shadowy fringes of his field of consciousness and never become clear enough to lead to a definite impulse of attack. As Lewin might put it, if the "potency" or focus-of-attention character of a work situation is sufficiently high, the relative potency of the interpersonal situation which gives rise to aggressive impulses necessarily remains low.

Whatever psychological terms may be used to describe or to interpret the situation, the fact is that in the experiments idleness often seemed to set the stage for aggression. For instance, Leonard's beginning of playful group aggression, on the day of the big water fight, was related to his lack of interest in the painting project which for a time continued to interest the others. He had nothing better to do than to play the clown and stir up a fight. Sam's considerable interest in his own work project kept him from participating in the group aggression until it was well under way. Later, under the democratic leadership of Mr. Rowe, this whole group became absorbed in work, and even Fred became so preoccupied with his soap carving that a direct provocation from the other group failed to elicit from him any response. Also, the relatively large amount of aggression in the laissez-faire situation could easily have been based partly on idleness, since in laissez-faire the boys had the greatest difficulty in establishing any continuous activity that would demand all of their time and attention.

POLITICAL COMMENTARY

It is probably no accident that modern totalitarian governments often not only require a long working day but also make great demands on leisure time. The right to a private life is one of the major casualties when a totalitarian regime takes over. Whether consciously designed as such or not, this may be one effective way of minimizing the chance of rebellion.

IMMOBILIZATION BY RESIGNATION

In the previous chapter it was suggested that resigning oneself to what seems to be inevitable may reduce frustration by a withdrawal of attention from the frustrating situation. "Mr. Rowe is too strict, but I can't do anything about it, and I'm having fun making this stool anyway." We can now go a step farther and consider another effect of resignation. Even if frustration exists and attention is focused on the frustrating situation, there may be no shifting of attention to possibilities of aggressive action if the autocrat who is doing the frustrating seems completely impervious to attack. Here it is not the inevitability of frustration but the impossibility of aggression that one becomes resigned to. It is as if a boy said to himself: "Mr. Rowe is too strict, but I can't hit him or do anything he doesn't like, so I just won't think about him unless I have to."

The rebelliousness of the Charlie Chan Club under Mr. Bohlen's autocratic leadership can be considered again from this standpoint, and especially the long conflict between Fred and Mr. Bohlen (see p. 119). Mr. Bohlen's handling of Fred was not characterized by decisiveness. He let Fred get away with a good deal, even though he did threaten (and would have carried out his threat, if Fred had gone too far) the ultimate sanction of exclusion from the club. It is more than possible, therefore, that something in Mr. Bohlen's manner gave those boys who were eagerly watching for it the impression that he was vulnerable. It is also likely that the impression they had gained of their previous leader, the extremely lenient and indecisive Mr. Rankin, carried over and influenced their perception of Mr. Bohlen. The fact that they had ridden roughshod over one adult leader probably made it seem more possible that they could ride roughshod over another.

The other of the two instances of large-scale aggressive action by a group—the one which occurred in Experiment I—was very different. It, too, occurred in autocracy, but in it there was no overt rebellion against the autocratic leader. The overt attacks were entirely directed against scapegoats. Here there is no reason to think that the leader was perceived as weak, but there is reason to think that he was perceived as lenient. The uninhibited character of the scapegoat behavior suggests that the children did not expect their leader to disapprove or to prevent it—and, of course, he did not. The case is of interest, however, as an example of how aggression can be canalized or restricted to a particular kind of object, if there is resignation to the impossibility of attacking another kind of object.

The other three experimental groups, all of which reacted nonaggressively to autocracy, without either rebellion or excessive scapegoating, apparently perceived their leaders as completely invulnerable to attack. They may even have assumed (incorrectly) that their leaders' unchallengeable power would be extended to the prevention of all quarreling among themselves (Lewin, 1951, pp. 207–211).

IMMOBILIZATION BY VAGUENESS OF THE IDEA OF AGGRESSION

If a person is to perform any voluntary act, two prerequisites are ordinarily necessary: (a) he must have some idea of the act and of how to perform it, and (b) he must want to perform it. Whether a person performs an aggressive act probably depends mainly on whether he wants to (e.g., whether he feels "mean" or resentful). But the first factor, whether he has some clear idea of aggression and of how to be aggressive, cannot be entirely overlooked. Aggression, like other forms of behavior, is partly a matter of "knowing how" and "remembering how" at the right moment. There is reason to think that in the experiments aggression sometimes failed to occur simply because the idea of it was unclear or far from the mind of the person in question. In the next chapter, on scapegoat behavior, the suggestion is made that aggression is ordinarily one of the simplest, psychologically most "available" forms of self-assertion, so that it is likely to be resorted to by a person who is in a self-assertive mood and whose psychological field has been reduced, by emotional tension, to its simpler and cruder elements. But is aggression always the simplest, psychologically most available form of self-assertion? Does it always come readily into a person's mind as a possible reaction to a disturbing situation?

In the most peaceable, conscientious, adult-value-centered children in the experiments, it is doubtful whether it did. Lyman, for instance, acted as if aggression by others simply bewildered him. On certain occasions, when he saw a particularly good opportunity to criticize, he did so ("Don't you think you've done enough destroying for one day?" and, to Fred, "You're a big liar"), but most of the time he acted as if his mind was simply not geared to either verbal or physical aggression. He could see the others being aggressive, but except when he was directly provoked, in ways that suggested an appropriate response, he apparently could not see clearly any way in which *he* could be aggressive.

If this is true, it would help to explain why the nonaggressive reaction to autocracy occurred in groups that were largely composed of conscientious boys. For boys like Eddie and Bill, submissive obedience and hard work were probably psychologically more available and clearly structured activities than aggression, as well as being more desired because of being "good" rather than "bad." And these two boys set the tone in the Law and Order Patrol, which reacted nonaggressively to autocracy.

It seems likely, too, that particularly clear and psychologically available ideas of aggression were an additional reason for the aggressive reaction of the Charlie Chan Club to Mr. Bohlen's autocratic leadership. This reaction occurred immediately after they themselves had developed, step by step, a more and more aggressive pattern of behavior in Mr. Rankin's laissez-faire group. Their destruction of the property of the "Monday gang," their big water fight with the Sherlock Holmes Club, and their continual bickering among themselves were still very fresh in their minds when Mr. Bohlen began his autocratic regime. The heightened need for self-assertion which presumably resulted from this frustration could therefore very easily find an outlet through the familiar aggressive channels. That is, ideas of aggression would naturally come into their minds first and most clearly, as ways of reasserting the ego status which Mr. Bohlen had challenged.

On the other hand, the Dick Tracy Club and the Law and Order Patrol experienced autocracy as their first club experience, and this probably meant not only that they accepted it with more equanimity but also that aggression did not come into their minds, immediately and vividly, as a possible course of action in this particular situation. Many of them had, of course, been more or less aggressive in other situations, but perhaps not recently, and certainly not in this particular East Hall attic and in this particular G-man-Club situation.

Breaking the Ice of Submissiveness and Nonaggression

The concept of "immobilization by vagueness of the idea of aggression" also offers one way of accounting for a striking fact which emerged again and again in the experiments: the *group* character of both aggression and nonaggression. Aggression was highly contagious within a group. So was peaceableness or nonaggression. If a group pattern of peaceable reaction to autocracy was once established, it tended to continue as if by its own momentum, but if the ice of peaceful conformity was once broken by a single conspicuous act of insubordination or aggression, disorderly behavior or aggression tended to become the group norm.

POLITICAL COMMENTARY

Historical examples are innumerable. In European history, for example, the ice of peace and political stability has been broken on a large scale only four times during the past two hundred years: during the period of the French Revolution and Napoleon (1789–1815), during the revolutions of 1848, during the First World War and the revolutions that followed it (1914–1920), and during the Second World War (1939–1945). In these periods disorder spread like fire, while in the long intervening periods of stability the ice was comparatively unbroken.

Three explanations suggest themselves:

1. *A need on the part of individuals to conform, buttressed by fear of punishment* (ostracism, or something worse) if they do not conform.

In the groups that reacted nonaggressively to autocracy, for example, each boy knew that if he were the first to break the ice and depart from the submissive, work-minded pattern of behavior he would make himself conspicuous as a minority of one in a group of five. Since there were no precedents to go by, he did not know how suddenly and severely the leader might crack down on him if he broke the pattern, nor did he even know how the other boys would react. Vaguely or clearly, then, he probably feared disapproval if he should break the pattern.

POLITICAL COMMENTARY

A dictator is not likely to be overthrown when he is able to inflict terrible punishment on whoever is the first to rebel, and when all individuals and small groups remain uncertain whether any others will join them—risking the same punishment—if they are the first to rebel. Hitler, Stalin, and others have been well aware of this and have deliberately heightened the potential rebel's sense of isolation by fragmenting the subjugated population and preventing, as far as possible, communication of discontent from one individual to another. Even communication from parents to children has been inhibited by recruiting the children to report on the "loyalty" of their parents.

From this it follows that even though a large majority of the people are discontented, "pluralistic ignorance" as to the real desires of the remainder of the population may keep the majority fragmented and unaware of its own strength. But, by the same taken, it follows that when this rigid pattern is broken and rebellion on a small scale occurs without being swiftly punished, the rest of the discontented may gather courage and (as in Hungary in 1956) an uprising may gather momentum until it is successful or the whole movement is drowned in blood.

2. *A perception of the leader as unchallengeable.* As long as a leader has not yet been successfully challenged, his image in the eyes of his followers is likely to have an aura of invincibility, over and above whatever other elements of hero-worship may exist. It seems likely that in each of the three groups that reacted submissively to autocracy the image of the leader carried some of this aura. On the other hand, in one group, the Charlie Chan Club, the autocratic leader never had such an aura, or quickly lost it. Fred's single-handed but half-successful defiance of Mr. Bohlen demonstrated to the group as a whole that Mr. Bohlen was vulnerable and his authority challengeable. Similarly, the tendency of the same group in laissez-faire to go farther each day in general lawlessness was based partly on the accumulating evidence that they could go far without incurring the wrath of Mr. Rankin. In both of these cases the ringleaders not only relieved their followers of any anxiety as to whether they would be conspicuous and would perhaps be punished if they followed suit; the ringleaders also demonstrated, to the satisfaction of their followers, that the adult was weak or lenient.

The aura of invincibility is of course closely related to the conscious fear of disapproval or fear of punishment, but it probably acts on a less conscious level, to keep even the *idea* of disobedience, or of aggression against the autocrat, from entering an individual's conscious thoughts.

3. *Vagueness of the idea of aggression.* Throughout this discussion there has been no invoking of the word "imitation" or the word "contagion" as an explanation of the mobilizing or immobi-

lizing of aggression. Since imitation does not occur automatically —since under many circumstances it does not occur—any use of it as an alleged explanation would only serve to gloss over a real and important psychological problem. Nevertheless it should be noticed that seeing another person do something can always at least put the *idea* of doing that thing into one's own mind. It makes this action-possibility clear and vivid. If, then, this action (or its perceived effect) is attractive—if it ties up with a motive that already exists in the individual—the individual himself is likely to perform the action and "imitation" is said to have occurred (Polansky, Lippitt, Redl, 1950).

This suggests an additional reason for the contagiousness of both aggression and nonaggression. Let us take, for instance, the rather consistent nonaggressiveness of the three groups that reacted submissively to autocracy. Two explanations of it have already been suggested: fear that disapproval or punishment would result from nonconformity, and the perception of the leader as unchallengeable. A third explanation can now be added: vagueness of the idea of aggression, or of the idea of disobedience, in the minds of these boys. Not one of them had himself been more than slightly aggressive in this place or in this club situation, and not one of them had seen any other boy be aggressive in this place or this situation. Their entire thought pattern was set in another direction, the direction of obedience, harmony, and hard work. While there was certainly a fair amount of frustration, at least in the Sherlock Holmes Club under Mr. Rankin's rigorous autocratic leadership, this frustration seems to have led only to a heightened level of emotional tension and not to even a clearly focused impulse of aggression against Mr. Rankin, since the very idea of aggression was somewhat alien and remote or not present at all in the mind of each individual boy.

In contrast, the idea of aggression and of "seeing how far we can go" in disobedience was rather constantly a clear and vivid one in the minds of all members of the Charlie Chan Club under both laissez-faire leadership and the subsequent autocratic leadership. One of them (Lyman) was very conscientious and consistently rejected the aggressive pattern set by the group. Another (Sam) was somewhat conscientious and usually rejected it. The other three (Reilly, Fred and Leonard) were relatively lacking in conscientiousness; each kept the ideas of aggression and of rebellion fresh in the minds of the other two, and each eagerly seized upon the example of the others to become more aggressive and more rebellious than he would have been on his own. Contagion and "giving the idea" did not create the energy which made them aggressive. That energy presumably came from self-assertive needs which existed before they ever entered the club situation (though the club situation may have intensified them). But the expression of these needs in aggressive behavior was apparently triggered or catalyzed by vivid ideas of aggression, and these ideas came in large part from seeing the aggression of others in the group.

POLITICAL COMMENTARY

As we have seen, stability has a tendency to perpetuate itself and disorder has a tendency to spread by "contagion," in large groups as well as in small ones. Whether the psychological forces at work are similar is a rather different question, but in this case there is no obvious reason to think that they are not similar. In large groups as in small ones there can be fear of punishment for nonconformity, leaders can have an aura of invincibility, and group thought patterns can be set which make the idea of internal violence (or of internal nonviolence) seem far away and unreal.

To Summarize

In contrast with the theory that frustration necessarily gives rise to anger and aggressive impulses, this chapter presents and defends the hypothesis that discontent can be immobilized—that is, kept from translating itself into even a clearly focused impulse of aggression. In autocracy this occurs:

When, spontaneously or by propaganda, the followers develop a feeling of hero worship toward a leader or leader-symbol.

When their attention is kept focused on continual activity, along lines that preclude rebellion.

When they are resigned to the futility or impossibility of aggression.

When even the idea of aggression is vague in their minds. This occurs: (1) when they themselves have never been aggressive in a situation like the present one, and (2) when no one else breaks the ice of submissiveness and nonaggression.

This "ice" ordinarily contains at least three elements: (a) a need to conform, buttressed by fear of punishment, (b) an image of a leader as unchallengeable, and (c) vagueness of the idea of aggression, as indicated above.

11

Aggression in Autocracy: Scapegoating vs. Rebellion

IN TWO of the autocratic groups, as we have seen, aggression was abnormally great. In one of them, the autocratic group in Experiment I, it was directed not at all against the autocrat but wholly against other members of the same group, and especially against two successive scapegoats, Tom and Joe. In the other, the Charlie Chan Club in Experiment II, some of the aggression was directed upward, in the form of rebellion against the autocratic Mr. Bohlen, but most of it, in this group too, went to scapegoats.

POLITICAL COMMENTARY

Although the situations are very different, the possible parallel with what has happened in certain modern dictatorships is too interesting to be ignored. In Hitler's Germany the almost incredible story of the gas chambers is a familiar one, though most of us prefer to forget it, and the story of Stalin's hounding of the "kulaks" and other alleged internal enemies is also fairly familiar. In two of the autocratic groups in the experiments similar persecution occurred, on a miniature scale, *without* being in any way directly fostered by the autocrat. On the face of it, this suggests that there may be something in the psychological structure of autocracy itself that makes for spontaneous persecution of scapegoats, and that this natural tendency plays into the hands of autocrats who, by merely encouraging it, can keep their subjects' hostility directed against hate objects other than themselves.

The possible political parallels are not, however, confined to Jews and kulaks. There is also the somewhat similar phenomenon of McCarthyism in the United States, and, in fact, *every form of irrational or partly irrational fear and hostility in the political world.* That is a large order. It includes a great deal of what goes by the name of race or class prejudice, and also a great deal of the exaggerated fear and suspicion of foreign nations that make the maintaining of peace or the establishing of world organization so difficult. Hitler found it easy to cultivate exaggerated suspicion not only of the Jews but also of the many foreign nations which were allegedly denying Germany a chance to live. Stalin cultivated not only hatred of the kulaks but also a mythology of a Wall Street which wants war and world domination. To understand scapegoating more fully is, then, to understand more fully a major element in the psychological background of war.

The psychological problem of scapegoating is inseparable from the problem of frustration-and-aggression, touched upon but not discussed in any fundamental way in the previous chapter. When a frustrated person attacks someone else who has caused frustration (e.g., an autocrat) the psychological connection seems clear enough. It can be regarded as a realistic effort to eliminate the frustration by eliminating its cause. But the connection is a puzzling one when a frustrated person attacks innocent bystanders who have not actually caused his frustration. It is at this point, too, that the problems of scapegoating and of frustration-and-aggression are inseparable from the problem of irrational hostility or hostile misperception.

In other words, the special problem presented by scapegoat behavior lies in its objectively unrealistic and seemingly purposeless character. Let us say that A hurts B, and B, instead of defending himself or attacking A, turns around and hurts C. What good does it do him?

The "common sense" reply is, "It makes him feel better; he's just blowing off steam." And the psychologist who talks profoundly about "displaced aggression" is actually saying essentially the same thing, except that he is substituting the word "aggression" for "steam" and "displacement" for "blowing off." As far as it goes, the explanation is certainly valid; B does "feel better." But, like many other explanations on the common-sense level, it does not go far enough. It would be interesting to know what the "steam" really consists of, where it comes from, and why it could not have been "blown off" just as effectively if B had simply shouted and waved his arms. Nor does the steam analogy explain why a normally purposeful human being should suddenly lose all sense of purpose and begin to act like a teakettle. The trend in psychology has been toward interpreting as much behavior as possible in terms of needs or goals (whether conscious or not), and it would be scientifically more satisfying if we could somehow integrate even this behavior into our general picture of the human being as a creature who is purposeful—and psychologically logical—even when objectively he is being most irrational.

The problem only becomes greater when one recognizes that, objectively speaking, scapegoating and other forms of irrational aggression are often not merely useless but actually harmful to the individual (or the group) that engages in them. The momentary satisfaction of venting malice is often paid for by a lasting injury to the standing of the individual in his group and, in relations between nations, aggression can be suicidal. Often the angry person seems almost willfully to put on blinders and refuse to consider consequences, though a few seconds later he may regret what he has done. Why?

Aggression as a Short Cut to a Feeling of Importance

The interpretation to be presented here is, in brief, that an impulse to aggression is likely to occur *whenever ego needs are especially strong and no other ways of satisfying them are, at the moment, psychologically available.* Such aggression is, in a sense, a short cut to a feeling of importance—a leap, often illusory, into the goal region of triumphant self-assertion.

Several of these terms call for definition, and will be defined in due course. It will be useful to start, however, with an example taken from the experimental record (p. 114). Becker, the "hostile stranger," insults the painting job that Reilly, Fred, and the others are doing. He calls it a "pretty sloppy job." At first, since work efficiency is not a primary basis of status or of self-esteem in this group, they react very good-naturedly. But, when he continues his attack in a "mean" way, they apparently see it as a wanton challenge to their *general* status. They rise to the challenge and resort to a vociferous verbal counterattack—"Hey, you're blind in one eye and you can't see out of the other!"—continuing as long as Becker is within earshot. And even this is not enough. There is apparently a residue of wounded self-esteem. The blow to their pride still rankles. Later in the meeting they engage gleefully in a large-scale water fight in which they are the chief aggressors, which is at the same time an assertion of their prowess against the out-group and a defiance of the adult club leader, whose wishes are blithely ignored when he attempts, rather mildly, to hold them in check.

There is probably no true "persecution of scapegoats" here. The only genuine hostility of the group was directed, realistically enough, against Becker. Nevertheless, the boys directed a certain kind of half-playful aggression against persons who had not hurt them or obstructed their normal activities in any way (the out-group and Mr. Rankin), and the satisfaction they got from doing so was, if our interpretation is correct, a direct satisfaction from the self-assertive acts themselves. These acts were not rationally chosen means to some other end. This end-in-itself quality seems as characteristic of their counterattack against Becker as of their attack on the outgroup and their defiance of Mr. Rankin. All three of these aggressive actions, therefore, can be fairly described as non-rational (not irrational, necessarily, but nonrational) in the sense in which that term is being used here.

How does this incident fit the short-cut interpretation of non-rational aggression?

If the interpretation implicit in our description of the events is correct, the dominant members of the Charlie Chan Club (Reilly, Fred and Leonard) had normal ego needs—i.e., needs for status both in the eyes of others and in their own eyes—which were mobilized and became acute as a result of Becker's challenge. Previously they had been in what will be called here a "status equilibrium." They had been coping with their environment in a normal, accustomed way, having fun, slapping paint around, showing off, joking, bickering, and reasonably pleased with themselves. Becker's insults disturbed this equilibrium. He intruded on their spheres, suddenly diminishing the stature of their egos in their own and each others' eyes, changing a situation in which they had been to a considerable extent masters of their own small worlds into one in which they felt subject to unpredictable harm, coming from outside, which they could not control. As in any disturbed equilibrium, forces directed toward restoring the equilibrium were accentuated. The boys felt a suddenly acute need to regain the status, the feeling of importance and personal adequacy, that they had lost. According to the present interpretation, this accentuated ego need is the essential basis of scapegoat behavior, and in fact of most nonrational aggression. Aggression is a major manifestation, but only one manifestation, of more fundamental ego needs, the goals of which are importance in the eyes of others and an inner sense of power to cope with the environment.

In the second place, no other adequate ways of restoring the status equilibrium appear to have been psychologically available to the boys, either immediately after Becker's insults or later, when they attacked the outgroup and defied Mr. Rankin. They were engaged in a pleasant painting job, but slapping paint around gives no great sense of mastery or of recognition, and Mr. Rankin (playing a laissez-faire role) did not seem to care whether they did well in it or not. Complex, roundabout paths to status, such as ambitious individuals often resort to when they do not feel subject to unusual stress, were probably not present in the boys' "lifespace" at all. Aggression was. Partly because the daily lives of the dominant individuals in the group were full of more or less good-natured tussling and word battles, this form of self-assertion was very familiar to them; it came quickly into their minds. Psychologically it was highly "available." According to the present interpretation, it is the combination of these two factors, a strong ego need and the nonavailability of any "outlet" other than aggression, that is explosive. When this combination exists, aggression normally occurs—whether it is rational in terms of other goals or not—unless strong inhibiting forces are mobilized against it.

In what sense, now, can their aggression be called a "short cut to a feeling of importance"?

It was a short cut in that, while giving them an immediate and vivid sense of their own power and importance, it did not, in any longer time perspective, increase their actual power or importance at all. It was a quick cashing in on certain kinds of power—the power to insult and hurt and destroy—that they already had. Like a self-glorifying daydream, it gave immediate ego gratification with no realistic thought about the relation of means to ends. In a sense it merely symbolized a restoration to their egos of power to cope with the environment, or reconfirmed, without increasing, their status. It was as if they were proving to themselves and each other, to the outgroup, and to Mr. Rankin that they were persons to be reckoned with, and not trampled upon as Becker had trampled on them.

If we now apply this general hypothesis to the specific case of genuine scapegoat behavior, what formerly looked like a mere purposeless "blowing off steam" now appears as genuinely purposeful behavior. A insults B. B for some reason cannot talk back, but the status which he had had, at least in his own eyes, is challenged, and there is an insistent need for some self-assertive act that will seem to reinstate it. He later finds himself in a situation in which he can assert his importance without too much risk—perhaps by insulting C—and he does so. Objectively nothing is accomplished, but subjectively the self has been asserted and an equilibrium restored. Steam has been blown off—yes. But the "steam" can be more usefully described as the disturbance of a status equilibrium, and its "blowing off" as the restoration of that equilibrium. Waving his arms and shouting could not have accomplished the same purpose; he had to prove his power and importance in a social context, and the simplest way to do that is, very often, aggression.

This hypothesis also puts the frustration-aggression problem in a new light. Why does frustration so often lead to aggression? One major reason now appears to be that frustration, *if it is felt as personal failure*, is always a blow to self-esteem. Like being the victim of aggression, then, it mobilizes a need to restore self-esteem, and one way of restoring self-esteem is aggression. A disappointment that was attributed wholly to the environment (such as an earthquake) should, according to this hypothesis, not produce as much aggression as a disappointment that is attributed to a failure of the self. There are illustrations of this also in our experiments. Bill's exasperation at the group when it did not follow his leadership is a cost in point. *He* was failing as a leader, and therefore felt an intensified need to assert himself against the group. There were also several instances of work failure followed by aggression:

Leonard can't find anywhere to saw, and tries to edge in on the box . . . , He is unsuccessful in getting in, and throws his saw on the floor.

Fred breaks his cast; is discouraged; goes on and tears up the whole thing. (Later in the same hour, he was the leader in destroying the work of the "Monday gang.")

The validity of the short-cut hypothesis is also supported, directly or indirectly, by four other generalizations based on the experimental data:

1. IN THE EXPERIMENTS THE SCAPEGOAT WAS NEVER TOO WEAK

In Experiment I, Tom and Joe, the two successive scapegoats in the autocratic group, were both boys who could hold their own against any of the others taken singly; and they both showed a fair amount of self-assertion themselves:

Tom: "I'm a lot smarter than you are. Boy-oh-boy, can I ever brag."
Harry: "I'll say you can."

Joe: "Sure, I've got three radios; I ought to know."
All the others: "You have not!"

In Experiment II, the one true scapegoat was Steve. He was the largest and heaviest boy in the group, and his favorite tactic when baited by one of the others (outside the club situation) was to get him down and sit on him. It may also be noted that the three physically weakest and least formidable boys in Experiment II (Lyman, Beaumont, and Van) never became scapegoats. It is of course likely that the code of good sportsmanship prevalent in this culture ("Why don't you pick on somebody your own size?") has something to do with the choice of scapegoats who are not too weak. At the same time, it also seems likely that the weaklings were not attacked partly because asserting physical superiority over them would add nothing to self-esteem or to status. Status and self-esteem are essentially relative, and to assert a relative superiority which is already taken for granted by all of the group can therefore (if the individual still has a grip on reality) do little or nothing to enhance or restore status. But when Jack the Giant Killer kills his first giant, his status is enormously enhanced. This way of looking at the problem brings out more clearly the difference between the blowing-off-steam hypothesis and the displaced-aggression hypotheses, on the one hand, and the ego-need hypothesis on the other. If the only requisite were to "blow off steam" or to "displace aggression," the easiest and safest object of aggression would presumably always be the one chosen; but if the need is for a restoration of status or of self-esteem, the chosen object is likely to be one who, without being actually too formidable, nevertheless has some aspect that is—or can be made to appear—strong and dangerous.

There is a real puzzle here, since the Jews in Hitler's Germany were in actual fact completely helpless, and most of us are used to thinking of helpless individuals or helpless minority groups (Jews, Negroes, kulaks) as the typical targets of a scapegoat attack. There is nevertheless much in the political world to support the hypothesis as formulated above—that for maximum satisfaction in scapegoating the chosen object must have some aspect that is, or can be made to appear, both strong and dangerous.

In the Nazi mythology the Jews of Germany were not helpless at all, but the diabolically clever representatives, inside Germany, of a powerful and very dangerous international conspiracy. As Hitler put it, "If, with the help of his Marxist creed, the Jew is victorious over the other peoples of the world, his crown will be the funeral wreath of humanity and this planet will, as it did thousands of years ago, move through the ether devoid of men." (Hitler, 1939, p. 65.) According to this extraordinary world picture, in curbing the Jews Germany was outwitting these sly creatures, who had been taking shrewd advantage of their immunity from physical violence to stab Germany in the back by more subtle means and to climb over a prostrate Germany to domination over the whole world.

Similarly, other scapegoats have often seemed menacing, in some way, to those who attacked them or discriminated against them. To many whites in the Deep South, for instance, there is something truly dangerous in the crude "animalism" which characterizes their image of the Negro. Those who discriminate against Catholics often see the Pope as a menace. When Stalin declared war on the kulaks he did not picture them as helpless but as the last great embodiment of capitalism in Russia, against whom he was protecting the poor peasants.

2. There Was a Close Relation Between Aggression and Other Indications of Need for Status

The most aggressive boys (Reilly, Fred, Leonard) were also as a rule the ones who ranked highest in "demands for attention." The nonaggressive boys (Eddie, Lyman) demanded attention much less often. This is consistent with the hypothesis that a general competitive, self-assertive need—which does not have to be related to specific frustrations—underlies both types of behavior. Aggression is one expression of the need for status, but it is by no means the only expression. Direct demands for attention represent an equally simple and psychologically very similar form of self-assertion.

3. There Was Much Good-Natured Aggression Which Could Not Be Attributed to Frustration at All

The behavior of Reilly, Fred, and Leonard before the "hostile stranger" appeared on the scene (pp. 111–4) is a case in point. In this group there was a very large amount of loud bickering over work materials which was difficult to classify as either pure "hostility" or pure "joking hostility." It was something in between. The term "good-natured aggression" is perhaps more accurately descriptive. These boys were having a good time. The only really frustrated boy in the group was Lyman, and he was not overtly aggressive. It would appear, then, that at least this good-natured type of aggressiveness is much more clearly related to the need for status (and to lack of inhibitions) than to any sort of frustration.

There is apparently a change in the quality of the behavior when real frustration and real anger are injected into the situation. For instance, when Becker's criticism of the Charlie Chan Club became "mean," their reaction became much more intense and personal, even though the words used were still the words of joking exaggeration: "Hey you. You can't see out of one eye and you're blind in the other." A similar change could be seen clearly in Fred, whose happy-go-lucky, joking aggressiveness changed to hot and sullen rebellion when he felt that the autocrat, Mr. Bohlen, was infringing on his freedom. And, similarly, there was probably more real hostility in the aggression of the poorly adjusted, chronically frustrated boys (Lyman, Beaumont) than in that of the rough-and-tumble, boy-value-centered individuals. When Lyman nerves himself to say "You kids quit this," or, "Don't you think you've done enough destroying for one day?" or when Beaumont drops out of the club in anger at the autocracy of Mr. Rankin (without a word of overt protest), the motivation seems to have a much more specifically hostile quality than when Reilly gaily declares, "We'll just sock you in the mouth then."

But this change in quality, important as it is, does not necessarily mean that ego needs are not the core of the matter in both cases. Reilly sought status continually, openly and naturally, sometimes by ostentatious verbal aggression, sometimes by direct demands for attention, and sometimes in other ways. Lyman's level of aspiration in regard to status was much lower; he was apparently very happy when in democracy he achieved a sort of equality of status with the other boys. But there is reason to think that his peevish protest against the overt aggression of the others ("You kids quit this") was also essentially a way—a fruitless, unrealistic way, objectively speaking, but still psychologically a way—of seeking to assert a superiority which he could not achieve otherwise. The whole laissez-faire club situation was an acute challenge to his ego; in the club he felt ignored and insignificant. But here (as he must have seen it) the other boys were proving themselves inferior to him in another frame of reference—the moral frame of reference. He perhaps felt half-consciously that he could gain status at least in the eyes of the adult leader by appearing as the sole champion of law and order, and by stressing the relative inferiority of the others in this respect. But the core of his hostile impulse was probably something simpler than any such calculation; it was probably a blind, primitive impulse to assert, against the hostile or indifferent environment, an ego which had too long been in eclipse.

4. Most of the Group Differences in Aggression Can Be Reasonably Interpreted in Terms of Different "Paths to Status," or in Terms of Heightened Ego Needs

In democracy and in the submissive reaction to autocracy, the most obvious path to status was to do good work. Praise for good work was forthcoming, both from the adult and (sometimes) from the other children. But in laissez-faire the path to recognition through good work was largely unstructured; much of the time, these work paths probably did not exist at all in the psychological environment of the boys. How, then, were they to get status? One path was always open, clear, and easy to take: the path of aggressive banter and physical horseplay.

Another difference probably consisted of the fact that achieving status by democratic leadership was a possibility which existed in democracy (and to some extent in laissez-faire), but not in either form of autocracy. In autocracy the adult leader monopolized all genuine leadership, so that the only way in which a child could directly assert himself in interaction with the others was by crude domination or aggression. He could not lead, but he could at least dominate, and—in the aggressive reaction to autocracy—that is what he did. The more subtle and socially acceptable techniques of democratic leadership—sensing the needs of the others, making good suggestions, integrating diverse purposes—gave place, necessarily, to direct self-assertion in competition with or in opposition to the others in the group.

There is also a likelihood that in laissez-faire and in the aggressive reaction to autocracy the ego needs themselves were heightened. In laissez-faire they were apparently heightened by the low "potency" of the work situation. Not being absorbed in work, the boys naturally turned their attention to the competitive social situation instead. A common group work project, or even parallel individual work projects, seemed to bring out friendly, cooperative discussion of the work rather than mutual competition. It would be a mistake to characterize the work solely as a "path to status" when interest in the work itself was genuine, as it was in democracy. In addition to the egoistic motivation there was also a genuine, self-forgetful absorption in the work, as a creative activity which was fascinating in and of itself. This high "potency" (i.e., high attention value) of the work situation as an alternative to status seeking was perhaps most dramatically shown in the Charlie Chan Club when, on the first day of Mr. Rowe's skillful democratic leadership, it became for the first time thoroughly absorbed in a creative activity:

The outgroup try to make this group mad by throwing something, and all they get in return is a jeer; Sam says, "Just wait till you guys get out of here. I pity you." . . .

Someone in the outgroup throws something at this group. It lights on Fred, but this time they fail to get a rejoinder.

In the aggressive reaction to autocracy the status needs were apparently heightened by the emphasis which the leader placed on the status difference between himself and the boys. As we have seen, both personal praise and personal criticism were more frequent in autocracy than in democracy; the leader promoted an ideology in which individual differences were stressed. And, in addition, he did it in such a way that *his* status was stressed. To some of the boys, who had not thoroughly adjusted themselves and resigned themselves to adult leadership or domination (e.g., Reilly and Fred), this seems to have served as a direct challenge. And even in Experiment I, in which the adult's autocratic role did not seem to be directly resented, it probably served indirectly to heighten the status-mindedness of the group.

The question naturally comes up: Did the same thing happen in the submissive reaction to autocracy? And if so, why did these groups show such a marked *reduction* in aggression, even as compared with democracy? Two psychological possibilities exist: it may be that status needs were heightened in even the submissive reaction to autocracy, but that their aggressive expression was almost wholly inhibited; or, on the other hand, it may be that the hopelessness of competing with or resisting the autocrat led to a drastic diminution of the status needs themselves.

EMOTIONAL TENSION AND THE SIMPLIFICATION OF THE FIELD

Before we leave the topic of frustration and aggression, another basic theoretical question should be considered: the psychological *simplicity* of aggressive behavior, and the way in which emotional tension, by simplifying the structure of the psychological field, tends to leave aggression as the only kind of self-assertion that is psychologically available.

The concept of the simplification of the psychological field as a result of emotional tension was first introduced by Dembo in her interpretation of her experiments on anger (1931). It is also closely related to the concept of regression as investigated by Barker, Dembo and Lewin (1941). The word "regression" is somewhat misleading, however, since to many persons it suggests a reversion to earlier behavior patterns, and emotional tension does not always produce reversion to earlier types of behavior; what it does always produce, apparently, is a reduction in the complexity of the psychological field that determines behavior at a given moment. The more tense and frustrated a person is, the more his thought processes are reduced to their simplest and crudest elements. Creative thinking tends to disappear, imaginative understanding of another person's viewpoint tends to disappear, remote goals tend to disappear, inhibitions based on an appreciation of remote consequences tend to disappear, intelligent weighing and choosing between various alternatives tends to disappear; and, as a result, the behavior that occurs is likely to be not the most intelligent or adaptive be-havior, but the most "available" behavior—the behavior that comes most quickly into one's mind.

The relation between all of this and the frustration-aggression problem is perhaps obvious. If, and insofar as, aggressive behavior is for a given person the simplest, most "available" type of behavior at a given moment, emotional tension resulting from frustration will necessarily increase the likelihood of aggression. And that is very often the case. Destruction is simpler than construction; a blind hitting out at the environment calls for less thought and planning than does careful building up. Picturing the world in terms of crude blacks and whites involves less complicated thought processes than does trying to make finer distinctions, to recognize ambiguity, to understand another's viewpoint, or to arrive at in-tegrative group decisions. We would conclude, then, that this is an-other major reason for the observed correlation between frustration and aggression. And, since there was apparently more frustration in both laissez-faire and in the aggressive reaction to autocracy than there was in democracy, this is probably another reason for the ag-gression observed in those groups. In laissez-faire and in at least some of the autocratic groups, the children were frustrated, for all of the reasons outlined in the previous chapter. Presumably, then, their level of emotional tension was higher, their thought proc-esses were simpler and cruder, so that when driven by their own ego needs they would be in some cases literally *unable to think* of any round-about path to status, and would in a sense have nothing left to do but to assert their egos through primitive aggression.

To Summarize

The psychological problem of scapegoating is a part of the broader problem of irrational or exaggerated hostility, which enters into many political situations including the psychological back-ground of war. It is a difficult psychological problem, scarcely solved at all by the glib phrase "displaced aggression."

Scapegoating can be best understood as one result of an accentu-ated ego need. An impulse to aggression is likely to occur when-ever ego needs are especially strong and no other ways of satisfying them are, at the moment, psychologically available. The aggression then serves as a short cut to a feeling of importance.

The experimental facts supporting this "short-cut hypothesis" include the following:

1. In the experiments the scapegoat was never too weak. He was always strong enough to make a successful attack on him appear to be something of an achievement.

2. Aggression was greatest in the boys who showed other signs of a strong need for status, e.g., demands for attention.

3. There was much good-natured aggression that could be more reasonably explained on the basis of ego needs than on the basis of frustration.

4. The large amount of aggression in laissez-faire and in the aggressive reaction to autocracy could be reasonably explained in terms of status-seeking competition and ego frustration.

One reason for the close relation between frustration and aggression is that frustration often represents a blow to the ego and an accentuation of ego needs. Another reason is that the emotional tension produced by frustration has a tendency to simplify the psychological field. The individual's thought processes are reduced to their simpler, cruder elements, reducing his capacity to see a "long way around" and increasing the likelihood of a resort to short cuts, including aggression.

12

Two Boys Who Made Democracy Harder To Achieve

DEMOCRACY is not only a question of objectives and methods; it is also a question of people—their individuality and their maturity. And because it is a question of people it is a question of homes.

This chapter and the next are about four individual boys, and the homes from which they came. Two of them, Reilly and Fred, were a net liability from the standpoint of democracy. They were largely responsible for the degeneration of the Charlie Chan Club from a would-be democracy to anarchic laissez-faire. The other two, Lyman and Eddie, were on the plus side. Lyman very feebly, and Eddie rather strongly, played constructive roles in combating laissez-faire degeneration and establishing democratic group atmospheres. A study of these boys, then, is likely to throw light on the personality characteristics that help to make democracy workable, and on the kinds of family background that promote the development of these characteristics.

In addition to their bearing on democracy, the case studies may be of interest from two other standpoints: (1) They illustrate how a rather full and quantitative picture of a person's behavior in various small-group situations may illustrate fundamental aspects of his personality. In this way they may contribute something to the art of individual personality study, as practiced by psychiatrists, psychologists, vocational counselors, biographers, and others. (2) Even apart from their roles in relation to democracy, Reilly and

Fred were conspicuous troublemakers, while Lyman and Eddie were conspicuously "good" boys. The contrasts between the two pairs therefore have a bearing on one of the most fundamental problems of social psychology: the nature and origin of that cluster of traits and attitudes which Freudians call the "superego" and ordinary people call "conscience."

REILLY

Club personality. Reilly's personality has been inescapable if the reader has dipped at all into the records of the Charlie Chan Club. It was Reilly, for instance, who gleefully shouted, "Let's make war!" at the beginning of the first big water battle with the Secret Agents; it was Reilly whose vociferousness, as much as Fred and Leonard's more aggressive horseplay, led to the complete disintegration of the group under laissez-faire leadership; and it was Reilly who led the sit-down strike against the autocratic leader, which was the one instance, in any of the clubs, of more or less organized rebellion against authority.

While he was heedless of adult values and adult wishes, he was very popular with the other boys. He was the best liked boy in his schoolroom, as determined by a sociometric questionnaire, and he had been elected president of his class. This is somewhat puzzling, since he asserted his personality as vigorously in competition with other boys as in competition with adults. "We'll just sock you in the mouth then" was a rather characteristic example of his conversation. His personality contrasts sharply with that of Eddie, who was the best liked boy in the other schoolroom from which the club members were selected. Where Eddie was conscientious, quiet, unassuming, and genuinely friendly with everyone, Reilly was exuberant, self-advertising, constantly bombarding the eyes and ears of the others with his demands for attention, and, as the statistics showed (i.e., the figures based on the content analysis of the stenographic record) he was relatively low in both friendly and group-minded conversation. He was not actually a leader in the sense that he showed any planning or organizing ability; he was too impatient and too lacking in time perspective for that. He was a leader only in the sense that he was liked, and that his headlong, self-centered activity was imitated by others in the group.

It would seem, then, that his somewhat surprising popularity was not due to the kind of warm liking which drew other boys to the quiet and unassuming Eddie. Rather, it seems to have been due to the fact that he was successful in getting a rather gullible public to accept him at his own valuation, while at the same time the absence of malice in his self-assertion kept it from arousing hostility in others. In spite of his competitiveness and essential self-centeredness, the group accorded him a sort of hero worship, perhaps largely because each of them would have liked to be the sort of vital and self-confident person, completely uncowed by adults, that he unquestionably was.

In the interviews he expressed a preference for his laissez-faire leader as compared with his autocratic leader, indicating, probably, that his need for orderliness was less strong than his need for free self-assertion. He also showed unusual frankness in his avowed preference for the boy-valued activity of playful "fighting," as compared with the adult-valued activity of working. In describing his autocratic leader he said, "We didn't have any fun then—we didn't have any fights."

The psychological processes lying directly back of this outward behavior—processes which call for some discussion before digging more deeply into their origins—do not appear to be especially complex. One can infer first a very general negative fact: Reilly was not noticeably motivated by any of the adult-sponsored values which were conspicuous in such boys as Eddie and Lyman—obedience, respectfulness, nonaggression, order, self-control, hard work. In a word, he was low in the broad trait cluster that is sometimes called "conscience" and sometimes "superego." (See discussion in Chapter 14.) Second, a very general, positive fact: he was motivated, to a high degree, by competitiveness, or desire for superiority in the eyes of the other boys. It was this competitiveness, not much shackled by any sort of conscientiousness, that made his behavior particularly disruptive of democracy. Third, his behavior is most intelligible if one assumes that he tended to perceive a male adult not as an object of obedience, respect, or hostility, but as an equal, with whom he could compete (or be friendly, as he was with his democratic leader) on much the same basis as with any of the other boys.

Home background. In each of the four cases presented here the material on behavior with other boys is particularly plentiful, while material on family background is relatively meager. In each case the latter consists essentially of one good interview with the boy's mother. These interviews, however, were so full of clues as to possible explanations of personality dynamics that they will be discussed here in some detail.

It seemed fairly clear that Reilly's mother did not like him, and that she felt helpless in relation to him. According to her he is impudent, irresponsible, lazy, impatient, and unable to stay long at one thing. He continually quarrels with his older brother and teases his younger brother. She blurted out these criticisms in a weary but almost defiant way. According to her, "Punishment doesn't do him any good. I used to lose my temper and whip him; I was pretty mean, I guess"; but he would be just as bad or worse afterward, so now she doesn't ever punish him. "He sasses me back, and I can't stand a sassy child." Sometimes he argues for hours at a time, she told us, "Maybe it's because I've given in to him several times," and he knows that arguing is a good way to get things. For a while he had an allowance, but "he'd borrow on the next week's allowance and then expect to get it just the same," so the plan was discontinued. He now gets money for movies at least twice a week; if his mother tells him he can't go, he often goes to his father and gets the money from him.

There are several indications that he likes and respects his father more than his mother. His mother says that he minds his father, although his father has "never touched him." Her only form of discipline now is to tell his father; "He hates it when I tell his father." Reilly himself has talked proudly about "my dad's hardware store." On the other hand, his father is extremely busy in the large hardware store which he owns. According to the mother, she is with Reilly much more than the father is.

Limited as these observations are, they provide a provocative basis for speculation as to the origins of the three central factors in Reilly's club personality that have been described above: lack of conscientiousness, competitiveness, and tendency to perceive a male adult as an equal.

Reilly's lack of conscientiousness and also his competitiveness can be accounted for, to a considerable extent, by the combination of his hostility to his mother and his ability to tyrannize over her. The hostility is evidently of long standing. In response to the whippings his mother gave him, a small boy would naturally react with hostility, and when he became able to win out in the struggle between them, he would naturally relish keenly the exercise of his new-found power. The normally affectionate relation between mother and son was apparently transformed into a power struggle. In such a context, conscientiousness could scarcely have the meaning of pleasing a well-loved parent. In his mind it probably acquired, instead, the meaning of meek subordination and loss of self-respect, while defiance of her and of the values that she tried to enforce upon him must have meant sweet revenge and triumphant self-assertion.

At the same time, the positive factors which in most boys produce some acceptance and absorption of adult values by the age of eleven apparently had little chance to operate as far as Reilly's relation to his mother was concerned. Feeling little love for her, he probably also felt little need to win her love by being "good" as she defined goodness; in his "lifespace" goodness was not, to any important extent, seen as a path to her love. There was also little reason for him to want to identify with her or to play a role like hers, since, after she began the policy of weak appeasement, her role must have seemed to him an unenviable if not a contemptible one. And as for the factor of sheer calculating prudence—getting tangible rewards and avoiding tangible punishments—it could scarcely operate to produce conformity to his mother's wishes, since he could so easily defy her and get away with it.

Since his relationship to his mother was so thoroughly unconstructive from a moral standpoint, the puzzle is, perhaps, that he was not a more thoroughly "bad" boy than he actually turned out to be. In fact he was well socialized in some ways. It will be remembered that when the group in which he found himself was quiet and absorbed in work, Reilly played the chameleon and became quiet and absorbed in work too. Even with adults he was by no means indiscriminately rebellious. His teacher did not think of him as a special troublemaker like Fred, and he got along very well with Mr. Rowe, his democratic club leader.

If this is a puzzle, one clue to its solution probably lies in his relation to his father. He liked, respected, and obeyed his father, though his father "never touched him." Not because of tangible rewards and punishments, apparently, as much as because of sheer affection for his father and need for his father's approval ("He hates it when I tell his father"). Reilly apparently had some real incentive to be good—as his father defined goodness. What is not so clear is just what his father's definition included. However, since the father was known to be burly, good-natured, and financially successful in a competitive man's world, and since Reilly too was eminently successful in the rough-and-tumble world of his own peers, it is plausible to suppose that Reilly did conform fairly well both to the pattern of what his father was and to the pattern of what his father wanted him to be. While not exactly a "good boy" as adults usually define goodness, he was something that his father may well have regarded as more important: a "real boy."

What still calls for explanation is his tendency to perceive a male adult not as a person automatically deserving obedience and respect, nor yet as a natural enemy, but as an equal. There is a paradox here since, as we have seen, he did respect and obey his father. Nevertheless an explanation of a sort can be found in the father-son relationship. Apparently the father is indulgent in money matters (if Reilly's mother tells him he can't go to the movies he often goes to his father and gets the money from him), and Reilly himself describes his father as "a little less strict" than Mr. Rankin, his laissez-faire club leader. These facts suggest that the father did not often demand obedience or outward signs of respect, and that he was easygoing enough and friendly enough not to evoke hostility. There was apparently, most of the time, a kind of man-to-man equalitarian relationship between them that was very pleasant for Reilly and that would lead him to look for a similar relation of overt equality in his association with other male adults. By perceptual assimilation he would then tend to see a friendly but firm club leader (e.g., Mr. Rowe, his democratic leader) as someone like his father. But by the same token he would see a not-so-friendly and dominating adult (e.g., Mr. Bohlen, against whom he led the sit-down strike of the Charlie Chan Club) as violating the expected pattern of man-boy relationships. As for a vacillating and impersonal adult (e.g., Mr. Rankin, his laissez-faire leader), he might fall outside the father pattern altogether and be assimilated rather to Reilly's image of his mother or his brothers, all of whom he regarded as natural enemies and natural victims in the power struggle which he saw as the natural pattern of life.

FRED

Club personality. Fred also is by now a familiar figure. One thinks, for instance, of his long and half-successful battle with the autocratic Mr. Bohlen (pp. 119–122), his booing of Sam's constructive ideas on division of labor (p. 113), his sullen kicking of the stool (p. 55), his barefaced lie when he was trying to get Lyman to do his work for him (p. 120), his use of clay as a new missile in the big water battle with the Secret Agents (p. 118), his mischievous grin when he willfully misinterpreted Mr. Rankin's belated efforts to stop that battle (p. 118), and also, perhaps surprisingly, his capacity to become absorbed in work in a democratic atmosphere: "Someone in the outgroup throws something at this group. It lights on Fred, but this time they fail to get a rejoinder."

In some ways Fred was different from Reilly. They differed, for instance, in appearance: Reilly's slick blond hair and neat clothes contrasted with Fred's unkempt, down-at-the-heels, happy-go-lucky appearance. They differed in the form of their self-assertion in the club situation: Reilly's self-assertion was more insistent and constant; Fred's was more playful and variable, ranging from mild, good-natured horseplay to deliberate destruction and openly hostile defiance of a disliked autocrat. Fred did not compete with adults, as Reilly often did, nor seek their companionship, as Reilly sometimes did; he ignored them when they left him alone, and defied them, with a kind of resentful bravado, when they were "mean" and did not leave him alone. There was much less of the calculating opportunist in Fred's make-up than in Reilly's, and more uninhibited emotion. For example, when he became hostile (as he did in the autocratic atmosphere, both in rebellion against the autocrat and in persecution of scapegoats) it appeared to be more genuine out-and-out hostility than Reilly ever showed.

On the other hand, if these two boys are compared with a conscientious boy such as Eddie or Lyman, it becomes immediately apparent that they have a great deal in common which is not characteristic of the conscientious boys. Both were self-assertive most of the time. Both lived decidedly in a boys' world rather than an adults' world; and in that boys' world both seemed to seek power or superiority more than approval as such or even friendship as such. Both were lacking in real interest in their work most of the time; both were lacking in time perspective, and found their concrete goals almost entirely in the immediate present. Both lived happily in the unstructured field of laissez-faire and reacted joyfully to the playful "war" situation. Both tended to perceive a typical adult as something alien to themselves. Both perceived an authoritative adult as a challenging barrier to the achievement of their goals, and both reacted to this barrier aggressively rather than apathetically.

Fred's quantitative scores, like Reilly's, bear out this picture. He stood highest in "frustration in autocracy" and "aggression in democracy"; he was the lowest in "interest in work," and "asking information of the leader" in autocracy, and "work-minded conversation with the leader" in both autocracy and democracy. Other high scores were in "enjoyment of fighting" (as expressed in the interview), "out-of-field conversation" in democracy, and "attention demanding" in both autocracy and democracy. Other low scores were in "work-directing" conversation in democracy, "friendly" conversation in democracy, and "group-minded" conversation in democracy. The picture is clearly one of a boy who, in his lack of the behavior cluster of conscientiousness or "adult-value-centeredness," stood with Reilly at or near the extreme of the entire group. In Freudian terms, both had remarkably undeveloped "Superegos."

Home background. Unlike Reilly's rather young and stylish mother, Fred's was a haggard, pinched, thin-faced woman of fifty or fifty-five, with the old-fashioned hairdress and forward-drooping head of a servant character in a play. As she put it, she had had "a hard life, a very hard life." She had borne eight children, of whom Fred was the youngest; her husband drank heavily, and for the past three years she herself had had to work as a maid in a hotel.

There was no bad humor in her pinched mouth, and no ill will in what she had to say about Fred. Nor, for that matter, was there evidence of any real ill will on his part toward her. On the other hand, there was also no evidence of any close, positive relationship between them. The mother seemed to take him and the other children (and grandchildren) more or less for granted as parts of her "very hard life," and her work during the day kept her discipline from being at all continuously effective. She showed no curiosity about the clubs or their purpose. "Even if all they did was kill time," she said, she would have been glad to have Fred belong, because the boys had nothing to do but play around the house after school when she was still at work, and "sometimes they get pretty wild."

The boys she was referring to here were the two youngest of her eight children: Jackie, who was twelve, and Fred, who was eleven. Jackie and Fred are "great pals—just great pals." "If one's in mischief the other's sure to be." But Jackie is likely to cry whenever he gets teased, and "Fred's an awful tease." Fred "is what you might call a happy . . . , just going from this to that all the time." Although Jackie is a year older, they are about equal physically. "I don't let them wrassle when I'm here, but of course when I'm not here I don't know what they do."

According to her, Fred's reaction to discipline is "all right"; he "understands that he's punished only when he has really done wrong." He was "whipped just this morning for not coming when he was called. I can't stand it for children not to mind. I don't want them to be the boss and me not." But she now uses sending to bed as punishment more than whipping; she doesn't "believe in whipping like some mothers do." She would whip Fred if he was impudent, "but none of my boys has ever sassed me back."

It is clear that there was little or no companionship between Fred and his father. The mother was free, though appropriately sad, in talking about her husband. "His failing is drink," she said with a sigh. He used to be a plumber, and now is doing janitor work. According to her, none of the children cares for him, "though I teach them to respect him because, well, he's their father." As she told the story, he once came home pretty "lit up," late at night, and Fred saw him come in. The next day Fred said something about trying a little liquor to see if it would make him the same way. Jackie answered, "All right, you do and I'll lick you till you don't know whether you're coming or going." Fred said, "Did you think I meant it?" The mother said, "I *hope* you didn't mean it, Fred," and he answered, "Of course I couldn't, Mother; I never could be like that." According to her, the boys see little of their father. She has "forbidden" her husband to discipline the children. "You see, he was so abusive to me." When their father is sick, none of the children seem to care, she says, but when she is sick they do.

There are at least two important differences between this picture and that of Reilly's family: the absence of any clear evidence of hostility between Fred and his mother, and the apparent absence of any significant, positive relationship between him and his father. At the same time there are at least two basic similarities: apparently neither boy has a very close or warm relationship to his mother, and not one of the four parents is able to maintain any constant and consistent type of discipline. Warmth and firmness are relatively lacking in the atmosphere of both of these homes. While Fred appears to have some affection for his mother and a good deal of respect for her whippings when she is at home, the relationship seems to be considerably watered down by her concern with other children and grandchildren, by her tiring work outside as well as inside the home, and by her tendency to self-preoccupation and self-pity. As for discipline, the father can provide none at all, and the mother cannot provide any when she is away at work. As she put it, when one boy is in mischief the other is sure to be, and while she is gone they "sometimes get pretty wild."

These background factors may be related to Fred's club personality in some of the same ways that were suggested in the case of Reilly. The most basic similarity is that *neither boy had any good psychological basis for accepting and absorbing (i.e., "internalizing") adult-sponsored values.*

For instance, the absence of a close and warm relationship between Fred and his mother probably meant that in his case, as in Reilly's, being good was not strongly desired as a path to love. There was apparently not much in his relation with his mother that would give him a strong desire to please her. It is more than possible, too, that some active hostility was mingled with his somewhat mild affection for her. She did not seem to the interviewer to be a very lovable woman, and her rather severe punishments were scarcely likely to endear her to him. If so, flouting her authority and her values must have had, to some extent, the meaning of personal triumph, in Fred's case as in Reilly's. The part of him that was hostile to her would exult in doing, in her absence, those things which she would whip him for if she were at home.

While Reilly could easily identify with his father and try to be like him, Fred could hardly want to be like either of his parents. His father, the most natural object of an eleven-year-old boy's hero worship, was a pitiable figure, "forbidden" by his wife to "touch her" or to discipline the children. Although Fred's suggestion that he might try a little liquor himself suggests some faint stirrings of identification with his father, he himself, according to the mother's story, disavowed the impulse immediately and said, "Of course I couldn't, Mother; I never could be like that." It is clear that his father-image was not attractive; on the whole, it was positively re- pellent. As for a possible identification with his mother, she too was scarcely a person to be hero-worshiped or envied. Although she clearly had more strength of character than Reilly's mother, her age, her sex, her appearance, and her "very hard life" probably combined to eliminate any unconscious need on Fred's part to be like her or to internalize her values.

Finally, the factor of sheer prudence—of reward seeking and pun- ishment avoiding—probably would not operate in Fred's case much more than in Reilly's. While his mother was at home he seems to have found it prudent to be reasonably good; his reaction to dis- cipline, according to her, is "all right," and "none of my boys has ever sassed me back." But when she was gone, in the afternoons, the chains were off and Fred could exultantly do as he pleased. There is also reason to think that his prudent desire to avoid being whipped or sent to bed was sometimes overbalanced by his tend- ency to make a game out of seeing how far he could go before be- ing slapped down. His not coming when called—an action which in this case did lead to a whipping—may well have been a case in point. Her punishments were severe but in the nature of things could not be consistently applied, and he evidently learned to take advantage of the loopholes between them.

The fact that Fred tended to *perceive an adult as an enemy* in- stead of as a potential companion, which was Reilly's tendency, can also be plausibly explained on the basis that Reilly's relation- ship to his father was closer than Fred's was. Neither Fred's father nor his mother, apparently, offered him any real companionship. For that he had long ago learned that he must look only to his peers; in fact, he seems to have learned to regard adults primarily as an intermittent danger to his normal life of having fun with other boys. In school as well as in the club (in both probably even more than at home) he had established a pattern of enhancing his status among other boys by actual defiance of the adult enemy.

Here too there was a similarity to Reilly, since Reilly also lived primarily in a boy's world, and Reilly's non-respectful competition with adults had much in common with Fred's disrespectful hostil- ity to or ignoring of adults. There were nevertheless some impor- tant differences. Reilly could "internalize" some adult values. Fred was more of an animal, more of a child, and less of a conforming, competitive member of his community. Reilly's father provided him with a bridge to his culture; Fred's father did not.

To Summarize the Picture of the Two Troublemakers

Along with elements which were different in the two boys and made each of them unique, there were also major underlying similarities in home background as well as personality structure. Both of them had failed to internalize and make their own, in any high degree, the cluster of values which adults normally try to inculcate in children; and in both cases this seemed to be connected, somehow, with a comparative lack of either warmth or firmness in the atmosphere of the home. Neither love, nor identification, nor prudence had led either of them to adopt the good-child role. For similar reasons, both of them very much wanted superiority in the eyes of other boys, and neither of them tended to perceive adults as automatically worthy of obedience or respect.

13

Two Boys Who Made
Democracy Easier To Achieve

LYMAN and Eddie both played constructive roles in the efforts of their clubs to create democracy in place of anarchy; both were allies rather than enemies of the adult leaders who were trying to do the same thing. In this they contrasted sharply with both Reilly and Fred, and a more thorough study of them, and of the homes they came from, is likely to be as suggestive on the positive side, in terms of the deeper roots of democracy, as a study of Reilly and Fred was on the negative side, in terms of the anarchic forces that democracy often has to overcome.

To be sure, there is something incongruous in linking so closely, in this discussion, two boys who in other respects were so different. Lyman was possibly the worst adjusted boy among the seventeen who were intensively studied, while Eddie was quite possibly the best adjusted. Lyman was a mama's boy and something of a sissy, while Eddie was a boy's boy and completely "regular." This contrast, however, brings out in sharp relief what they had in common. They both showed the cluster of perceptions, attitudes, and actions which can be called a highly developed "conscience," and they both showed the basic family pattern which appears to furnish the best soil for the development of conscientiousness.

LYMAN

Club personality. Lyman, the unboyish misfit in the Charlie Chan Club, will be remembered for his physical immobility (p.

111), his bewildered silence while the others were shouting and bickering (p. 109), his tendency to think about faraway subjects while the others were preoccupied with the immediate situation (p. 128), his protests against group aggression: "You kids quit this," and "Don't you think you've done enough destroying for one day?" (p. 117), his gain in self-confidence during autocracy (p. 120), and especially his gain during democracy (p. 128).

He may be remembered also as one of the three boys (Lyman, Van, and Beaumont) who, although they were physically the most inadequate boys in any of the clubs, never became scapegoats. The aggression of Reilly, Fred, and Leonard was nearly always directed against each other, against their autocratic club leader, or against the Secret Agents on the other side of the tool chest, rather than against Lyman. Even when he petulantly protested against their collective aggression the other boys scarcely seemed to hear him; and even when he bragged about his marks in school, as he did on two or three occasions, they showed no irritation. One reason, as suggested in Chapter 11, may have been that no one could gain in status by "picking on" a boy as obviously lacking in physical prowess as Lyman was. Another reason, perhaps, was that even on the rare occasions when he bragged or criticized he did not actually provoke the hostility or challenge the status of any one other boy. The rest of the group apparently accepted him (when they thought of him at all) as somewhat queer but harmless.

This curious kind of acceptance was shown not only in their behavior toward him but also in their choices as expressed in two sociometric questionnaires. In the first one, involving all the boys in the schoolroom (p. 17), he came out only slightly below the average of the group, although the typical attitude toward him was indifference rather than either acceptance or rejection. In the second questionnaire, given to the five members of this club on their sixth meeting day (in the laissez-faire atmosphere, in which he was most ill at ease), he came out third, or exactly in the middle of the five boys. He was liked slightly better than Sam, the hardest working boy in the group, and decidedly better than Leonard, one of the three troublemakers, whose overdone horseplay made him actively objectionable even to those who were troublemakers like himself. (The order of popularity was: Reilly, Fred, Lyman, Sam, Leonard.) In fact, when Reilly was asked in an interview who he considered the best club member, he nominated Lyman for that position, saying that Lyman "never gets into trouble; he always does what us kids like."

His maladjustment showed itself not in being disliked but in his strange immobility and his lack of emotional contact with the group. When they were joyfully exploring some new play materials he was likely to be leaning awkwardly against a post, looking at them with a blank expression on his face. When they stopped work to loaf, or to shout their disrespect at the Secret Agents, he would still be plodding away with a hammer or a paintbrush. When the others rushed in a body into the clubroom, racing with each other to see who would get there first, he was always lagging several paces behind. His language was more bookish than that of the others; for instance he once laughed at someone's misfortune, saying, "That's rich!" His movements were awkward and his speech had a certain plodding, labored quality in comparison with the fluency of the others. There was usually no expression on his face except a kind of wide-eyed, childlike placidity.

According to the statistical records he fell far below the average of his group in total amount of social interaction, with low scores also in "friendly approaches received" and in the proportion of his own conversation classified as friendly or playful. Instead, his meager conversation tended to take the form of asking for information about the activity in progress—one of the safest and most modest forms of conversation—and of "out-of-field" talking. This out-of-field conversation, occurring chiefly under democratic leadership when the group was most harmonious and he was most adjusted to it, seemed to reflect his lack of strong interest in the immediate club situation and his preoccupation with the schoolroom—an area in which he had greater security, apparently, than he had in any of the club situations. In short, the whole picture was one of rather extreme lack of emotional contact with the group.

What was going on behind that placid face of his? What might be the psychological causes of this kind of behavior? It was impossible to tell, with any certainty, but some tentative inferences can be made. It seems fairly clear, for instance, that one factor was simple bewilderment. To him, the play world of the other boys was an "unstructured field"—a pathless wilderness. It was a good thing for him when an autocratic adult leader, and later a democratic leader, clearly defined the situation and ended his bewilderment.

One of Lyman's important goals, then, was a clearly structured field. Another, probably, was physical security, including the security of his clothes as well as his body. It was noticed, for instance, that he did not participate at all in either of the "wars" of his group. He stood behind a post and ducked even when no one was throwing at him. It seems likely that he associated the confusion of the boys' play world with danger to his own poorly coordinated body, and disliked it all the more on that account. Probably it also involved, in his mind, the disapproval of his mother. In an interview he expressed repeatedly his dislike of Leonard, who "caused a fight with the other club, and I got a scolding." He said that he had had on new clothes, and his mother was very upset at first. But most of the clay and water came out, so "she is all right now." He added that "the fight hurt me," and he also expressed dislike of Fred, who "is always acting up, and picks fights." (He liked Sam, the hard worker, best, and Reilly next.)

The inferred psychological factors, then, which need to be accounted for if possible in terms of Lyman's home background, include the following: his strong conscience, including a special dislike of all forms of aggression; his lack of psychological contact with other boys; his need for a structured field; his physical immobility and need for physical security.

Home background. Lyman's mother was a plain woman of perhaps forty, with strong features and a tight mouth, expressionless except for a humorless smile. She was voluble in her interview, and painted a most idyllic picture of her relationship, not only with Lyman but also with John, who was three years older than Lyman. It was plain, though, that she felt much closer to Lyman. "There's only one thing I regret," she said, "I regret that I don't have nicer things to give Lyman—toys and things like that." "John is more his daddy's boy"—out working with machinery in the shop, while Lyman stays home. Lyman likes to "potter around home." He has a pet hen and pet pigeon which he feeds. He picked them up in the alley. He's satisfied with rather meager things—a flower garden, for instance, with four rows of zinnias. He "likes to help me in the garden." He has no regular responsibilities, though "he helps whenever I ask him. He is a very willing little chap." He is usually home

in the afternoons, and "has never had a desire to go out evenings."
He was "good" even as a baby; he "wasn't one of those squawky
babies." "I never did punish Lyman—outside of admonishing him."

His relationship to his teachers appeared to be similar to his relationship to his mother. "We've had three of his teachers at home
recently. They're all crazy about his work in school. He's had 38
E's (excellent), and all the others G plus." In general he appeared
more at ease with women than with men.

His relationship to his father seemed rather tenuous. When
asked whether Lyman was with his father much, his mother said
"No—really no." Now that the father is operating the shop, "we
hardly see him at home." It is John and not Lyman who works
with his father in the shop. Here, too, the mother painted a somewhat idyllic picture. The father "comes in so quietly" and he's so
nice to the children. "Mrs. Langley thinks he's just a wonderful
father." He doesn't drink. He is with John the most, but "thinks
the world of Lyman too." The father was like the mother in that
he had never spanked Lyman. Yet there were signs that Lyman was
not at ease with his father. "The worst thing his daddy ever said
to him was 'That's enough, Lyman,' and he got smaller and smaller
and sobbed a little, and that was all." Lyman himself saw his father
as very strict. When asked in an interview whether Mr. Bohlen
(his autocratic club leader) was more strict than his parents, he
answered that Mr. Bohlen was not as strict as his mother and "not
half as strict" as his father.

As for the relation between Lyman and his older brother John,
it too seemed less idyllic than the mother at first tried to make it
appear. She began by saying that they got along together "very well,
for brothers," but she went on to say that they don't play together
much, and that the two boys are "exactly opposite." John is interested in doing things; he takes home books and Lyman reads them.
Lyman will be sure he's right before he argues with John, but John
flounders around and argues with him just for the sake of arguing.
"John will sometimes argue until he has to be swat down." The
mother's only criticism was of John, and also her only description
of conflict. Lyman, she said, "isn't a bit sassy," while John is.
"When John was little I did considerable switching. Dr. Kimball
told me I was wasting my time and temper, and it did seem like
he got along just as well when I gave him plenty to do." "When

my husband is with John he has no fault to find with him. It's his idle times that are bad with him."

Instead of playing with John, Lyman played with Howard Storey (a boy in one of the other clubs, who was small, scatterbrained, and probably even lower in economic status than Lyman himself) and sometimes with Lester Millen, the son of a professor. With other boys, according to the mother, Lyman "is more of a reserved type. He'll rebel if they are doing something he doesn't approve of. Sometimes he'll say, 'Mother, I didn't go with so-and-so because they were doing something you wouldn't approve of.'"

The economic status of the family was not especially low, but their straitened circumstances were apparently a rather recent thing, and rather important in the mother's eyes. "Before we came here we had a large place and several friends. Now we're cooped up with Grandma and Grandpa, and Lyman doesn't have much of a chance," since she is unable to give him "toys and things like that."

From these facts there emerges a fairly coherent picture of a strong-minded woman who was holding tightly to her favorite son and who seemed to have no insight into his failure to adapt to a boy's world, or her own possible part in that failure. She could not see that she had made him a "mama's boy." Nor did she seem to realize that her dominating ways might conceivably have something to do with the fact that her husband was so often out of the picture ("we hardly see him at home"; he "comes in so quietly"), and that John too is so often away with his daddy. One can speculate that the home is somewhat cheerless for both John and his daddy, that she in turn does not get much affection from them, and that there are also problems in her relationship with "grandma and grandpa." If she does lack other sources of affection this would help to account for her clinging to Lyman, and her inability to see the harm that her clinging probably did to him.

Another problem is why Lyman himself also seemed quite unaware of the extent to which he was a "mama's boy." He could not see himself through the eyes of the other boys. Although physically in a boy's world during at least some part of each school day, he judged that world only from the outside, so to speak, in terms of his mother's values, without seeming to realize that in the other boys' eyes he and his values might appear equally strange. One may hazard the guess that he could not see this partly because he did not want to see it, and that he did not want to see it partly because his relationship to his mother was too necessary to him to permit itself to be subjected to realistic scrutiny. His relation to his mother, in turn, may have been emotionally important to him partly because he had so few other sources of affection. He seems to have been somewhat afraid of his father ("He got smaller and smaller and sobbed a little, and that was all"), and his older brother too was not much of a companion to him.

His conscientiousness was at bottom a life pattern of contented conformity with his mother's wishes, dating from early childhood (he "wasn't one of those squawky babies"; "I never did punish Lyman, outside of admonishing him"). He gladly conformed to the rather firm pattern his mother provided; in fact he seemed to have had his chief satisfactions inside this little island of her approval. In his world "being a good boy" was definitely a path to his mother's love, which mattered to him enormously, and her values were the ones that he would naturally "internalize."

Even the normal tendency of a boy to identify with his father did not seem to be in evidence in Lyman's case. The father was a somewhat unsuccessful breadwinner, and his role in relation to the mother also was not particularly enviable. (One wonders whether the mother might "swat down" her husband too if he should dare to drink, or if he did not "come in so quietly.") Lyman, therefore, had little reason to want to identify with or to imitate his father, and even if he had wanted to imitate him there would have been, apparently, no pattern of vigorous male independence for him to imitate. His mother's image was the only glowing one in his small psychological world. It is understandable, therefore, that he tended to feel ill at ease with all males, including his adult male club leaders, who most nearly resembled his father.

EDDIE

Club personality. One surprising fact is that Eddie, the other outstanding "good" boy to be discussed here, was as well integrated in his own peer group as Lyman was poorly integrated in his. In addition to being good he was also a "real boy" in every way in which Lyman was not. In fact, the sociometric questionnaire showed that he was the most chosen boy in the schoolroom from which the Law and Order Patrol was selected (p. 17). He was quiet, hard-working, nonaggressive, and not attention demanding, yet quite capable of holding his own physically or engaging in rough-and-tumble horseplay when the occasion arose (p. 57). He will be remembered as an ally of Bill, the would-be dictator, against the disruptive influence of Finn (pp. 105–6); yet he never participated in this quarrel enough to antagonize Finn, and was elected, by a majority which included Finn, to succeed Bill in the role of commander-in-chief. It was characteristic of him that even in this role he almost never asserted his authority, but was quite content to let Mr. Rankin, the new democratic adult leader, exert whatever leadership was needed.

Eddie will also be remembered as the one boy, out of twenty, who preferred autocracy to democracy. It was he who said, "Mr. Rowe was the strictest, and I like that a lot. Mr. Davis and Mr. Rankin let us go ahead and fight, and that isn't good. . . . A club leader ought to keep us from loafing." (Actually there was little or no actual fighting under Mr. Rankin, the democratic leader. What Eddie was reacting against must have been primarily the nonviolent feud between Bill and Finn, which came to a head during Mr. Rankin's period of leadership and which resulted in the election of Eddie himself to take Bill's place. Although it brought him glory, Eddie apparently regarded this whole episode as both "fighting" and loafing, and therefore unworthy. The fact that he was the son of a National Guard officer might perhaps suggest that a militaristic atmosphere in the home brought about his preference for autocracy. This explanation is of course an attractive one to believers in democracy who are also opposed to "militarism." Unfortunately, it is by no means the whole story. Considering his relations with other boys as well as with adults, Eddie was also one of the best adjusted boys, if not the best adjusted boy, in the entire experiment. Does this mean, then, that a good adjustment brings about a preference for autocracy, or perhaps that a preference for autocracy makes for good adjustment? Obviously the question calls for closer analysis, with careful definition of terms such as "militaristic," as well as a closer look at the actual relationship between Eddie and his parents.

About his club behavior there is not much more to be said. His degree of focus on work was outstanding, as evidenced by high scores in work-oriented conversation, by his expressed preference for "the work part" of the club as compared with the "play part," and by his strongly expressed dislike of the laissez-faire atmosphere. He also expressed a wish to be the best worker in the club rather than the best liked or the one who directs things. In school, similarly, his teacher gave him high ratings in obedience and in absence of teasing and quarreling.

It seems evident that he was entirely different from Reilly and Fred in his habitual way of perceiving adult authority. To him an adult was self-evidently a person to be obeyed and respected (perhaps depending to some extent on how the adult behaved) rather than challenged, circumvented, ignored, or treated as an equal.

2. *Home background.* Eddie's mother was an exceptionally pretty woman of from thirty to thirty-five, who talked very freely and apparently frankly, with good humor and vivacity. It was evident immediately, too, that in this family, unlike the families of Reilly, Fred, and Lyman, the two parents were harmonious and very similar in their ways of handling their three boys, so that a separate treatment of Eddie's relationship to his two parents would not be appropriate. Harmony between the parents was evidenced partly by what the mother said directly about their relationship— "I'm rather a tomboy; I ride horseback with my husband, usually, on Sunday morning"—and partly by her characteristic use of the pronoun "we" rather than "I" in discussing their handling of the boys: "We are very strict," "We don't take them out at night," "We don't spare anything to give them a good time." She also said that she and her husband don't need to discuss questions of discipline much. "He and I agree so much that either he takes care of them or I do."

There is no doubt about the firmness of this discipline. "My husband has been captain of the cavalry troop, and has treated his children as privates in the guard. They've been brought up not to talk back. My brother-in-law thinks that we're terribly strict—that the kids don't have any fun. But we're *always* doing something for them . . ." The boys don't play much with the boys in the neighborhood. "I don't entirely approve of the neighborhood." Eddie's friends come from further away. "I've never allowed my children to go out of the yard, and if they go anywhere after school they come home first and tell me." There is also no doubt about the two older boys' approval of strict discipline. (Eddie, eleven, is the oldest; Jim is nine and Roger six.) Both Eddie and Jim belong to the

Drum and Bugle Corps. "Both the boys like the discipline there; it's very strict. They'll say, when some boy is penalized, 'Yes, but he deserved it.'" "Eddie's very conscientious—in some ways I think a little too much so. If he destroyed something he'd come himself and say, 'Mother, I won't go to the show tomorrow.'"

At the same time, there is equally little doubt that the parents' despotism—if it can be called despotism—was benevolent. After making the above statement that "we're always doing something for them" the mother went into detail. "They see every parade, carnival, circus, and everything else that comes along. I've always felt that this home was as much theirs as ours. My husband brought home two army tents once. There are seventeen birds in the house, and now two sets of baby birds." The father doesn't have a great deal of time to spend with the children, since he works eight hours a day at the Biology Building and the rest of the time at "the guard" (the local National Guard). But he's very fond of children. "He'll take the children with him sometimes. He goes with them to the Drum and Bugle Corps. He'll stop and play ball for five minutes at noon. In winter they'll lay for him with snowballs. They talk over the baseball and football situation every noon —college teams, and their own."

And in view of the relatively mild character of the punishments described by the mother, and the general respect which she showed for the differing personalities of her boys, it is even doubtful whether the word "despotism" is appropriate at all. With all of its firm consistency and its strictness on some points, the discipline does not seem at all severe compared to that found in other families of the community. When asked what she would do if one of her boys were late in coming home she said that she would first hear his story. "That has happened," she said. "When there was no excuse, they stayed in the house and couldn't play ball with the other boys. That was quite a punishment." When asked what she would do if they destroyed anything intentionally she said "they'd be severely punished—I'd send them upstairs." "There's only one thing I've ever slapped them for; it's when they laugh at me when I scold them. If they're impudent I make them sit on a chair until they see there isn't any headway to be gained that way. It's very, very seldom."

Eddie was also less thoroughly in sympathy with all forms of discipline than the evidence presented up to this point might suggest. "Physical discipline arouses his anger. He can't seem to take physical punishment. He can be ridiculed or shamed; he can't stand that. But if I raise my voice he gets stubborn." (It may be noted that Mr. Rowe, the autocrat whom Eddie liked better than his democratic leader, never raised his voice or used physical punishment. If he had, Eddie's resentment of these things was such that he probably would have preferred his democratic leader.)

In some other respects also he was far from docile. "His biggest fault is stubbornness—bullheadedness. His father and I are both that way too. He can be coaxed to do anything, but if you force him he won't do it, or if he does he won't do it right. . . . It's very hard for him to cry. Only if you shame him; not if he's hurt." This, surely, is not a picture of a boy whose spirit had been broken by "militaristic" handling.

Among the brothers themselves there was apparently at least a normal amount of friendliness. According to the mother there had been "a great amount of cooperation." "Among themselves there's a good deal of argument, but they take each other's part if anyone else has anything to say."

The family atmosphere seemed to be one of frankness and mutual confidence. "All our children are decidedly truthful." "Eddie criticizes too much. He's very critical. He not only criticizes others; he criticizes himself." "Of course we've always treated our home life as an open book; whatever concerns one concerns all of us. If anything happens, Eddie tells all of us about it."

The picture as a whole was "autocratic" or "militaristic" only if firm insistence on obedience is regarded as automatically, by definition, "autocratic" or "militaristic." It was neither autocratic nor militaristic if certain other criteria are applied: the parents' love for their children, their regard for the wishes and individual personalities of their children, the absence of continual or overfrequent supervision, the absence of oversevere punishment, and the ability of the children to communicate freely with their parents. In all of these ways Eddie's home was "democratic." There was even a notable absence of false dignity on the part of the parents; the boys felt free to fire snowballs at their father when he came home to lunch. In fact, the "strictness" of the parents had been purged of almost everything that might make it repugnant to a boy like Eddie, and had been an integral part of a pattern of life to which, as a whole, he could only react with approval and pride. The parents appeared to be basically happy and well-adjusted themselves, devoted to each other as well as to the children, and exceptionally successful in maintaining their children's friendship as well as their respect. The economic status of the family was evidently somewhat higher than that of most of the other families whose children go to the same school. For these and other reasons, including the father's dashing role as captain of the cavalry troop, the boys must have been immensely proud of their family and sure of its superiority to most of the other families in the neighborhood. It is quite understandable that, in such a context, "strictness" should seem to Eddie a desirable form of adult behavior. Strictness to him meant his family, and his family meant everything that was wonderful and fine.

To Summarize the Picture of the Two "Good Boys"

Eddie, in sharp contrast with Lyman, had great rapport with his peer group. He was a boy's boy where Lyman was a mama's boy.

Nevertheless, he closely resembled Lyman in his conscientiousness; he was "good" in the ways in which adults define goodness for children.

In his case, as in Lyman's, this goodness coincided with both firmness and warmth on the part of the significant parents. In Lyman's case his mother was by far the more significant parent; in Eddie's case both parents were highly significant.

It would seem that for both boys goodness came to be valued as a path to their parents' love.

In addition, both boys must have identified with at least one of their parents, and "internalized" their parents' values to an unusual degree.

14

Notes on the Nature and Growth of Conscience

CONSCIENTIOUS individuals such as Eddie and Lyman are likely to contribute to the effective working of democracy, while self-assertive individuals such as Reilly and Fred are likely to have a disruptive influence. Unless constrained by autocratic controls, a group composed mainly of Reillys and Freds often becomes sheer anarchy. In order to develop the kinds of individuals who can make democracy work, then, as well as for other good reasons, it is worthwhile to consider what makes a child conscientious. The last two chapters considered this question in terms of case studies; this one approaches it somewhat more systematically.

NEEDED: *A psychological explanation of conscience (internal standards) as distinguished from conformity (external standards)*
It is relatively easy to give a psychological explanation of the prudent, opportunistic type of imitation or social conformity. For instance, Reilly's chameleon-like behavior, boisterous when the other boys in the club were boisterous and hard-working when they were hard-working, is intelligible in terms of his desire for the approval of these other boys, and perhaps also in terms of a generalized, functionally autonomous imitative tendency (Miller and Dollard, 1941). The real challenge to psychology—a challenge which few psychologists have seriously taken up—is to explain, in naturalistic terms, why some people, some of the time, are guided by internal moral standards that do not depend directly on social approval or any other ulterior goals. Why did Eddie resist the general demoralization of the Law and Order Patrol and keep on working after

the others had stopped? Why did Lyman, timid as he was, stand out against the destructiveness of the troublemakers who predominated in the Charlie Chan Club, and brave their disapproval by asking, "Don't you think you've done enough destroying for one day?" Why does anyone hold to standards of honesty even when honesty does not seem to him to be "the best policy" in terms of tangible, external goods such as money or group approval?

In answer to such questions it is easy enough to say that "moral standards of the group tend to become internalized," or that "many individuals develop a need for self-approval as well as for social approval." But such formulas, valid as they may be, only push the problem a step further back. Other questions remain: How are moral standards internalized? What is the origin of the approving and condemning "self" that is implied when "self-approval" is invoked as an explanation? Why are some people more "inner-directed" than others? Or, as a Freudian might put it, where does the superego come from?

The experiments do not contribute much toward solution of this problem, but they do offer some sidelights on it, and these sidelights are brought together in the present chapter.

A Definition of Conscience, and Some Data on Whether It Is One Thing or Many

A first step is to define, with some care, what is meant here by the key word "conscience."

Some definitions are arbitrarily laid down; others emerge from accumulated research. While both types are legitimate it is fortunate that our definition of conscience can be of the latter type—a nonarbitrary empirical definition, based on accumulated correlation data. At least fourteen investigations (thirteen in addition to the present one)[1] have shown significant positive correlations between traits that are ordinarily regarded as "moral": nonaggression, honesty, modesty, perseverance, hard work in school, etc. That is, a person who is high in any one of these traits is likely to be at least

[1] See, for example, Webb (1915), McDonough (1929), Hartshorne, May & Maller (1929), Pinard (1932), Howell (1933), McCloy (1936), Richards & Simons (1941), Ackerson (1942), Kremer (1942), Sanford, Adkins, Muller & Cobb (1943), Lovell (1945), Cattell (1950), MacArthur (1951). The cluster has been given many names, "will" and "persistence" being two of the more prominent ones.

above average in most of the others. For the purposes of this discussion, then, conscience is defined as the *psychological processes that lie back of the traits in this cluster and that account for the intercorrelations between them*. This definition is empirical in that it forces us to pay attention to the available correlation data. At the same time it leaves the door open for theorizing and for further investigation as to just what psychological processes do "lie back of the traits in the cluster" and "account for the intercorrelations between them."

This definition also has the advantage of calling attention to facts which have actually solved the old and troublesome problem of whether "conscience" is a single trait or a mere word illegitimately used to cover a number of unrelated traits. Many psychologists have hesitated to use the old-fashioned word "conscience," or the new-fashioned word "superego," on the ground that the facts calling for explanation were too complicated and diverse to be covered by any one word, and that if any over-all term is used it should be one that is naturally plural in form (e.g., internalized moral values) rather than singular. The statistical facts would seem to constitute convincing evidence that the truth does not lie at either extreme. "Conscience" is obviously not a single unitary trait; the correlations between different moral traits are by no means high enough to permit any such assumption. At the same time it is not a mere word for many unrelated traits; the correlations are much too high for that. Instead, it is a *cluster* of related traits. As long as the word is recognized as merely a convenient label for this cluster and for the psychological processes that lie back of it, no one needs to have serious qualms about either the word "conscience" or its Freudian equivalent, "superego."

Both the size of the often-demonstrated correlations and the nature of the correlated traits can be illustrated by the data of the present experiments. The core of the cluster—the behavior measures that correlated most highly with each other—consisted of three characteristics: nonaggression (measured in two independent ways), persistence in work (three independent measures), and—surprisingly—contentment in autocracy (two independent measures). The average intercorrelation of these seven measures was .60.[2] A number of other measures correlated positively with the

[2] This average correlation of .60 is surprisingly high when one considers that the average self-correlation or reliability coefficient of these three characteris-

core traits; these correlations, though usually less than .60, were almost all positive, and their average size was .47. The other correlated characteristics were: obedience in school, not demanding attention (two measures), respectful aloofness from the democratic leader, frustration in laissez-faire (perhaps because of its lack of structure, lack of time perspective, and lack of constructive achievement), and friendliness with other boys in autocracy (perhaps as a reflection of contentment in autocracy). The clustering together of all but two of these might have been anticipated on the basis of other research, the two exceptions being "contentment in autocracy" and its obverse, "frustration in laissez-faire." The clustering of these two with the others was a new finding, and an unexpected one, since there is nothing obviously "moral" in a preference for autocracy.

Conscience May Not Be Wholly Admirable

An additional advantage of the naturalistic definition suggested here is that it provides a safeguard against over-rosy views of conscience. As the Freudians have long insisted, the superego can be a tyrant; there are hazards in being too conscientious, or conscientious in the wrong way. The evidence just presented tends to support the Freudian view in one respect. It suggests that conscientiousness may carry with it a kind of docility that makes for a too-easy adjustment to autocracy.

---

tics (e.g., the correlation of one measure of persistence-in-work with another independent measure of persistence-in-work) was only .63. Roughly speaking, the small difference of only three points between these two figures suggests how little is specific to a trait such as nonaggression or persistence, while the figure .60 itself suggests how much they have in common. (Speaking more precisely and technically, most of the variance is attributable either to random errors of observation and variability of behavior or to the general conscientiousness factor; very little of it is attributable to specific factors involved in the three traits as such.) If corrected for attenuation, the intercorrelations would be very much higher than .60.

Readers are reminded that the population consisted of only 17 boys, so that none of the figures mentioned above can be regarded as at all precise. However, when N is 17 a correlation of .61 is significant at the 1 per cent level. Since each of the core characteristics is represented within the core by at least two independent measures, so that there are at least eleven correlation coefficients involving each trait, each coefficient adds something to the combined statistical significance of the whole. It can therefore be regarded as highly probable that each of the three "core characteristics" is in some degree a part of the conscientiousness cluster, though not necessarily part of its core.

This possibility is illustrated by all four of our case studies. Eddie, one of the conspicuously good boys, was the only one who actually preferred his autocratic leader to his democratic leader, while Fred, one of the conspicuous troublemakers, was the outstanding rebel against Mr. Bohlen's autocratic rule. Does this mean —if our democratic philosophy is sound—that something was wrong with Eddie and right with Fred? As for Reilly and Lyman, which was better, Reilly's lusty, irreverent self-confidence or Lyman's mama's-boy timidity?

A number of things could be said on the other side. For instance, the kind of autocracy represented in these experiments was not actually very bad, and Eddie's enjoyment of it was therefore not a very serious blot on his character. In fact, it offered much that laissez-faire did not offer; if the good boys typically preferred it to laissez-faire, this might not be a matter of docility as much as of a quite healthy enjoyment of structure, time perspective, and constructive achievement. It might be recalled, too, that there was nothing weak in Eddie's character, and that Lyman, though overdocile in relation to his mother, showed a rather startling courage in challenging the destructiveness of his harum-scarum companions. Nevertheless, the possibility remains and is worth thinking about. It may well be that, though many good boys are not Lymans, many others share some of his timidity and his oversensitivity to adult standards as compared with boy standards.

SOME EVIDENCE ON WHAT TYPE OF DISCIPLINE ACTUALLY IS A HAPPY MEDIUM

It has become something of a commonplace to say that there is a sensible halfway point between the rigorous old-fashioned type of discipline and the over-permissiveness of some modern parents. The only thing wrong with this eminently sound idea is its vagueness; the notion of a happy medium covers so many different things in the eyes of so many different people. Even Fred's mother, who had just whipped her boy for not coming when he was called, said, with obvious self-satisfaction, "I don't believe in whipping like some mothers do." Many a blunder in childrearing has appeared, in the eyes of those who committed it, in the shining raiment of a happy medium. It is useful, therefore, to descend from the high level of abstraction represented by terms such as "happy medium" and to discover more exactly and concretely where the happy medium actually lies.

In these experiments there are two relevant lines of evidence. One consists of the main outcome of the experiments: that, in one type of recreational situation, "democracy" (defined in a good deal of concrete detail in the previous chapters of this book) is "better" (in terms of immediate group morale and individual satisfaction) than either a permissive laissez-faire or a form of autocracy that was not actually very rigorous. In addition, there is a type of evidence which, though much less concrete and detailed, is much more directly relevant to the problems of parents: the evidence that "conscience" (defined by a specified constellation of behavior traits) is significantly correlated with a certain pattern of parental behavior. This evidence differs from the other in two major ways: it deals directly with *parents'* behavior rather than club leaders' behavior, and it makes use of a more fundamental, long-term criterion of what constitutes "success" in an adult's handling of a child. Instead of using immediate group morale or individual satisfaction as criteria, it focuses on the long-term question: Does a parent's discipline achieve its avowed purpose of producing a "good" child—"good" not from immediate fear of punishment or hope of reward, but from the force of internal standards?

The pattern of parental behavior that appears to be most conscience building is not actually a midpoint on any single dimension. It is not just halfway between old-fashioned rigor and new-fashioned over-permissiveness on a single scale of rigor or harshness of discipline. The evidence suggests that this one-dimensional way of defining the problem is misleading. As in the case of "democracy," which on closer examination proved to be not a midpoint but a near-maximum in each of two different dimensions (see Chapter 8), so in this case it is necessary to distinguish at least two major dimensions: *firmness* or consistency of discipline and *warmth* of affection (which is completely inconsistent with harsh, oversevere forms of discipline such as whipping). On neither of these dimensions is a midpoint indicated as best. Instead, the ideal apparently involves going rather far toward one extreme in firmness or consistency, and very far toward another extreme in warmth of affection. If there has to be an oversimplification and an abstraction of parental wisdom in terms of only one or two words, the abstraction should not consist of the one word "moderation" but of two words, "firmness" and "warmth."

What these terms can mean, more exactly and concretely, and what effect they can have on a child's character, are suggested by the case studies. Eddie's parents were both warm and firm, combining the two with apparent ease and extraordinary success. Eddie developed one of the stoutest, most internalized consciences in the entire group. Lyman's mother, the one adult who mattered most to him, was similarly firm, and her warmth, though perhaps neurotic in origin and misguided in expression, was unbounded in amount. Lyman, too, developed a stout conscience, and though it, like the attitude of his mother toward him, might be regarded as in a sense neurotic, it was unquestionably genuine. By contrast, Reilly's mother was both hostile and weakly over-permissive; his father supplied some warmth but was in some ways equally over-permissive. Reilly became an aggressive, attention-demanding, sometimes thoroughly obnoxious boy. Fred got no affection or discipline at all from his father, and though his mother whipped him she gave him neither steady control nor steady affection. The outcome was a willfully rebellious, capriciously troublemaking youngster.

These examples serve at least to show that warmth can go with firmness, while coldness can go with too much lenience. Eddie's parents and Lyman's mother were "new-fashioned" in their warmth and "old-fashioned" in their firmness. Fred's parents and Reilly's mother were the reverse, "old-fashioned" in their coldness[3] and "new-fashioned" in their weak over-permissiveness. Both pairs, therefore, might be plausibly described as variations on the theme of a combination or compromise between old and new. Yet the outcomes were a world apart. In terms of conscience building, the evidence suggests that Eddie's parents and Lyman's mother chose the best from both old and new, while Fred's parents and Reilly's mother chose the worst.

The evidence by no means comes only from these four cases.

[3] Actually there is no good evidence that old-fashioned parents were any less warm, on the average, than parents are today. What is really meant here is that a hundred years ago there was less talk about the mental-hygiene value of affection than there is now, that there are probably more over-permissive parents today, and that a strong conscious belief in the importance of affection is one reason for the over-permissiveness of many modern parents.

The experiments provide also a fair amount of statistical evidence. Chiefly on the basis of interviews with their mothers, the home backgrounds of seventeen boys were rated in terms of warmth and firmness. Each of the two experimenters made an independent rating based on all the data, and these two ratings were averaged. These ratings were then correlated with the seven core components of the conscientiousness cluster described above, i.e., various independent measures of nonaggression, persistence in work, and contentment in autocracy. The average correlation of the estimates of warmth with these seven measures was .46, with a range from .13 to .76. The mean correlation of the estimates of firmness with the same measures was .34, with a range from .05 to .51. (While these raw correlations are not large, the true correlations are in all probability higher, since presumably the true correlations were reduced by the roughness of the estimates of parental warmth and firmness, and also by the fact that no one form of club behavior was a perfect measure of the conscientiousness cluster as a whole. If corrected for attenuation, the correlations would be considerably higher than the raw coefficients given here.)

This statistical evidence, like the case studies, is not based on enough cases to be very convincing if taken by itself. Fortunately, however, there is in this case, as in the case of the evidence for a "conscientiousness cluster," a large amount of supporting evidence from other studies. Most familiar, probably, is the finding of the Gluecks (1950) that in the homes of delinquents there is a striking amount of inconsistency of discipline and lack of affection. But this is only one of a considerable number of similar findings. Others include, for example, Burt's findings (1925) of a high proportion of "lax discipline" in the homes of delinquent children as compared with a control group of non-delinquent children from the same neighborhood; the finding of Hewitt and Jenkins (1946) that there were sizable correlations of two clusters of delinquent behavior with "parental rejection" (lack of warmth) and with "parental negligence" (lack of firmness); the finding of Sanford et al. (1943) that "the conscientious-effort syndrome" had sizable correlations with stability of the home, including "steady, quiet discipline," "acceptance" of the child in the home, and "affectionate training."[4]

[4] See also Zucker (1943), Cass (1952), Lesser (1952), Whiting & Child (1953), and Wittenborn (1954). An interpretation similar to that presented here is offered by Sears, Maccoby, and Levin (1953).

There is nothing new in our emphasis on the conscience-building effects of both firmness and warmth. But, by the same token, these can be regarded as two of the most solidly established of all psychological generalizations, grounded as they are not only on common sense but also on a large amount of systematic research.

SOME EVIDENCE THAT SEVERE DISCIPLINE DEFEATS ITS OWN END

A recurrent and striking fact in the case studies is that conscience building is associated only with "firmness" in the sense of consistency and not at all with "firmness" in the sense of severe discipline. If anything, the boys who undergo severe punishments in their homes are on the average less conscientious than those who do not.

For example, it was the troublemakers Reilly and Fred, not the good boys Eddie and Lyman, whose mothers spoke of "whipping" them. According to Reilly's mother, "I used to lose my temper and whip him; I was pretty mean, I guess." But as she herself put it, "he would be just as bad or worse afterward." Fred's mother had "whipped him just this morning" for not coming when called; the fact that he did not come when called, together with his rebelliousness both in school and in club meetings, suggests that her discipline was as ineffectual as it was severe. By contrast, Lyman's mother "never did punish him—outside of admonishing him." It was Lyman's less tractable brother John who had been "switched," and here again, as in the case of Reilly, there is direct evidence of its futility. "When John was little I did considerable switching. Dr. Kimball told me I was wasting my time and my temper, and it did seem like he got along just as well when I gave him plenty to do."

The clearest and most interesting case, however, is that of Eddie. The word "whip" did not seem to be in his mother's working vocabulary at all; her word was "slap," and in the interview it occurred only once: "There's only one thing I've ever slapped them for; it's when they laugh at me when I scold them." Otherwise her punishments were nonphysical: staying in the house and not playing ball with the other boys ("That was quite a punishment"), being sent upstairs (she called this "severe punishment"), or sitting on a chair. "If they're impudent I make them sit on a chair until they see there isn't any headway to be gained that way. It's very, very seldom." There could hardly be a clearer case of firm, consistent and effective discipline without physical severity. And even here there are indications that corporal punishment made the situation worse rather than better: "Physical discipline arouses his (Eddie's) anger. He can't take physical punishment."

While this may seem out of line with the abundant evidence that "firmness" of discipline promotes the development of conscience, it is certainly in line with the equally abundant evidence that warmth of affection promotes conscientiousness. Severe discipline, and especially severe corporal punishment, apparently tends to create in the ordinary child's mind a feeling that the adult is hostile to him, and—whatever the psychological reasons for this may be—a feeling that the adult is hostile seems to work powerfully against genuine absorption or internalization of the adult's moral standards. At best it produces a prudent external conformity. Perhaps this is because a kind of psychological gulf is created between adult and child. Perhaps it is because the adult's approval is no longer so greatly desired—as if the child said to himself, "Why should I try to please *him?*" Perhaps it is because the feeling of being rejected causes the child in turn to reject the adult, and to rejoice in thwarting or circumventing the adult's will. In any case it seems clear that, in defining more concretely what is meant by "firmness," severity should be excluded. The kind of firmness that promotes conscientiousness apparently includes the consistency, immediacy, and decisiveness of punishment whenever punishment is clearly indicated—not its severity, and, most emphatically, not severity of physical punishment.

Why Firmness Matters

If the idea of firmness is purged of all overseverity, its power to build conscience becomes relatively easy to account for in terms of clear and firm boundaries of the psychological "space of free movement." This has already been discussed in the description of democratic leadershsip (Chapter 3, pp. 46–9) and does not need to be repeated in detail here. Suffice it to say that a clear and firm barrier is not a challenge to the child's exploratory urge, nor is it an invitation to him to pit his will against that of the adult. On the other hand, an ambiguous boundary line, made hazy by an adult's vacillation or lack of enforcement, is both a challenge to exploration and a challenge to a contest of wills.

Of course the challenge to a contest of wills is intensified when, as in the cases of Reilly and Fred, the child is also hostile to the adult, so that a potentially affectionate and companionable relationship has been transformed into a power struggle. The most trouble-breeding, conscience-destroying kind of adult-child relationship is, apparently, that in which a basic power struggle has developed and the adult is weak and vacillating. Reilly's mother epitomized it when she said that he sometimes argues for hours at a time: "Maybe it's because I've given in to him several times." With all of her hostility she was nevertheless an appeaser, and her appeasement, like her hostility, merely stored up trouble for the future.

However, even in a reasonable and amenable child like Eddie or Lyman—a child who does not see the world basically as a power struggle and who does not see adults as enemies to be conquered or circumvented—there is apparently a conscience-building value in the child's knowing just how far he can go. Most children welcome such stability and definiteness of psychological structure, and when limits are clear the child has a tendency to put out of his mind, as inherently "bad" and to be avoided, those things that he is sure will lead to trouble with the adult. At first, undoubtedly, this is a matter of prudent, conscious avoidance of punishment or disapproval. (In a child as sensitive to adult disapproval as Lyman, "admonishing" is punishment enough.) But, as time goes on, the adult's standards may become internalized in the sense that what the adult has forbidden acquires a more or less permanent aura of "badness," a "negative valence," that clings to it even when no adult is present to disapprove. Perhaps also the amenable child's mind tends to economize energy and avoid trouble and confusion by focusing only on what it sees as permissible and therefore "good."

In addition there is the whole question of how adults are perceived. If the child learns to perceive adults in general as vulnerable, vacillating, easy to bring around by whining, arguing, or passive resistance, then even without any hostility he may continue the pattern of getting his way by such methods. The over-indulged type of spoiled child is not necessarily hostile to his parents; he may merely see them as exploitable and fail to respect them—or their ideas of what is good and bad. Such an adult is also not likely to be (as Eddie's father was) the object of hero-worship or of admiring imitation. This brings up the even more basic problem of identification.

Why Warmth Matters—The Problem of Identification

The question of why a parent's affection promotes conscientiousness in a child is more puzzling than it appears to be at first sight. It is easy enough to see why a child needs love in order to be happy and secure, but why does he need it in order to be good?

One possible reason has been suggested in the case studies: that a loved child may see good behavior as "a path to love," or a way of getting more love, and may therefore gradually come to value good behavior as an end in itself. Lyman, for instance, could be described as emotionally dependent on his all-too-loving mother; her approval and disapproval mattered a great deal to him, probably too much; and if one infers that the behavior she approved came to have in his eyes a permanent quality of self-evident goodness while the behavior she disapproved came to have a quality of badness, then his internalizing of her standards might be said to be fully accounted for.

The inference is in fact a reasonable one, since there is a good deal of evidence that what might be called "the spreading of goal character from end to means" is a very common psychological process. That is, a means apparently always tends to be seen as good-in-itself when it has functioned for a long time as a means to an end that is regarded as good. If, then, good behavior functioned through many years of Lyman's childhood as a means to the end of his mother's love and approval, one might expect goodness, defined as his mother defined it, to become for Lyman an end in itself.

On the other hand, as a complete account of what is going on, this has at least one serious defect: it does not explain why the approval of a loved parent should be sought any more than that of an unloved parent. Lyman is again a case in point. He was not at all close to his father, yet three words from his father hurt him acutely. "The worst thing his Daddy ever said to him was 'That's enough, Lyman,' and he got smaller and smaller and sobbed a little, and that was all." Obviously he cared very much about his father's disapproval—perhaps precisely because he was less sure of his father's affection than of his mother's. Why, then, would he not try even harder to keep his father's approval than to keep his mother's? From this standpoint, if a parent wants to give his child the strongest possible motivation to be "good," one might suppose that he should not give unconditional love at all, but only love that is strictly dependent on and proportional to the goodness of the child's behavior. Yet the evidence suggests that this is not the case; the evidence suggests that the stronger and warmer a parent's affection for his child is, the more the child is likely to develop conscientiousness. To account for this it is apparent that one must look for some other psychological process, perhaps a less rational one, on a deeper emotional level.

Freud suggested another answer when he invoked the mechanism of "identification" with parent figures as an explanation of the growth of the superego:

> Here we have that higher nature, in this ego-ideal or Super-Ego, the representative of our relation to our parents. When we were little children we knew these higher natures, we *admired* them and *feared* them; and later we *took them into ourselves.*—(*The Ego and the Id*, p. 47; italics ours)

Freud's metaphor, "We took them into ourselves," deserves serious consideration. What he seems to mean is that, without any rational basis for doing so, and perhaps without any conscious desire to do so, a child tends to accept as his own (i.e., to internalize, or "take into himself") the standards of another person on whom his attention is focused and who seems to him to be both admirable and powerful. Presumably the same process occurs in all cases in which hero worship is combined with admiring imitation, but the commonest and most important example of it is a child's relationship to his own parents. (It will be noticed that this version modifies Freud's version in that perception of the other person as powerful is substituted for Freud's term "fear." In our own case studies what seems to matter is respect for the parent's power, moral as well as physical, rather than actual fear. Eddie's parents, for instance, inspired respect but not fear. The only clear example of fear was Lyman's fear of his father, and there was no evidence that he identified with his father.)

In this somewhat free translation, Freud's hypotheses do seem to fit most of our case studies. To Eddie, his romantically military father was a wonderful person; he was the sort of person that any boy would "naturally" want to be like and the strictness that he stood for was obviously good also. Reilly's hail-fellow father apparently had much the same obviously-to-be-imitated quality in Reilly's eyes, while his mother must have seemed to him to be a petulant weakling whom he had no desire to resemble and whose standards he could treat very lightly. Fred had the growth-stunting misfortune of not possessing either a father or a mother whom he would want to resemble or whose standards he would want to take seriously. His mother was a harried drudge with little time for affection, and his father was a drunkard, intimidated by his wife. Lyman was at least equally unfortunate. Afraid of his father and turning his attention far more to his mother, he had only a feminine parent figure with whom to identify and around whom to build his ego ideal. In all of these cases the evidence suggests that there was a kind of gravitating of the child's self-image toward his image of a loved and respected parent—a form of gravitation not wholly, and perhaps not even mainly, dependent on a need for that parent's approval, but operating also directly by virtue of the powerful and rather puzzling process which is here called identification.[5]

Is It Fear or Perception of Power That Promotes Identification?

If identification of a child with a parent is the chief process by which a parent's values are internalized by a child, it becomes important to understand how this type of identification works, and what conditions promote or interfere with it.

One of the two factors that Freud suggests as a basis for identification is fear. We have suggested that perception of the parent as powerful, or respect for the parent's power, should be substituted for Freud's term "fear," citing the case of Eddie, who respected but did not fear his parents, and of Lyman, who feared his father but did not identify with him. This is not far from Freud's hypothesis. Fear of another person normally involves two aspects or components: a belief that the other person is hostile (wanting to do harm), and a belief that the other is powerful (able to do harm). Freud's hypothesis seems wholly acceptable as far as the second of these two components is concerned. If a child is often frightened by a parent, it does seem reasonable to suppose that he may de-

---

[5] The word "identification" has been used by various writers in various senses; the particular sense in which it is used here is suggested by the above discussion, and can be formally defined as merging or linkage of the self-image with the image of another person, and also the imitative tendency, or tendency toward increasing resemblance, that is ordinarily associated with this linkage.

velop a wish that he could change places with the parent, and be the safe and powerful inflictor of harm rather than the weak and helpless receiver of it. Even while recoiling from his unchallengeably powerful parent, the child might envy the parent's power and unconsciously pattern himself after that parent, as if unconsciously reasoning, "If I can only make myself resemble this parent in other ways, I will be like him in power also." This conception of envy as a basis of identification—i.e., wanting to be like another person because the other is *fortunate*—is implicit or explicit in much psychonanalytic theory, and on the whole it seems acceptable enough. At least insofar as the child's perception of possible human roles is limited to only two, the role of the powerful harm-inflicter and that of the weak harm-receiver, it would seem that he must almost inevitably be drawn to the safer and more powerful role of the harm-inflicter, and might then identify with a harm-inflicting parent.

What the evidence seems to refute, however, is the idea that the other component of fear, the perception of another person as hostile, could have a positive relation to identification. If affection for a parent promotes identification with that parent, and acceptance of that parent's values, as the evidence clearly demonstrates that it does, then hostility to the parent should interfere with identification. If, for instance, Reilly's mother is hostile to him as well as weak, her hostility as well as her weakness should repel him. It should (as obviously it did) promote a power struggle in which he took delight in defying his mother whenever possible and in not taking over her values. It should (as it did) feed his competitiveness and self-assertion, not his morality. In his lifespace it should (as it apparently did) create a gulf—a *dis*-identification—between him and her.

It would seem, then, that Freud's fear hypothesis ought to be modified; the envy-of-a-powerful-person element in fear apparently promotes identification, while the hostility-to-a-hostile-person element in it does not.

Respect is something different. A child can see and respect his parents' power, envy it, and try to be like those who have it, without fear and without hostility. Eddie and his brothers were companionable enough with their father to "lay for him with snowballs," yet Eddie identified with the values of his "very strict" father and mother to such an extent that "if he destroyed something he'd come himself and say 'Mother, I won't go to the show tomorrow.' " The practical implications of this tendency to identify with power are far-reaching. It is another and a most important reason for firmness of discipline. The advantages of firmness in terms of setting clear and substantial limits to a child's action have already been discussed. In addition, it now seems evident that firmness matters because it creates in a child's mind an image of parents whose power he wants to share and whom he will therefore, consciously or unconsciously, try to resemble (Lippitt, Polansky, Rosen, 1952; Pepitone, 1950). Appeasement and vacillation, such as Reilly's mother showed, give the child a parental image that he cannot respect or envy and that he is therefore unlikely to pattern himself upon in other ways. On the other hand, strength of moral conviction and rigor of enforcement, such as Eddie's parents showed, create a pattern that a child is likely to take pride in ("My father's real strict") and that in the long run he will tend to make his own.

Of course a child's envy of his parents' power is not by its own nature a good thing. If Eddie's parents had been vicious in other ways his envy of their power could only have promoted his internalizing of their vicious characteristics. But with ordinary parents who are reasonably well-intentioned human beings this is not a problem. Most parents can legitimately, with all due humility, take it for granted that any enhancement of their child's identification with them will be more good than bad in its long-run effects. Even while thwarting a child's will, a firm parent who is also loving can take comfort from the reflection that he is giving his child an object lesson in strength of character and is making his own image a more attractive one in the child's eyes.

The Implications of Hero Worship—Absorption of the Values of Those Who Are Loved and Respected

The other of the two factors suggested by Freud as a basis for the development of conscience is the admiration of a child for his parents. "When we were little children we knew these higher natures, we admired them . . . and later we took them into ourselves."

With this one can only agree. In fact, Freud's word "admire" suggests a way of combining into one broad statement the two most important generalizations of this chapter: that a child's *love* for his parents (based largely on their love for him) promotes the growth of conscience in him, and that a child's *respect* for his parents (often based largely on the firmness of their discipline) also promotes the growth of conscience in him. These two generalizations have something in common: in both cases the child sees his parents in a strongly favorable light. A parent's warmth makes a child see him favorably in terms of affection, and a parent's firmness makes a child see him favorably in terms of power. The common element, then, is *favorable perception*, and the two basic generalizations—that warmth promotes conscientiousness and that firmness promotes conscientiousness—can be looked upon as special cases of a single broader generalization: that *a person tends to identify with, and internalize the values of, those whom he perceives very favorably.*

In other words, when hero worship exists, there is a tendency to absorb into one's own value system the values (as perceived) of the person or persons who are hero-worshiped. This way of putting it is broad enough to include both love and respect for power, in any relative proportions, and it is broad enough to include every object of a child's hero worship as he grows up. While the parents (one or both of them) represent for most children the first and by all odds the most important objects of hero worship, the same process may also occur with an older brother or sister, a gang leader, a teacher, a national hero (Lincoln, Hitler, Lenin), a religious figure (Mary, Jesus), or a conception of a personal God.

There is nothing new or startling in this favorable-perception theory. It is little more than a formal statement of the old saying that "imitation is the sincerest flattery." It is not as commonplace, however, as it deserves to be. The process in question has not been generally and clearly recognized by behavioral scientists—perhaps because many tend to explain every kind of behavior as a means to some end, and this is not necessarily a matter of means and ends at all. The theory does not assume that the function of identification is to get anything, such as approval. There is implicit in it the notion of a need or motive of identification, the goal of the motive being an increased linkage with another person or resemblance to another person, but this goal is self-sufficient, an end in itself, not a means to any other end. According to this theory Lyman got a direct satisfaction from being like his mother and conforming to her values, a satisfaction that was not wholly derived from feeling that she approved of him; it was at least partly a simple satisfaction in feeling close to or in harmony with goodness as represented by his mother. This pleasure lay in *being* something, rather than in getting something or having something. Or, as a sociologist might prefer to put it, the good-boy role, the role of being-a-good-son-of-my-mother, was for Lyman an end in itself.

Actually the theory implies three different processes, which, though they are intimately related to each other, should be separately recognized:

First, there is admiration—*favorable perception*. Lyman sees his mother as loving or powerful or both; her image in his mind becomes "good."

Second, there is *identification*. By a kind of psychological gravitation which does not necessarily involve any conscious self-seeking or calculation of means in relation to ends, Lyman is drawn toward the image of the mother he admires; his conception of himself is linked to his conception of her. He "identifies" with her, which means that—by a process that is largely or wholly unconscious—a unit is formed in his mind that includes himself and her, with all of her values, and the whole unit is now favorably perceived. The whole unit—my-mother-and-I-and-the-values-we-represent—is seen as good. Of course at this stage the process is a pleasant one for him; he thinks more highly of himself because he is now identified with her and her values. "We" are now superior beings, in his eyes, and "our" values are superior. If there is an element of unconscious goal seeking or pleasure seeking in the process, the goal and the pleasure lie in the enhancement of the ego that comes from identifying with an admired person. It should be emphasized again, however, that the ego enhancement is directly satisfying; it is an end in itself, not a means to some other end.

Third—and this is where a psychological process that is less generally recognized comes into play—there is *coherence and behavior-determining power in the perceptual unit formed by identification*. This unit has a kind of momentum; it tends to maintain its own integrity, and behavior inconsistent with it tends to be rejected. For example, in Lyman's mind fighting and wanton destruction were inconsistent with the unit "my-mother-and-I-and-the-values-we-represent"; the temptation to participate in a fight or in an act of wanton destruction would have meant—if he felt it as a temptation at all—a tearing loose of his self-image from this tightly integrated unit. Of course there were overtones of "Mama wouldn't like it if she found out," but this thought was not necessarily decisive, especially when the situation was such that Mama would probably not find out. According to the present theory another major factor —in many situations the decisive factor—was that to Lyman it would have seemed utterly incongruous and unnatural for *him* to engage in wanton destruction. It would have torn apart the most important unit in his perceptual field: "my-mother-and-I-and-the-values-we-represent." In other words, this theory makes use of the Gestalt psychologists' idea that there is a self-maintaining tendency or strain toward congruence within *any* well-established unit in the perceptual field.[6]

The favorable-perception theory, then, links together three ideas which, considered separately, are at least implicit in much present-day psychological thinking: (1) It makes explicit the rather obvious but rarely stated idea that love and respect for power are both forms of favorable perception. (2) It states explicitly the idea, implicit in Freud's thinking, that favorable perception is the main reason why a child identifies with, or "takes into himself," one or both of his parents and their values. (3) This in turn is explicitly linked with the Gestalt idea of a strain toward congruence in any established perceptual unit.

This way of putting it brings out the idea that identification and value absorption are to a large extent unconscious and involuntary. Lyman probably never decided that he wanted his self-image to be pulled into the orbit of his powerfully attractive mother-image, but his self-image was pulled into her orbit nevertheless. A person does not ordinarily choose his identifications or his values; he is caught by them. He may be made unhappy by them, but they are there— as real as his animal appetites, and often at least as strong.

In the light of the favorable-perception theory a number of other

---

[6] This aspect of the favorable-perception theory does not stem from Lewin, although, like other Gestalt psychologists, he would probably have found it quite acceptable. It is related rather to Köhler's concept of perceptual "requiredness" (1938), to Heider's development of the basic Gestalt concept of a "strain toward uniformity" or strain toward congruence within a perceptual unit (1946, 1958), to Osgood's theory of "congruity" (1955) and to Festinger's theory of "consonance" and "dissonance" (1958). Under various names the recognition of factors of this sort is an increasingly important element in present-day psychology.

psychological processes become more understandable. For instance, there is something inappropriate in the word "envy" as an explanation of the fairly well-established tendency to identify with those who are powerful, or fortunate in some other way. There is something strained in the speculation that a person "unconsciously reasons" to the effect that "If I can make myself be like that person in other ways, I will be like him in having power also." If one breaks away from the inveterate tendency of many psychologists to reduce all psychological dynamics to means-end terms, and assumes only that respect for another person's power is one form of favorable perception, it begins to seem quite natural that a person should be attracted toward, and identify with, those whose power he respects. Eddie did not necessarily ask himself "How can I get power like my father's?" nor give himself—even unconsciously—the silly answer, "I can have his power if I am like him in other ways." It is enough to assume that Eddie tended to link himself psychologically with what was attractive, and that power was an attractive aspect of his image of his father. Such attraction is neither logical nor illogical, since in this realm logic is irrelevant. It is simply a special case of the primary principle in terms of which all identification is to be explained.

One further aspect of the matter remains to be clarified: Why is it that a parent's values are dragged along, so to speak, in the process of identification? Let us say that Lyman found his mother-image strongly attractive in terms of two qualities, warmth and strength. Why should this cause him to internalize any of her characteristics other than these two qualities? Why did he also internalize the whole cluster of her moral standards, including such values as nonaggression, nonattention-demanding, obedience, hard work, and truthfulness?

The answer seems to lie in the process of spreading of favorable perception—a process which is familiar to psychologists in another context under the name of "halo effect." If one trait of an individual is highly regarded by another individual, other traits are likely to be more highly regarded than they would have been otherwise. This too links up with the Gestalt principle of a strain toward consistency. According to this principle there is a tendency to be consistently favorable or consistently unfavorable in evaluating any thing or any person. If the main aspects of it are seen as good, the goodness seems to spread and there is a tendency to regard other aspects of it as good also; if the main aspects are seen as bad, the badness seems to spread in a similar way. "Black-and-white thinking," in which enemies are seen as completely black and friends as completely white, is a case in point. It is not surprising, then, that a child's favorable perception of some of his parents' characteristics, such as warmth and strength, should spread and make him also perceive favorably certain other characteristics of his parents, including their moral values.

It is by this process, apparently, that a parent's moral values first begin to seem in the child's eyes to be inherently good rather than merely representing what he has to do to get the parent's approval. Without needing to put any of it into words, it is as if the child said to himself "Daddy thinks it's good; Daddy is good; so it must really be good." This is at least the first step toward absorbing or "internalizing" Daddy's values. If then there is also an identification of the self with the parents, so that a perceptual unit is formed consisting of me-and-my-parents-and-the-kind-of-goodness-we-represent, the spread is likely to continue, so that all of this unit is favorably perceived. The moral values attributed to the parents are attributed to the self too and become a source of pride. Eddie begins to take pride not only in having an honest and hard-working father but in being honest and hard-working himself; any violation of the code of honesty and hard work begins to mean a disruption not only of the family image but of the self-image also. When this occurs, the process of conscience building is well on its way to completion—as far as the parents' contribution is concerned.

The Broadening of Conscience

It seems clear that the core or nucleus of conscience is established in the home, and perhaps throughout life this core is what matters most. A good deal, however, depends on what is added to the nucleus. In a child like Lyman, conscience seems to remain a mere nucleus, home-bound and limited almost entirely to the values inculcated in the home. On the other hand, in a child like Eddie conscience apparently becomes broader and more flexible—without becoming weaker—by identification with persons and groups outside the home. Eddie, like Lyman, was a thorough member of his family, proud of it and identified with its values. Unlike

Lyman, he was also a thorough member of his peer group, proud of his place in it, and identified with most if not all of its values.

Those who develop this broader kind of conscience are evidently, on the whole, more mature individuals. They are also, from the standpoint of democracy, better citizens. In the process of broadening, their consciences necessarily lose some of the undiscriminating docility and rigidity that a purely home-bound conscience has. Conflicts are set up; identification with "my-family-and-the-values-it-represents" necessarily conflicts at times with identification with "my-gang-and-the-values-it-represents." Lyman has to get his clothes wet and dirty if he is to join in the big water battle with the Secret Agents. This conflict of identification is at the same time a conflict of group memberships and of group loyalties—with a particular type of conscientiousness derived from each membership. Out of the resolution of such conflicts is likely to come a more individualized and independent conscience, as well as a more discriminating and effective one. In resolving the conflicts, the growing child is more or less forced to do some thinking about what he believes the more important values to be, and to downgrade or eliminate those that seem to him "unreasonable"—that is, in conflict with other values that he sees as more fundamental. It is probably at such times, if at all, that the process of conscience building becomes voluntary and, in some sense, self-determined. When loyalties conflict, the individual may perhaps rise above both of the conflicting standards and become, to some extent, the architect of his own value system.

From the standpoint of democracy it is fortunate when this occurs, since democracy needs individuals whose values are rooted both in the family and in the peer group. It needs them if family-rooted values are to be effectively lived by persons who are emotionally in touch with their peers, and it needs them if there is to be real thinking, by individuals, about what values are most important. With peer values alone, the child is apt to be a Reilly or a Fred, shallow, other-directed, seeking fun and popularity without even caring whether "things go right," from a more than momentary standpoint, in the peer group itself. With family values alone he is likely to be a Lyman, overly docile in relation to adults (including autocratic adults), shallow in a different way, and ineffectual in dealing with the "real world" of his peers. With both kinds of values well developed and in balance, he is an Eddie, strongly committed to those more fundamental values (e.g., friendliness) which are emphasized by *both* the family culture and the peer culture, and yet, having survived and surmounted many past conflicts, capable of looking at each new conflict with the perspective of an autonomous individual.

SOME LOOSE ENDS

The notes presented above are far from covering the nature and growth of conscience. Nothing has been said, for instance, about a rather different type of identification—*empathy*—which involves feeling with or for others, without regard for whether it is morally "right" to do so. Nothing has been said directly about the momentum of the self-image—the tendency to conform to an established self-image (the "black sheep of the family," the stammerer, etc.) regardless of whether this image is approved or not. Almost nothing has been said about religion, or about how political ideals are acquired. Many unsolved problems remain; for instance: Does the identification process work the same way for identification with the peer group as for identification with parents? Is the child who is conscientious in terms of family values or family loyalties likely to be more conscientious about peer-group loyalties than the child whose family roots are shallow—and therefore involved in more serious emotional conflict when the two kinds of loyalty pull in different directions? To what extent are values conscious or verbalized, and how important, in determining behavior, are the verbalized, explicit values as compared with unverbalized, implicit ones? Granting that actions speak louder than words, and that example is more important than precept, are there nevertheless some occasions when precept makes a difference? Important as they are, none of these points can be discussed here, since the experiments and the case studies shed no direct light on any of them.

SUMMARY, AND IMPLICATIONS FOR DEMOCRACY

The development of internal moral standards, as distinguished from external conformity or approval-seeking, is a process that calls for psychological explanation, although few psychologists have seriously attempted to explain it.

While "conscience" is not a single or a simple thing, moral standards do have a tendency to hang together; a person who is conscientious in one respect tends to be conscientious in others also.

While conscientious people typically have a need for order and constructive activity that enables them to avoid anarchy and achieve democracy, the same need for order may make them over-docile in autocracy.

The parents whose children become conscientious are likely to be those with the greatest warmth of affection and the greatest firmness or consistency—not severity—of discipline.

Very severe discipline, and especially "whipping," usually defeats its own end. It cuts at the root of the feeling of closeness, or iden-tification of a child with his parents, that is the main source of conscience.

Firm, consistent discipline promotes the development of con-science in two ways: by preventing a struggle for power, and by making the parents seem strong in the child's eyes, which in turn tends to make the child identify with them and absorb their values.

Warmth of affection on the part of parents promotes the devel-opment of conscientiousness in a child by directly promoting the process of identification. Perhaps even more than the desire for a parent's approval, identification with the conscientious parents leads to a child's "internalizing" their values—i.e., making their values fully his own.

Freud thought that a child's fear of a parent promoted the de-velopment of conscience (the superego). The available evidence suggests that fear does not do this, though perception of the par-ents as powerful does.

The internalizing of the values of a parent (or of any other ob-ject of hero worship) apparently has three elements or aspects:

a) Strong "favorable perception"—i.e., love, or respect for the parents' power, or both.

b) Identification or linkage of the self-image with the parent image and with the parents' values.

c) Coherence of the new perceptual unit which contains the self-image and the parents' values, and rejection of behavior incon-sistent with this image, not only because the behavior seems in-herently bad but also because it seems incongruous to associate such behavior with oneself.

One implication is obvious: to develop conscientious individuals who are able to make democracy harmonious, workable, and efficient, parents (and teachers) need to combine warmth of affection with consistency of discipline. Needlessly severe discipline, antidemocratic in its essence, is also antidemocratic in its effects.

Another implication is less obvious: since conscientious individuals are especially likely to be repelled by the confusion and the cross-purposes of anarchy, they are especially in need of making a clear distinction between orderly autocracy and orderly democracy. If this distinction is not clear in their minds they may be especially ready to accept a dictator who insists that his own rule is the only alternative to anarchy.

15

The Psychological Core of Democracy

THE characteristics of democracy considered up to this point, such as majority rule, and "low goal and means control," have all been in a sense external. They are mere forms of behavior. Closer to the heart of the matter is the question of the spirit or psychological core of democracy. What kinds of persons and relationships are capable of making democracy work? What are their values, their characteristic attitudes? For parents and teachers this is a basic question. To a large extent it is these values and interpersonal orientations, rather than the outward procedural forms of democracy, which must be fostered in the growing child if he is to become an effective democratic citizen.

Everyday observation, supplemented by the experimental data reported in this book, suggests that the psychological core of democracy consists of an interrelated cluster of values, beliefs and relationship skills in which general conscientiousness is very important (see above, Chapters 13 and 15).[1] More specifically, the following six values appear to play a central role:

[1] The factor analysis approach gives some support to this generalization; for instance, the important research of Cattell, Saunders, and Stice (1953) finds that one cluster of intercorrelated variables includes not only group aspects of democracy, such as "commonness of purpose" and "feeling free to participate" but also personality variables such as "deliberate will control" and "positive character integration." Haythorn et al. (1956) also present evidence that "authoritarian personalities" tend to put their mark on the groups in which they participate.

1. OPEN-MINDEDNESS

An example of a closed mind in laissez-faire:

Here (in the painting of the poster) there is an excellent chance for division of labor, because the group now has a common goal, but so far there is no indication that the former attitude of competition is going to be replaced by one of cooperation. There is a dispute over color, Reilly insisting on having his way. . . . Sam suggests that one of them make everything red and one of them blue. This is almost the only instance in which this group has made an effort at organization and division of labor. Fred boos him. (And apparently no one else even notices the suggestion.)

Interest in the new task continues for a while, but, in the absence of real pride in group accomplishment, the activity disintegrates rather easily under the impact of hostile criticism, an activity vacuum is created, and the big water battle with the Secret Agents is the result.

An example of open minds in democracy:

Reilly has another suggestion, when Mr. Rowe asks for more. He says "Let's make some spears and bows and arrows." Fred is practical now: "Well, I don't know." Reilly explains, "You could use willow. We could use cheap wood." Leonard has actually paid attention; he follows up Reilly's suggestion: "You can buy arrows to make."

Free speech is widely recognized as an essential element in genuine democracy, but what is not always recognized is that free speech is only the most elementary and indispensable aspect of a much more inclusive value—the value of listening to "the other fellow's point of view." We cannot learn what is in others' minds, and think constructively with them, if their mouths are gagged, but neither can we do it if they are talking freely and we are too arrogant or too preoccupied to listen. The grim determination of a Hitler or a Stalin to wipe out an opponent's thought by physical force is only the ultimate, most terrible manifestation of an attitude that is met every day in our own society in its milder forms— a mere dislike of listening to an uncongenial point of view, or an indifference to anyone's viewpoint but one's own. "Fred boos him . . ." Democracy cannot function harmoniously and efficiently unless its members share, in a relatively high degree, each other's goals and ideas (see above, Chapter 11). Without Fred's listening to Sam there can never be the partial consensus which is called a majority, and democracy, in the sense of majority rule, cannot emerge out of the chaos of laissez-faire. But even if a 51 per cent majority is achieved, the group as a whole cannot function harmoniously and efficiently if the 49 per cent do not listen to, do not understand, and therefore inwardly rebel against the decision of the 51 per cent. Nor can it function intelligently if the 51 per cent are pursuing an unwise policy and are unwilling to listen to the wiser counsels of the 49 per cent. Nor can either the 51 per cent or the 49 per cent think their way through to a creative, integrative solution, embodying the valid elements in both points of view, unless both the majority and the minority are actively, receptively, appreciatively listening to what "the other fellow" has to say.

On the other hand, the discussion of spears and arrows by Reilly, Fred, and Leonard is an example of the kind of genuine receptivity —and democracy—which can develop when egoistic self-assertion does not block it. Effective practical discussion involves cooperative exploration of objective reality ("You could use willow"; "You can buy arrows to make") and often it also involves cooperative exploration of subjective reality (the varying beliefs of individuals, their varying goals, their varying usage of key words). Everyday experience suggests that the attitude which is most conducive to such exploration is a leisurely, wondering, seeking, reality-centered, non-self-centered attitude. When such an attitude prevails, discussion can lead to decisions that are wise, insofar as they are based on a broad and thoughtful appraisal of both objective and subjective reality; and it can lead to united action, since the decisions arrived at do integrate most of the individual purposes within the group. The relation between nonreceptivity and the clash of egos is well illustrated by the following incident:

Finn (in disgusted tone): "Aw, why don't we have a majority?" (He means a majority vote.)

Bill stands in back of the table, separated from the rest of the group, and begins to name the other officers, ignoring the fact that there is any controversy over the method of choosing them.

Interpretive comment: This ignoring of Finn's democratic impulse by Bill is apparently the beginning of the long feud between them, which comes to a head several meetings later.

All this has implications for parents and teachers that are worth considering. One of the simpler implications might be that the civilized taboo against interrupting is a good one that should not be abandoned even by parents who pride themselves on being permissive. To wait until another person has had his say is not mere good manners; it implies an attitude that is basic to democracy.

Mr. Rankin, to the group: "Do you know what a regular army is like?"

Finn: "I don't."

Hamil: "I do. They have drills and. . . ." (He is interrupted by much loud and somewhat irrelevant conversation.)

Mr. Rankin: "We ought to listen to what Hamil has to say, and take our turns." (The volume goes down considerably.)

Hamil: "My father was in the army, and it's no roses either."

Another implication might be that listening can be taught by example as well as by precept. Mr. Rowe's sensitivity to the ideas and interests of the obstreperous Charlie Chan boys and his drawing out of the ideas of the inarticulate Lyman were major civilizing factors in the atmosphere of the group. It was his example more than any preaching of democracy which made possible the practical, mutually receptive discussion of spears and arrows quoted above.

A more fundamental implication, however, has to do with the basic character structure of the child. The psychological feat of receptively listening to a new point of view, while not abandoning one's own viewpoint, calls for a kind of inner strength which is by no means universal. It is more difficult than the docile listening to simple orders which is characteristic of the apathetic reaction to autocracy, and also much more difficult than the stubborn clinging to one's own individual point of view which is characteristic of laissez-faire. In both docile listening and stubborn individualism there is only a single mental focus, while the democratic combination of listening and individualism calls for a double mental focus. Two versions of reality must be held in the mind simultaneously while the implications of each are explored and compared. For as long as this weighing and comparing lasts, reality is seen as ambiguous, subject to two different interpretations, either of which may turn out to be true. In a sense it is like seeing double, and, like seeing double, can be acutely uncomfortable. What is needed, then, is a psychological make-up which does not defend itself against this discomfort by simply blotting out one idea and clinging blindly to the other one. "Fred boos him . . ." Fred's mind at this point was not the leisurely, wondering type of mind which can easily "tolerate ambiguity" (Frenkel-Brunswick, 1954). Fred was intent on his single-minded enjoyment of what he was doing. He was in no mood to stretch his mind to take in Sam's suggestion and compare it critically with the existing plan of action.

If this analysis is correct, it implies that the ability to suspend judgment, to "tolerate ambiguity," and to recognize the inevitably tentative character of most knowledge should be a major goal of education in a democracy. Of course this runs counter to the strong urge of most young people to have immediately the ultimate and final truth. Children want to know "the answers," and it is often intolerable to them to contemplate the thought that no final answers exist. Like adults, they have a need for clearness of psychological structure. But if parents and teachers have a long-range point of view and want the child to function effectively as a democratic citizen ten or twenty years later, it may be necessary for them to frustrate this need by freely saying, "I don't know" on many occasions, or even by deliberately confronting children with some of the ambiguities and some of the many-sided controversial questions which the real world contains.

For instance, the typically innocuous, wholly noncontroversial nature of "social studies" in American schools on the elementary school level may need to be considerably changed if this aspect of citizenship is to be effectively taught during the most formative years. A considerable change in this respect might not result in a net loss even from the standpoint of the child's satisfaction if enough use is made of another characteristic of youth—its strong curiosity about the real adult world and its capacity for enthusiastic broadening of its own horizons. If the exploration of diverse viewpoints on hotly controversial issues is presented as an intellectual adventure and an exciting challenge—without too much confusion, and with a readiness on the part of adults to express clearly both their own opinions and the opinion of those who disagree—then the building of this basic element in the democratic personality structure may utilize, instead of frustrating, the emotional needs of the children themselves.

2. SELF-ACCEPTANCE AND SELF-CONFIDENCE

Lyman's timidity in laissez-faire:

Seems to be most inadequate and dependent—can't find anything to do by himself . . . Still just watching . . . Watching, and would like to join, but doesn't quite know how.

Lyman's self-confidence in democracy:

Lyman is talking more than he ever has before in all the rest of the time together. . . . The change that has taken place in him in the last two meetings has been quite phenomenal. . . . The group has responded to him and has directed questions and kidding in his direction where formerly they just plain ignored him.

Interpretive comment by observer: Autocracy was better for Lyman than laissez-faire, because it was more orderly and gave him something definite to do. But democracy was much better still, because it was at least as orderly as autocracy (to which his group reacted aggressively) and because in the friendly, cooperative atmosphere he became a more genuine group member.

In these small clubs, the kind of timidity and apathy originally shown by Lyman was rare except when the whole group showed the apathetic reaction to autocracy. In small groups which are not autocratically controlled, even the more backward individuals usually have some real chance to participate and to develop self-confidence through participation. The question of apathy becomes acute, however, in almost any group of more than twenty or thirty people. In such groups it is fairly typical for an active nucleus of only a few individuals to take nearly all of the initiative, to carry the burden of group discussion and action, while an actual majority sits back and does little. There are then twenty or thirty or many thousands of Lymans instead of one.

The experiments illustrate also how group self-confidence, based on successful group achievement, contributes to group morale and motivation. It will be remembered that when the Law and Order Patrol was just beginning to integrate itself under laissez-faire leadership the jerry-built table which the boys had made broke down, and the resultant loss of pride and group self-confidence had much to do with the continual failure of efforts at integration from that time on. (See Chapter 7.)

There is a paradox in the fact that democracy depends on the simultaneous existence of both pride and humility. As we have seen, there can be no really integrative group discussion unless there is the kind of humility that makes genuine listening possible. At the same time, there must be at least the kind of pride that makes an individual ready to assert his own point of view until facts have convinced him that there is a better one. There must also be the kind of pride or self-confidence that makes it possible to arrive at an individual "point of view" in the first place. Listless self-distrust is as inimical to creative thinking as arrogant self-assertion. However, the paradox is more apparent than real, since it is clear that *genuine* self-acceptance and self-confidence lead not to a decreased but to an increased ability to listen to others. The fully self-confident person can pass easily from enthusiastic presentation of his own ideas to an appreciative, open-minded listening to the ideas of others.

From all this it follows that parents and teachers are contributing to democracy as well as to mental hygiene when they try to develop self-confidence in timid children such as Lyman. In view of what leaders can do to transform laissez-faire into democracy, it is perhaps even more important to develop the right sort of self-confidence in potential leaders such as Eddie.

In developing self-confident leadership, what particularly needs clarifying in the minds of parents and educators is that there is nothing wrong in merely persuading or influencing another person. Perhaps no one has ever put into words the idea that mere influence or persuasion is autocratic, and yet the wide prevalence of passive, do-nothing behavior on the part of a great many potential leaders in our society suggests that there is implicitly, in the back of their minds, an assumption that a self-assertive influencing of others is at least semi-autocratic. Many people act as if they assume that in order to give complete freedom to others they themselves need to be completely passive. But if our experiments prove anything they prove that this is not true. A large part of the adult's role in democracy consisted of frankly influencing the children's behavior. There was not only information giving (as in laissez-faire); there were also guiding suggestions in great variety, stimulation of self-direction, clarifying of alternatives, giving of time perspective, and direct teaching of the values and skills of democracy. And the results fully justified this more active leader role.

Other examples from everyday life come easily to mind. One is the teacher who leans over backward to avoid expressing his own honest opinion on controversial issues. Another is the counselor who prides himself on being "nondirective" and who consequently gives neither direction nor legitimate leadership. Still another is the chairman or discussion leader who has no well-prepared agenda, and who feels that he is being democratic when he allows a discussion to wander far afield or to waste time in needless argument over nonessentials.

POLITICAL COMMENTARY

The political situations in which some potential leaders are not self-confident enough are many and varied. One of the most crucial is the weakness of democratic leadership in technically undeveloped parts of the world which are subject to Communist infiltration or conquest. In China, Indochina, Iran, and elsewhere there has been a tragic absence of strong indigenous leadership to which the common people could turn with confidence that they were not kowtowing to Russia, to America, or to their own landowning aristocracy. One of the great tests of Western leadership of the free world, during the coming years, may well lie in our ability to foster, without coercion, the development of vigorous, well-trained, genuinely democratic (though probably anti-Western) leadership in countries that have not yet developed a firm democratic tradition.

Another political example is the lingering inhibition connected with the vigorous use of "propaganda" by the Western world. It is certainly true that we in the more democratic world should not stoop to some of the deceptive propaganda techniques used by our less democratic opponents, but surely there is nothing evil in the mere effort to communicate and to make ourselves and our policies understood. As Wallace Carroll put it: "In the debates of the United Nations, Americans failed to utter a single phrase which stirred the imagination of mankind, and when the Russians used the international platform with some success, the Americans could only bleat that the Russians were making 'propaganda.' As if it were a crime to put a persuasive case before the peoples of the world!" (1948, p. 379)

3. REALISM

Another integral part of the democratic value cluster is a respect for facts. Democracy works best when there is a shared feeling of responsibility for continuous reorientation to present and possible reality.

When Fred stopped booing Sam's constructive ideas and began listening to them (under democratic leadership) why did he do so? If open-minded listening is a crucial factor in the workability of democracy, it follows that the reasons for listening represent an important psychological problem.

There were probably two reasons: the new atmosphere of respect for the personalities of other group members (Fred was more aware of Sam as a human being like himself, and not merely as a competitor), and at the same time a new keenness of interest in getting a work project that would be practical and reality-oriented. Too many tables had broken; too much paint had dripped in places where it was not wanted. The impact of objective reality on the nebulous plans of the boys had been a sobering one, and with the subsidence of the personalized competitive atmosphere which characterized this group's reaction to both laissez-faire and autocracy (note Fred's happy-go-lucky egoism in laissez-faire and his sullen rebellion against Mr. Bohlen in autocracy), realistic work-mindedness tended to take its place. Fred listened to Sam not primarily because he was interested in Sam but because he began to care about whether his own ideas were in line with reality, and listening to Sam was a way of finding out.

At several points the findings of the experiments bring out reality-orientation as an aspect of democracy. The democratic leader himself was strongly reality-oriented, as was shown not only by his information giving but also by his guiding suggestions, stimulation of self-direction, and promotion of creative group discussion which clarified group goals and established time perspective. We have seen how the fragmentary, step-by-step character of the knowledge given in autocracy contrasted with the more integrated knowledge and longer time perspective developed in democracy. We have seen the need for the "humility of the true scientist" who is willing to recognize specialized knowledge in others and either obtain it for himself or delegate responsibility to those who have it.

We have also noticed the seemingly self-contradictory fact that democracy flourishes when pride is combined with humility: the kind of humility that makes genuine listening possible combined with the kind of pride that makes an individual ready to assert his point of view until the facts have convinced him that there is a better one. The seeming contradiction has been partly explained by the idea that genuine pride or self-confidence does not require self-assertion for its own sake and therefore is consistent with genuine listening. A further explanation can now be added: the person who listens at the right time and contributes his own ideas at the right time is likely to be the person who forgets his own ego most completely and becomes most completely absorbed in the reality aspects of the situation. Merely having the right balance of humility and self-assertiveness cannot tell him *when* to listen and when to contribute. Only absorption in the reality-situation can do that. The democratic alternative to listless apathy on the one hand and competitive status-minded argument on the other has been defined here as "a wondering, seeking, fact-centered, non-self-centered" attitude. The key word here is "fact-centered." Even good will is not essential (although an absence of ill will *is* essential, since ill will interferes with fact-centeredness). The person who contributes most to effective group discussion is not necessarily the one who is most brimming over with good will for the group; at certain times it may be the one who forgets the egos of other group members (along with his own) in his absorption in getting at the facts and finding out how the group's action can be most realistically adapted to the facts.

On the other hand, there are other times when "forgetting the egos of other group members" is fatal. Not only objective reality but also subjective or psychological reality (the differing personalities and needs of different group members) is relevant to group efficiency. The Charlie Chan Club might have made much more progress toward its own real goals if it had been capable of tactfully handling the mischief-maker, Leonard. At its best, the "shared feeling of responsibility for continuous orientation to present and possible reality" includes a shared feeling of responsibility for realistic evaluation and improvement of the democratic group process itself, including those individual attitudes which are most directly relevant to group efficiency. Conscious group self-evaluation, or evaluation of group process by the group itself, is an art which has recently begun to be systematically cultivated. [Lippitt (1949), Thelen (1954), Lippitt, Watson, and Westley (1958).] Experience has shown that its rewards can be great, both in terms of enhanced group effectiveness and in terms of individual satisfactions —satisfactions from a sense of individual growth and self-understanding as well as from effective participation in a new sort of group process, on a deeper emotional level than a purely action-oriented group is likely to explore.

At least one educational implication of this emphasis on realism is clear. It implies that the affinity between the democratic spirit and the scientific spirit, in the broadest and best sense of that word, is very close. The humility of the true scientist, in the face of the immensity of the facts he does not know, is psychologically akin to the humility of the true democrat in the face of the emerging ideas of other group members. Each must have a capacity to suspend judgment, to tolerate varying versions of reality, to be wary of dogmatic, emotionally satisfying oversimplification. It follows, then, that insofar as education promotes either the scientific spirit or the democratic spirit it is to some degree promoting the other also.

4. Freedom from Status-Mindedness

Status-mindedness in laissez-faire (at a time of strong effort to become autocratic):

Bill: "Eddie can be captain. I'm inspector general. You (Van) can be colonel-lieutenant, and sergeant for you (Finn), and the rest of you can be just lieutenants." (Hamil has been omitted from the specific naming, either on purpose or by mistake.)

Finn: "Aw, why don't we have a couple of privates? Anyhow, I'm second lieutenant. (To Hamil) You're just a plain leevie—that's what we call lieutenants at home."

Hamil sits alone and looks as though he is about ready to cry. There have been some remarks tossed around about lieutenants being the lowest rank, and he isn't even sure he is that. He feels completely isolated.

Absence of status-mindedness in democracy:

Eddie has just been elected "dictator" of the Law and Order Patrol, which is now under democratic adult leadership. "Eddie goes right to work quietly and makes no use of his position. He is entirely work-centered and answers quietly the two or three work questions that are asked of him." (Note the contrast between this attitude and either Bill's self-assertion or Van's childish dependency. In spite of his new title, Eddie's behavior is wholly in keeping with the democratic atmosphere of the group.)

Among other things, these two examples illustrate the possible inefficiency of wasting time on questions of status, as Bill did when he was handing out military ranks, and the possible efficiency value of ignoring status, as Eddie did when he "answered quietly the two or three work questions that were asked of him" instead of throwing around his rank as "dictator."

In addition, the first example illustrates another social loss when a whole group focuses on matters of status: the self-indulgent pleasure of those whose status is high (e.g., Bill) is at least equally balanced by the unhappiness of those whose status is low (e.g., Hamil). If there are captains and inspector generals, someone else must always be "just a plain leevie."

Finally, the evils of the hierarchical mind are illustrated by the tendency to group disruption which was implicit in Bill's functionless doling out of military ranks. The end of the incident shows more clearly its disruptive effect:

Hamil to Finn (trying to sound boastful): "I'm special on the job!"
Finn and Hamil make some comments to the other club.
Bill (to Finn and Hamil, pounding the table): "Order! Come on, turn around and listen."
Hamil: "Well, what am I?" (i.e., what rank)
Bill (ignoring the question): "Now if you'll wait we'll plan to get together at certain times for special arrangements, and we want to cut all laws and reports out of the newspapers. . . ."
(It will be remembered that Bill's grandiose impracticality, uncorrected by good communication with other more realistic members of the group, led to a disorganization of the Law and Order Patrol, and that a major additional factor in this disorganization was the running feud between him and Finn. This feud was largely due to Bill's arrogance, which in turn was related to his inveterate status-mindedness.)

The word usually used for this element in the democratic value cluster is equality. One would ordinarily say that Eddie showed a "spirit of equality" when he refused to act superior even when elected dictator, and that Bill showed a spirit of inequality when he organized the group along military lines and, in doing so, dealt highhandedly with both Finn and Hamil. But the word "equality" does not quite hit the mark. It is a fine, ringing word, but not quite precise enough for careful psychological analysis. What tended to happen in the democratic groups was not that the boys assumed themselves to be equal to each other and to the adult. When they thought about the matter at all they recognized many real inequalities. What occurred was, rather, *an escape from the whole equality-inequality frame of reference*—a tendency to forget about all questions of superiority, inferiority and equality except when such questions had some functional relation to what was going on. In both laissez-faire and autocracy, on the other hand, the boys tended to seize upon individual differences (real or imagined) and to focus attention on them needlessly, whether they had functional meaning or not. In a sense, important differences of status existed in democracy. What varied according to the nature of the group atmosphere was not status but status-mindedness. The term "freedom from status-mindedness" is cumbersome, and does not have the satisfying emotional overtones of "equality," but there does not seem to be any other term that expresses as well what needs to be expressed.

The distinction is probably clearest in the behavior of the democratic adult leaders themselves. A democratic leader did not assume that he was equal to the boys he led. In his guiding suggestions, his clarification of alternatives, his explanation of democratic procedures, he accepted and fully played a role which was appropriate to him as an adult who had special experience and knowledge of "how a good club goes." When the occasion called for it, he also could and did exert authority. In these ways he accepted his naturally differentiated adult role. The democratic leaders differed in this respect from the laissez-faire leaders, who in a sense deliberately denied and abdicated their natural adult role. Like certain parents and teachers, the laissez-faire leaders lost the natural dignity and authority of their position by weakness in enforcing control where control was needed, and by unreadiness to express confident judgments on matters with regard to which their experience was actually much greater than that of the boys. As might be expected, the boys in the laissez-faire groups sensed the artificiality of such forced equality, and they did not like it. They wanted an adult to be an adult.

Yet, although the democratic leaders did not deny their natural dignity and authority, that dignity and authority was very seldom in their minds. As we have seen, they took off their coats, they sat or squatted, they shared the boys' interests, they laughed at themselves, they paid attention to the boys' own ideas, they found themselves talking in the friendly, informal ways that were classified as "jovial and confiding." They worked in much the same way that the boys worked. An example:

> Mr. Rowe is working too. There is a very nice relationship between him and the group. There is no conflict, and he seems to be able to work right on, yet keep control. . . . Mr. Rowe seems to be having the most fun of all.

It will be noticed that he was able to "keep control." This important type of inequality was implicit in his role, and if the occasion had called for it he could have been firm. But most of the time questions of dignity or of control were simply not in his mind. He knew that his dignity did not depend on anything as artificial as dress or posture or needless aloofness, and he knew, most of the time, that the minimum of dignity necessary in order to "keep control" was not at the moment a point of issue.

A closer analysis suggests that the kind of status-mindedness which flourished rankly in laissez-faire and autocracy, and tended to disappear in democracy, has three main aspects:

a. *A tendency for thoughts of status to spread into situations where they are not appropriate.* When Van recognizes Eddie's expertness in the work and asks him a work question, this is in a sense a recognition of inequality, but it is not status-minded in the present sense of the term, since it serves a definite practical need. Or when an adult enforces his authority over children on those occasions when firmness is necessary, this too is functional and not necessarily status-minded. On the other hand, when Bill handed out military ranks he was being status-minded because this behavior had no real function.

b. *A tendency for thoughts of status to spread from part of a personal image to the image as a whole.* To think of a person as superior or inferior *at* something or *in* some situation is not usually status-minded. To think of him as a generally superior or inferior person usually is. Bill looked down on Finn and Hamil as persons; he had no eyes for their actual good qualities or abilities. Since human qualities and abilities are usually fairly specific, the tendency to stereotype individuals as totally superior or inferior makes for inefficiency, since it interferes with finding, for a given function, the person who is actually best for that particular function. In addition, as we have seen, a single simple hierarchy or class division tends to produce both generalized arrogance at the top, such as Bill showed, and generalized apathy or nonparticipation at the bottom, such as Hamil showed. Both are destructive of morale and of free, friendly communication within the group.

c. *An unusually strong desire for status.* Bill's extraordinary maneuvers to keep his position as commander-in-chief constitute one case in point, and another is the generalized, unproductive competitiveness which characterized both laissez-faire and the aggressive reaction to autocracy.

It is true that such unproductive competition may be satisfying to those who win, and that there may be a certain zest in the competition itself. These psychological gains, however, seem definitely overbalanced by the frustrations of those who lose or are anxious about losing (Hamil seems "about ready to cry"), and by the whole group's loss of time and emotional energy which could be spent on other, more productive and solidly satisfying activities. When competition takes the form of competition in socially productive activities this is of course not necessarily true. But a desire for status *as such,* more than for achievement or creative activity as such, means a perennial possibility of seeking status by short cuts—aggression, attention demanding, or the kind of underhanded maneuvers resorted to by Bill; and these short cuts, while they may indeed gain status for the individual (as they apparently did in the case of Reilly), are clearly a net loss to the group as a whole. The energy required to handle individual status striving, and keep it from disrupting the group, probably makes up a large part of what Cattell calls "maintenance synergy" (1951).

5. FAIRNESS

Self-assertion, without regard for fairness, in laissez-faire:

Reilly: "No, you guys are going to use green."
Leonard: "Who said we weren't going to use blue? We can use it if you can."
Reilly: "We'll just sock you in the mouth then."
Leonard: "Oh, yeah?"

Fairness in democracy:

Mr. Rowe rises and gets knives with brightly colored handles, one for each group member. They run after him and eagerly divide up the knives.

Lyman does not follow the group and does not get a knife. Fred points out this omission loudly and the cry is passed on by Sam, so that Lyman is provided for. This is the first sign of interest in anyone but themselves I've almost ever seen in the group.

These examples suggest another kind of "spirit of equality" that seems to flourish in a democratic atmosphere: *equality of rights and opportunities*. Reilly denied such equal rights when he pre-empted the blue paint. Fred and Sam took equal rights for granted when they saw to it that Lyman got his share of the knives.

In Fred and Sam there were probably two psychological factors operating: a need for closure or completeness of a psychological pattern (in this case the pattern of a-knife-apiece-for-five-boys—a pattern which also represents the concept of fairness that is sanctioned in our culture), and an identification with or sympathy for Lyman as an individual (as if Fred said to himself, "If I were Lyman I'd want a knife too"). Probably both of these mechanisms tend to operate whenever they are not counteracted by a strong spirit of competitive self-assertion, as they were in the case of Reilly when he said, "No, you guys are going to use green. . . . We'll just sock you in the mouth then." Reilly cared little about the completeness of any perceptual pattern, whether culturally sanctioned or not, and he certainly did not put himself in Leonard's shoes and imagine, sympathetically, how Leonard would feel if denied an equal opportunity to choose his color. If Reilly imagined what was going on in Leonard's mind at all, he must have imagined only Leonard's discomfiture and taken a triumphant delight in it. His own mind was probably dominated almost completely by the urge to assert himself in competition with other members of the group. Generalizing, then, one can set up the hypothesis that there are psychological forces making for equality of rights and opportunities (at least in our own culture and in other cultures that are more or less like it in this respect) which tend to predominate whenever they are not overbalanced by factors making for competitive self-assertion. The latter tend to predominate both in laissez-faire and in the aggressive reaction to autocracy.

POLITICAL COMMENTARY

If the above hypothesis is correct, it has some bearing on the question of how the Communist ideology can be most effectively opposed.

It suggests that many persons tend to regard equality of economic rights and opportunities as an important aspect of democracy. If this is true, it follows that our non-Communist definitions of democracy will gain in popular support throughout the world, as compared with the Communist definition, to the extent that our practice is clearly superior to Communist practice in this respect. We are not likely to get far in the conflict of ideas if we focus only on majority rule and individual freedom as the "true" meaning of democracy, and ignore or soft-pedal the question of equality of economic rights and opportunities. Anti-Communist democrats will have to think about something more than freedom if they want the full support of the many millions who, either from self-interest or from a sense of fairness, care a good deal about this kind of equality.

Both self-interest and the sense of fairness are illustrated in the incidents described above. Leonard's protest against Reilly's behavior was not a matter of principle. He was a boy of Reilly's own stripe, and he was merely refusing to be outdone by Reilly when he said, "Who said we weren't going to use blue? We can use it if you can." On the other hand, Fred and Sam, who loudly asserted Lyman's right to equal treatment when Lyman failed to assert it for himself, were standing on a principle. They wanted an underdog to get fair treatment, and in the absence of any personal involvement on the other side—they already had their knives—they went out of their way to see that he got it. There is a possible analogy, here, with pro-underdog movements in politics. Such movements are usually supported by a coalition of Leonards —i.e., articulate underdogs bent on securing equal rights for themselves —and Freds and Sams who, without being underdogs themselves, have some preference for procedures that seem to them to be fair all around.

It may also be noticed that there was never any demand by the boys for equality in the products of their work. Whatever Sam made himself was assumed to be rightfully his, regardless of how much better it might be than what was made by Reilly or Fred. The old Marxian ideal of "from each according to his ability and to each according to his need" had no counterpart in the psychology of these boys. What they defined as fairness was not material equality in general but equality of material *rights* (e.g., rights to share equally in those goods which were not earned but freely distributed), and *opportunities* (e.g., the opportunity to choose one's own color of paint).

Insofar as this distinction may have any relevance to the political scene, it suggests that there would be no particular advantage, even from the standpoint of competition with the Communist ideology, in an abandonment of free enterprise or free competition in the West. The kind of inequality that is brought about by fair competition is not likely to be much resented. What might make a great difference, however, would be an extension of present efforts to see to it that economic competition is fair as well as free. Those who do not inherit land or capital or easy access to higher education have an unfair disadvantage as compared with those who do. But there are methods within our competitive democratic system to correct such inequalities: land reform, inheritance taxes, social security, adequate scholarships for poor but able students. By pressing forward with such things as these we anti-Communists can take from the Communists their last strong talking point. We can at least greatly diminish the appeal of the Communist "definition of democracy" both to the self-interest of those who do not now have their share of opportunity and to the sense of fairness of those who have more than their share.

And if we do it, there is no reason why we should not also talk about it. If our definition of democracy is broader than the Communists' definition—if it includes majority rule and individual freedom as well as equality of opportunity, while the Communist definition focuses only on equality and evades honest discussion of the other two ingredients—then we might as well say so. To those who assert that the Western democracies have no "idea" comparable with the Communist idea, we can answer that our "idea" includes all that the Communist idea includes, and a good deal more besides. (White, 1958)

6. FRIENDLINESS

Sullen hostility in autocracy:

Fred is definitely sullen and responds to Mr. Bohlen by muttering under his breath. . . . He is getting madder and madder and is kicking things about. He kicks the stool under the sign. . . . Everybody is yelling at once, but Fred is the most objectionable.

Competitive hostility in laissez-faire:

Leonard and Reilly accuse the other group of having taken the paints. Leonard says, "You robber! Give us that back." They got it. . . . Everyone quarrels about just what part they are going to paint. Every boy for himself.

Friendliness in democracy (same group as above):

Lyman goes to the water and floats his model, calling Reilly to see. Reilly actually comes over. Sam follows, and for the moment they are all around the bucket. . . . Reilly has never worked so intently on a project, or been so friendly. He is not even making a special effort to attract the leader's attention, which is new for him.

While these are selected quotations, they illustrate a tendency borne out by the statistical findings: there was a higher level of friendliness in democracy than in either laissez-faire or the aggressive reaction to autocracy (see pp. 80–84). The absolute amount of friendly behavior was also higher in democracy than in the apathetic reaction to autocracy, though because of the generally damped-down level of social interaction in this atmosphere the relative proportion of friendliness was as high as in democracy. It seems clear, then, that in these situations friendliness tended to be one effect of democratic leadership. Reilly "actually comes over" and looks at Lyman's model in the bucket.

But it is worthwhile to consider also some ways in which friendliness can be a cause of other attitudes that make a workable democracy possible. Good will—or at least an absence of ill will—can promote every one of the five values we have considered as components of the democratic value cluster:

a) It tends to promote courteous, open-minded listening. Fred does not listen to Sam when he sees him only as a competitor; he "boos him" and tries to outshout him.

b) It can promote self-confidence, especially in insecure persons like Lyman, who blossomed in the congenial atmosphere of democracy.

c) While good will does not necessarily promote realism, ill will certainly tends to destroy it. There was nothing practical or realistic in Fred's mood when he kicked the stool under the sign.

d) Status-mindedness melts and disappears in the warmth of real friendliness. The following incident could scarcely have occurred if, under democratic leadership, a new mood had not taken the place of the long feud over Bill's status as commander-in-chief:

Bill holds up his piece with a laugh. "Look, Mr. Rankin, I might make a bed out of this." Finn admires it: "Well, nice going, Bill." . . . Bill later returns the compliment: "Oh, that's good, Finn. That's a good idea. Mine's too weak."

e) As for fairness, the incident of the knives, already quoted, shows how the new attitude of friendliness throughout the group seemed to promote a concern over whether Lyman got his share of the knives. This may have been because of a new awareness of the group as a whole, so that there was a new need for completeness of the pattern a-knife-apiece-for-five-boys; or it may have been a matter of a new friendliness toward Lyman as an individual and a new awareness of how he would feel about it.

The evidence indicates, then, that friendliness is an integral part of the value cluster which tends to flourish in democracy and which is, in turn, necessary if democracy is to be workable and efficient. The French implied this association when they stated their revolutionary ideal as including not only liberty and equality but also fraternity.

One further question, then, deserves careful consideration: how can genuine friendliness be promoted in a group? These things are worth considering:

HONESTY ABOUT THE NATURE AND SOURCES OF ILL WILL

A distinction needs to be made immediately between the superficial kind of friendliness that comes from consciously and directly cultivating it and the deeper sort that does not need to be cultivated. There is even a danger that setting up friendliness or good will as a conscious goal may result only in a hypocritical suppressing or denying of hostilities which need to be honestly seen in order that their causes can be overcome. It is here that an ethical-religious approach most needs supplementation by a psychiatrically oriented approach. The building of a friendly basis for democracy does not call for bottling up natural resentments, carrying them along indefinitely, and turning one's eyes away from both them and their natural causes. It calls for emotional honesty. As many psychiatrists and group therapists have learned, genuine good will is likely to be promoted by bringing out suppressed hostilities under circumstances conducive to an objective evaluation of them and their causes. What is needed is to let in the air and sunlight on anxieties and hostilities which fester all the more when they are kept out of sight.

ELIMINATING THE SOURCES OF ILL WILL

For instance, in the laissez-faire groups two major sources of unproductive competition, and consequently of occasional ill will, were the absence of a clear sense of group purpose and the absence of satisfying achievement. This lack was a real, objective source of frustration and therefore of aggression. In such a case promotion of good will could be successful only if it took the form of getting the group involved in constructive activity and helping it to be successful in that activity. That is what the later democratic leadership did in both groups.

Other sources of ill will may be discovered: unfairness in the distribution of goods or of recognition or of opportunity to contribute creatively to a group goal; breakdowns in two-way communication; ambiguity in the definition of roles; procedures which needlessly focus attention on status and on competition for status; needless impersonality and mechanization; problem individuals who need understanding help or who are, perhaps, inherent misfits and need to be removed from the group. Whatever the sources may be they need to be first diagnosed and then treated.

EXAMPLE AND CONTAGION

Psychological warmth, like physical warmth, tends to spread, but, unlike physical warmth, it does not diminish at its source in the process of spreading. Instead, the quickening of warmth in another is likely to bring back a reverse wave of warmth from him, so that the total amount of friendliness grows by mutual reinforcement. This occurred in the reaction of the boys to their democratic leaders, as contrasted with their reaction to either their laissez-faire or their autocratic leaders. It also occurred between the boys themselves. The extraordinary interchange between Bill and Finn, quoted above, is a case in point. After their long feud the stage was set for friendliness by the removal of objective causes of hostility, including the idleness of the group and Bill's misfit position in the role of commander-in-chief. But what directly kindled friendliness in Bill's hard and anxious heart was Finn's impulsive compliment, "Well, nice going, Bill." Bill's later reaction was both friendly and entirely out of line with his normal status-mindedness: "Oh, that's good, Finn. That's a good idea. Mine's too weak."

LONG-TERM EFFECTS ON PERSONALITY

Bill's new friendliness is one of several indications that democracy had a good effect on the boys themselves—"good," that is, in terms of the six traits that have just been discussed: openminded-ness, fairness, friendliness, etc. It is impossible to tell from the evidence at hand how lasting and fundamental these effects were. Of course it would be unreasonable to expect that an experience as short in time as this one (an hour a week for six weeks under democratic leadership) would bulk large among the formative influences in the life of any one boy. But suppose it were multiplied by a thousand. Suppose that a democratic atmosphere characterized most of the groups in which a child took part during his formative years: home, school, club, gang. Would this foster in him all of the basic values and personality traits described in this chapter? The chapter has focussed on these values and traits as factors in producing democracy, or in making democracy work. Does this relationship also operate in reverse, with democracy, made possible by these traits, reacting back on the individuals who compose it and reinforcing in them the characteristically democratic traits and values?

Although not yet fully established, this seems a plausible hypothesis, consistent with everyday observation, and also with the accumulating evidence that "authoritarian" parents tend to re-create themselves in the form of authoritarian children.[2]

To Summarize:

The evidence suggests that six of the basic psychological conditions that foster the development and maintenance of a democratic social system are:

1. Open-mindedness to influence from others.

2. Self-acceptance or self-confidence in initiating one's own contributions and expressing one's needs.

3. Realism about the objective nature of task situations and interpersonal situations.

4. Freedom from status-mindedness.

[2] See Frenkel-Brunswik (1954), Frenkel-Brunswik and Havel (1953), Block (1955), Bird, Monachesi and Burdick (1952), Harris, Gough, Harrison and Martin (1950), Hart (1957), Lyle and Leavitt (33), and the recent summary of the evidence by McCandless (1958). For more direct studies of the effects of autocratic and democratic behavior on the part of parents, see, for instance, Radke (1946) and Baldwin (1948, 1949). For general discussion of the "authoritarian personality" see the major work by Adorno, Frenkel-Brunswik, Levinson and Sanford (1950) and the review of subsequent research by Titus and Hollander (1957).

5. Fairness about equality of rights and opportunities.

6. Friendliness and good will in attitudes and actions toward others.

It seems likely that these traits or values tend to foster democracy and that democracy, in turn, tends to foster their development in the individual.

16

Obstacles to Effective Democracy: Apathy and Over-Conformity

BOTH apathy and over-conformity might be called diseases of democracy. It is not that they are especially characteristic of democracy; if anything, they are probably more characteristic of autocracy. Yet each of them is likely to be present most of the time, in some degree, and to the extent that they are present they keep "the psychological core of democracy" from being as healthy and vigorous as it could be.

APATHY

Since self-confident participation is a part of the core of democracy, democracy cannot be itself when the freedom to participate remains a mere form and when, in actual practice, most of the individuals remain alienated and isolated from the decision-making process.

Apathy of many sorts, however, is conspicuous in the United States at the present time. On every hand there are expressions of concern about it: "voters' apathy," "workers' lack of interest in production," "public highway litterbugs," "lack of international-mindedness," "parental neglect." A variety of surveys support the conclusion that a majority of citizens belong to no community groups, the majority of those who do belong are inactive, and a small minority in the community belong to and exert active leadership in a large number of groups.

In looking at this situation Riesman (1950, p. 3) comments:

> The complexity of society, its segmentation, the difficulty of comprehending it, the consistent failure to have it act the way they would like it to act—all these factors induce political apathy. At the same time general political apathy is itself one of the main factors "causing" the apparent inelasticity of society.

Fromm (1955, p. 339) amplifies this:

> The average voter is poorly informed. While he reads his newspaper regularly, the whole world is so alienated from him that nothing makes real sense or carries real meaning. He reads of billions of dollars being spent, millions of people being killed; figures, abstractions, which are in no way interpreted in a concrete, meaningful picture of the world. The science fiction he reads is little different from the science news. Everything is unreal, unlimited, impersonal.

Two facts seem to make the problem of noninvolvement more serious for democratic groups than for autocratic groups. First, external compulsion can be, and is, more easily mobilized to enforce participation in carrying out decisions (not in making them) when such obedience is desired by the leaders in authoritarian systems. In the absence of voluntary cooperation, an autocrat can more readily fall back on the simple device of "You do what I say." Second, the core of democracy, as described in Chapter 15, involves active, creative interaction in exerting and accepting influence, in selecting and using leadership resources, and in taking cooperative action. The health of a democracy depends on certain kinds of participation that might actually be fatal to a dictator. Therefore the pathology of non-involvement is more serious for the democratic group.

An attempt to diagnose the causes of apathy is obviously in order. Here are some of its possible causes:

Remoteness. For a long time Lyman did not really participate in the life of the Charlie Chan Club because he did not feel himself to be a regular member of it. His life's center of gravity did not lie in the boy group at all, but at home, "pottering around" with rabbits and zinnias under the fond eye of his mother. When he was physically in the group he was nevertheless separated from it by a kind of psychological gulf.

As far as civic and political groups are concerned this kind of remoteness seems to be, at least in the United States, the rule rather than the exception. And this is understandable. In their training and growing up, the child and adult receive little opportunity to become aware of the larger units of local, national, and international community as concrete realities to relate to or contribute to, and from which to receive satisfactions. In fact, for many persons even the small face-to-face groups involved in community activities have hardly become realities, in the sense that they are objects on which to focus attention and concern. Consequently there is a lack of identification with, and internalization of, these social units as objects for loyalty and as sources of support for action and growth. So the efforts of community leaders to appeal for participation and responsibility strike no responsive chord in the majority of community members.

One way to prevent the development of remoteness is to draw the growing child into groups of all sorts, especially on his own level, in which he can participate in a meaningful way, and to encourage him to participate in them fully.

Another less obvious remedy is to promote, in the life of adults, a two-way connection with significant social networks. At the present time the individual citizen and the small group have a difficult time relating to the structure of the community or nation in a way that makes participation a meaningful process. As one citizen put it, walking home one night from a discussion of foreign policy, "Why should I spend my energy learning about these problems? My opinions can't go any place or do anything." The night before, this same individual had been much involved in a TV audience-participation program in which viewers were invited to phone in, collect, their opinions on a topic. He made a phone call and enjoyed seeing his idea "get added to the hopper."

Many persons do belong to local units of national organizations, but the communication process between local and national levels usually does not provide the experience of "our ideas being wanted and listened to," or the experience of getting any return message that shows that personal or local-unit opinions were received and considered, used or rejected. The "American genius for invention" could certainly provide a battery of social inventions to provide a two-way linkage between membership and leadership, citizen and government, on many matters that would benefit from widespread consideration and action.

Self-distrust. Lyman was apathetic and nonparticipating not only because of his sense of detachment but also because he felt inade-quate; he did not know whether his contribution was worth any-thing or not. In the same way, millions of citizens have the feeling "What do *I* know about politics?" or, in smaller groups, "Let the other fellow do it; he's better at it than I am."

Surely such self-distrust is in most cases based largely on previous experiences. As children grow up, in the company of parents, teach-ers, and older children, they are likely to have a great many experi-ences that are frustrating or punishing rather than supporting and rewarding. So it is natural that they should become impressed with their own inadequacy and unworthiness. Sensitive teachers and parents, recognizing this problem of being little, weak, and un-skilled in a big, demanding world, have learned many ways of teaching without deflating, and of supporting and guiding without blocking and frustrating. (There are many examples of these tech-niques in the case materials of Chapters 3, 4, and 7, and the ques-tion of self-confidence is discussed at some length in Chapter 15.)

Above all, sensitive teachers and parents encourage participation itself. When a child shows initiative in a group or tries to influence others they do not discourage him by needlessly pointing out his awkwardness or his mistakes. Instead, they show interest and pleas-ure and accept his suggestions when it is at all practicable to do so. That is, they try to see to it that his influence attempts are re-warded, by success where possible and in any case by serious con-sideration.

Another necessity, if the sequence of failure, self-distrust, and apathy is to be prevented, is to learn to choose tasks that are realis-tically possible to accomplish. One unpublished study of the work of mayors' committees on intergroup relations showed that in many communities a typical sequence in the life of such a committee was: initial enthusiastic membership with vigorous plans for action; selection of the problem of housing discrimination as the first prob-lem to work on; the experience of failure in efforts to make head-way on the problem; drop in the morale of the committee; drop in participation by many of the committee members. The committees unrealistically chose the toughest problem to work on first, at a time when they were least equipped with the skills of action.

Vagueness of democratic ends. In the preface to this book, Kurt Lewin reported his observations of the lack of clarity about democ-racy of "the student at Harvard or Columbia, or at Iowa or Berkeley." Another concerned observer, Eduard Lindeman, writing about the same time, reports:

In recent months I have tried an experiment with several classes, including adults, undergraduate and graduate students. In each case I presented to these classes a list of the arguments which are now being advanced for the purpose of demonstrating that democracy is no longer a feasible or desirable form of government. After presenting these various arguments I then asked the students to propose appropriate rebuttals in defense of the democratic process. To my great surprise I discovered that these students were not prepared to furnish such defenses. On the contrary, the anti-democratic arguments left them in confusion and consequently their initial responses were primarily emotional in character and could not have been accepted as logical supports of the democratic idea (1956, pp. 44, 49).

One obstacle to active psychological involvement in the ideas and affairs of democracy is the widespread tendency to keep the reflective analysis of democracy off the agenda of our deliberations. In educational groups, in work groups, and in planning and policy groups "democracy" seems to be to some extent a tabooed word; it is sometimes regarded as a symptom of "tender-mindedness" or "starry-eyed idealism." But is it actually "tender-minded" to try to make clear what it is we stand for? And is there actually anything "tender" in strength of conviction? The Communists obviously don't think so. They are not embarrassed about declaring what they want, or their conviction that it is good. Communism is a religion in this sense. To be sure, insofar as Communism or any other religion is dogmatic and not accessible to facts, we have a right to be skeptical about its assumptions. But a distinction is needed between the dogmatism that often accompanies religion and the great strength inherent in the religious person's clarity about his goals and values. While the believer in democracy may well try to avoid dogmatism, pomposity, and sentimentality, he will be a more effective advocate of democracy, both at home and abroad, to the extent that he achieves the clearness of purpose and strength of commitment characteristic of the religious person and the Communist.

This clarification will not be achieved solely by more vigorous discussion about the meaning of democracy. Participation in, and analysis of, democratic and nondemocratic life situations will do more to tie concepts to concrete ways of living and to sensitivities about "what it is we stand for" and "what we disapprove of and will rebel against."

A student council in a high school was transformed from a sorry experience in learning cynical non-involvement defenses to an active enthusiastic democratic system by having an opportunity to experience a frustrating authoritarian adult-controlled procedure, and a contrasting experience of freedom and responsibility, with time for reflective analysis of the differences in the feelings and consequences of the two situations. This is only one example of the many innovations that may be needed in the school and family to make the goals of democracy more real.

Vagueness of democratic means. When preoccupation with democratic ends results in forgetting or glossing over the complex, ever-changing problem of how to reach these ends, it too can lead straight to discouragement and apathy. If a child is to become an effective participator his parents and teachers cannot indulge in an idealism that focuses only on the values of democracy and not on the skills that make it possible.

Often the first important step in learning the skills of participation is the discovery that *good intentions* and *motivated effort* are not a guarantee that one's actions will be appropriate or adequate. This assumption seems to be a natural and frequent mistake of the young child, the adult citizen, and the leader. The child is often hurt or frustrated when his awkward efforts to make friendly contact or to "get into things" are reacted to with hostility, rejection, or no attention. Seldom does he learn that the problem is his lack of action skills in communicating his friendly intentions. For him either "the others are naughty" or "I'm no good." These interpretations provide no basis for wanting to try again, or for doing better next time. Leaders of groups get caught in this same problem. Feeling confident that the followers ought to do what they ask because "I have their welfare at heart (i.e., good intentions)," the leader often uses very inappropriate means of eliciting participation of the group members, and is righteously indignant at the apathy and resistance of "those ungrateful people." Therefore, learning to think about one's behavior as a language or means of communication is a very important step toward learning to act effectively.

Perhaps the greatest help in improving the skills of action is the opportunity for practice in realistic situations in which the actor is not "playing for keeps." The use of such procedures has been described in the extensive literature on role playing, psychodrama, and "skill-practice" exercises. (Lippitt & Hubbell, 1956.)

In addition to the danger of discouragement and apathy resulting from lack of skill, there is the further, more serious danger of a resort to undemocratic or unethical means to achieve "democratic" ends, if democratic means are not clearly available. A dominant preoccupation with gaining a particular goal often results in insensitivity about the choice of appropriate means of action toward the goal. It is very human to justify the use of undemocratic means-behavior when a leader feels sure that his purposes and intentions are "for their welfare."

Bill is a case in point. He was in some ways an unusually conscientious boy, and partly for that reason he was so intent on holding office—which he thought would make things "go right"—that he resorted to transparent chicanery in order to get votes. A great deal of the history of the Communist movement illustrates the same human tendency. Most autocracies, perhaps, involve at least an element of genuine idealism as to ends, with lack of skill and clarity about democratic ways of reaching those ends, and therefore a resort to highhanded methods.

Maintaining a coexistence of democratic ends and means. The need, then, is for individuals who can give simultaneous loyalty to democratic ends and democratic means, with clarity of both and neither sacrificed to the other. As Lindeman puts it, democracy involves "the discipline of the partial function of ideals. . . . A complete functioning of ideals is rarely, if ever, possible under democratic conditions . . . precisely because democracy must carry the weight of its diversities, its differences."

This is a difficult discipline for the political leader, or the schoolteacher, or the parent—another state of balance or creative conflict, like the balance between self-confidence and humility (discussed in Chapter 15). This means-end balance requires discontent with the imperfect present, based on goal images of an improved state of affairs, but an emotional acceptance of the imperfect present and enthusiastic participation in any small step of becoming. Again Lindeman contributes a vivid image of what this implies:

My meaning will, perhaps, become clearer if I say that what I am urging is that the search for the good life be made an adventure, a mass "game" in which everybody participates, a "game" in which the players agree in advance to abide by certain rules and that, so far as possible, they will not keep their eyes fixed on the ultimate goal, the "score," but rather upon the enjoyments and satisfactions attendant upon the exercise. . . . Those who get their fun out of traveling and not out of arriving will be the healthier ones. (1956, pp. 340, 40.)

OVER-CONFORMITY[1]

The fact of conformity pressures on the member from the group, as a weakness of American democracy, has long been a concern. More than a hundred years ago (1835) a friendly visitor and critic, Alexis de Tocqueville, wrote:

I know of no country in which there is so little independence of mind and real freedom of discussion as in America. . . . In America the majority raises formidable barriers around the liberty of opinion. . . . The majority no longer says "You shall think as I do or you shall die" but it says "You are free to think differently from me and to retain your life, your property, and all that you possess, but they will be useless to you, for you will never be chosen by your fellow citizens if you solicit their votes; and they will affect to scorn you if you ask for their esteem. You will remain among men, but you will be deprived of the rights of mankind. Your fellow creatures will shun you like an impure being; even those who believe in your innocence will abandon you, but they should be shunned in their turn."

Riesman (1954) adds:

The point is that the individual is psychologically dependent on others for clues to the meaning of life. He thus fails to resist authority or fears to exercise freedom of choice even when he might safely do so.

Some of the critics of conformity even go so far as to assume, or imply, that membership in strong groups is bad because "groupism" is destructive of the development and expression of individuality.

This view is, as we see it, extreme and one-sided. Certainly the creativity that characterizes democracy at its best is forfeited if the group idolizes itself and individuals tamely assume that what the majority does or thinks is necessarily right. Yet it also seems clear that certain kinds of conformity are legitimate and necessary. The development of larger and more complex social organizations presents the democratic society, and the democratic citizen, with a

[1] Many of the ideas summarized in this section are drawn from Cartwright and Lippitt (1957).

number of mutual problems. Society needs leadership and creativity in the development and maintenance of improved conditions of life and modes of living, but it also needs individuals who will accept the discipline of interdependence. Individuals need the opportunity to develop a unique identity and a sense of power to reflect, decide, and act; but individuals also need freedom from isolation—a sense of security rooted in close relations with others.

What needs to be deplored and diagnosed, then, is not conformity as such but over-conformity—automatic, indiscriminate, slavish imitation of the group, at the expense of the creative powers of the individual. The distinctions needed may become clearer in the course of the following attempt to analyze three of the roots of over-conformity.

1. *Group insistence on conformity.* One of the mistaken notions held by some of those who correctly view with alarm the problems of conformity pressures in our society is the idea that loyalty to a cohesive group necessarily implies a uniformity of behavior among the loyal members of the groups. Loyalty to the group does imply adherence to the standards of the group, but many groups have developed standards which expect and support variability of behavior pattern on the part of members. In many mature groups there is consensus in placing a high value on each member contributing his own type of resources to the welfare of the group, or performing at his own unique rate or level. Individual conformity to this group standard would presumably be greater the more cohesive the group. But conformity to such a group does not imply uniformity, or inhibition of individual differences. Educational experiments with classrooms of young children have shown that group standards of this type can be developed and maintained with great benefit to the mental health of the members and the productivity of the group.

2. *Self-distrust.* Just as self-distrust was found to be a major source of apathy, so it appears to be a major source of over-conformity. The person who assumes that the group is better than he is necessarily tends to defer to the group's judgment (Gorden, 1952). And a major source of self-distrust is a lack of stable, secure group membership.

This is another reason to reject the theory that "groupism" is necessarily at war with individualism. It has been observed in children's groups that those with the most emotional acceptance and those with the most influence status are psychologically freer to respond spontaneously to their own interests, and to the opportunities presented by new situations (Lippitt, Gold et al. 1959). The psychological situation seems to be one in which "because we like him what he does is O.K." rather than "we like him because he stays in line and only does things that are O.K." This type of basis for freedom suggests another way in which groups may promote, rather than stifle, individuality. A person who is a secure, accepted member of at least one group may be more free to be himself than a person who is not a secure, accepted member of any group. At least he is more likely to have the kind of self-confidence that makes for the best, most balanced type of creativity. From this standpoint, what is needed for maximum individuality is not to discourage group formation and loyalty to groups, but to build more and better groups, so that more individuals can have secure group membership.

3. *Too few groups and subgroups.* Another line of investigation has shown that lower group-wide pressures to uniformity of opinion and behavior result when members of the group perceive that the group is composed of persons differing in interest and knowledge. Under these conditions subgroups may easily develop with a resulting heterogeneity within the group as a whole. It has been noted that even finding one other person who "sees things the way I do" greatly strengthens the readiness to be independent in perception and opinion formation (Asch, 1952).

This suggests a third reason for over-conformity: the individual dissenter may feel, unrealistically, that he is wholly alone in his dissent. Lyman's rebellion against the standards of the Charlie Chan Club was futile and left him discouraged partly because he was alone in it. If even Sam had formed a little subgroup with Lyman, united in opposition to the destructiveness of the majority (Reilly, Fred, and Leonard), both would have gained in courage to be themselves. Even as it was, Lyman drew courage from the fact that another small group—his family—stood behind him in disapproval of the club's dominant behavior pattern.

These examples illustrate the broader generalization that membership in a number of groups makes it possible for an individual to exercise freedom, and develop individuality, in choosing between a variety of values and expectations. Each person is a member of many groups, past and present, and is influenced by many other "reference groups" to which he does not belong. A study of older adolescents discovered that the young people could name from twenty to forty "important groups and persons that influence my opinions and behavior in decision situations." This phenomenon is what has led some personality theorists to view personality as an "internal society" composed of representations of the diverse interpersonal and group relations which the individual has had and now has. Each individual, according to this view, has a unique internal society and makes his own personal synthesis of the values and behavior preferences generated by these affiliations (Solomon, 1959).

The various membership loyalties of an individual may relate to one another in various ways. A past group (e.g., family) may exert internal pressures which are in conflict with the values of a present membership group. Or two present groups may have expectations for the person which are incompatible. Or an individual may move back and forth, from one group to another (e.g., the family and the classroom; or the home and the office) keeping the two loyalties, and consequent value systems, separated and unintegrated in the personality system.

Every group is faced with deviancy inclinations of each member, deriving from his other loyalties. These pressures may be creative or destructive for the welfare of the particular group. And the group, to maintain itself and its functions, must generate loyalties and conformity pressures which may be supportive or disruptive of the integrity of the particular individual member.

This double focus on the individual and on the group seems to be one of the consequences of trying to think about the dynamics of democracy and its improvement. The welfare and efficiency of the group are important values. But, if it is a group committed to democratic values, then the growth and health of the individual are also central values. So in looking at this multiple loyalty phenomenon as an aspect of the conformity problem, it is necessary to look both at how the group copes with divided loyalty, and at how the individual personality copes with multiple loyalty. The improvement of democracy will depend on creative, interdependent solutions to both problems.

Observations of individuals working on the multiple loyalty problem suggest that there are authoritarian, anarchic, and democratic types of solutions by the "internal society" of the individual.

In the authoritarian internal solution the individual lets one membership or loyalty (e.g., to mother, to the organization) dominate his values, ideas, and behavior in all group situations, making him an inflexible, deviant, and unloyal participant in most group contexts. Or, the individual lets "the group I am in now" be the dominant determiner of values and behavior, making him a dependent, slavish follower of what he perceives to be the expectations for him in each group.

In the anarchic internal solution the individual says "a plague on all you groups" and is loyal primarily to the impulse inclinations of the self. This solution may result in uncommitted unpredictable membership, or in withdrawal from group affiliations.

The democratic internal solution involves more tension and hard work, because it requires that relevant conflicting loyalties to the self and to others be taken into account in working out creative compromises as the basis of value formation and action. This is comparable to the "double mental focus" discussed in Chapter 15 (pp. 226–7). Such a solution means that the personality is constantly involved in a process of becoming, of changing, but also of maintaining personal continuity.

The democratic group, or society, has a great deal to gain from supporting its members in working on the democratic internal solution to personal identity and personality formation. This means acceptance of divided loyalty, of indecision and self-searching, and openness to challenge and change. Democratic group processes and personality processes are mutually supportive in creating a situation of creative conformity rather than constricted uniformity.

17

How Satisfying Is Democracy?

Erich Fromm's phrase "escape from freedom" sums up one of the more frightening aspects of dictatorship in the modern world: the frequent tendency of human beings to relapse into a passive, dependent, irresponsible acceptance of a slavish role, without resentment and often even with relief. People have often put chains on themselves voluntarily, or at least have acquiesced without a murmur when others put chains upon them. It would be sheer wishful thinking, then, to generalize too far on the basis of the fact that certain groups of eleven-year-old children, in certain specific circumstances, preferred democracy to autocracy. Even their preference had definite limitations (see Chapter 9). Actually, history and everyday experience, as well as a number of systematic experiments, have shown that both reactions are possible and frequent—that some people, in some circumstances, prefer democracy, while other people in the same circumstances, or the same people in other circumstances, prefer autocracy. What is needed, evidently, is not to demonstrate once again this much-demonstrated fact, but to attempt the more analytical task of trying to discover more about what kinds of people, in what kinds of circumstances, find their needs satisfied in a more or a less democratic type of organization.

As a preliminary oversimplified picture, to be modified and elaborated as the evidence is further examined, we suggest the following highly unoriginal hypotheses:

1. That *some feeling of participation* in group decisions is generally satisfying. Even children, and even the lowliest subordinates

in any organization, tend to enjoy the sense that when decisions affecting their welfare are to be made, and when they have definite feelings on the subject, their feelings are at least known and given some weight. Other things being equal—e.g., efficiency being equal —"government by the people" is satisfying.

2. That a leader's *consideration* for the welfare of his followers is likely to be appreciated, and obvious lack of it is not easily forgiven. Other things being equal, "government for the people" is satisfying.

3. That consideration for the followers' welfare normally implies *freedom from needless restrictions*. While rational restrictions and compulsions, clearly rooted in the need for efficient performance, may be accepted willingly, there is often quick resentment of those that appear to be irrational or based on purely selfish motives. As a minimum, *freedom of communication*, including freedom of communication upward in any power hierarchy, is normally desired.

4. On the other hand, *clearness* of roles and role expectations is as important for satisfaction as it is for group efficiency. Confusion and needlessly prolonged indecision, as in the laissez-faire experimental situations, are important aspects of the kind of "freedom" from which most people want to escape. They are bad enough in themselves; they are worse when misunderstanding of what others expect results in compounding confusion with ill will. Where clearness of roles calls for frank recognition of an inherently autocratic power structure, or of the inherently autocratic elements in an otherwise democratic power structure, it is still far superior to a blurring of perception of that structure by a pretense of being "democratic."

5. *Accomplishing effectively* what the group wants to accomplish is very often an overriding need of most of the group. Many frustrations may be cheerfully accepted once they are seen as means to this end. Lack of participation in final decision making, lack of freedom to "socialize" while on the job, being forced to work hard and long—all these and more may be taken in stride if a leader or leading group appears to be preoccupied with securing the safety, the economic welfare, or the competitive success of the group as a whole.

6. Finally, it is clear that *group norms*, both in a culture as a whole (e.g., the German, Japanese, or Russian culture in compari-

son with the American) and in the past experience of any particu lar organized group, have a great deal to do with what subordinates will expect and regard as appropriate.

These generalizations are on the whole confirmed, but also modi- fied in some respects, by the experimental evidence that has been accumulating in a number of different areas: in business and in- dustry, in military groups, in education, and in groups constructed specifically for the purpose of experimentation.

Participation promotes satisfaction. Of all the generalizations growing out of the experimental study of groups, one of the most broadly and firmly established is that the members of a group tend to be more satisfied if they have at least some feeling of participa- tion in its decisions. The first experiments confirming this com- mon-sense observation began several years before the experiments reported in this book. They were the famous studies of the Har- vard group (Mayo, Whitehead, Homans and others), beginning in 1927, on morale and productivity in the Hawthorne plant of the Western Electric Company (see especially Roethlisberger and Dickson, 1939; Homans, 1941). The most dramatic of their early findings was the steady increase of productivity—and of satisfaction —in a group of working girls who, in the course of an experiment on rest pauses and hours of work, began to feel that they were important and valued members of a group. "A change in morale had been observed. No longer were the girls isolated individuals, working together only in the sense of actual physical proximity. They had become participating members of a group . . ." (Roeth- lisberger and Dickson, 1939, p. 86). Other investigations in a busi- ness or industrial setting have usually led to similar findings. For instance it has been found that increased participation leads to a marked reduction in employees' emotional resistance to changes in industrial techniques (Coch and French, 1948); that a feeling of involvement in decisions on the job is related to a reduction in turnover (Wickert, 1951); that shop stewards and foremen can promote favorable attitudes by involving workers in joint activities (Jacobson, Charters and Lieberman, 1951); that in a sales group assumption of decision-making functions leads to higher morale (Babchuk and Goode, 1951). Kahn and Katz (1953) generalize that "the full motivation of workers in a complex organizational system can be tapped only when some system of functional rep- resentation assures them of an element of control in the larger organization as well as in the primary group." A particularly interesting finding is that, in a series of decision-making conferences in government as well as industry, the feeling of *opportunity* to participate mattered more than the amount of actual participation (Marquis, Guetzkow and Heyns, 1951).

In a military setting, Stouffer and others (1949) discovered that when a discussion group was led by an "informal" leader—that is, one chosen by the men themselves—it was likely to be more satisfying than when led by an equally competent man who had not been chosen by the group. In an educational setting, "student-centered" classes have on occasion been judged by students to have more "social and emotional value" than instructor-centered groups (Faw, 1949) or to be more generally enjoyable (Wispe, 1951; cf. Adams, R. G., 1943–46, and Robbins, Florence G., 1952). And in experiments on communication networks both Leavitt (1951) and Heise and Miller (1951) found that satisfaction was usually greater when the nature of the network, or the position of the individual in it, permitted a maximum of participation.

All of this evidence lends support to the one simple conclusion stated above—that, other things being equal, participation promotes satisfaction.

The seemingly negative evidence, of which there is a good deal, can on the whole be explained by the fact that, in many situations, "other things" are not equal. Other major factors, loaded in the scale on the other side, may outweigh the satisfaction value of participation.

There is, for instance, the frequent tendency to admire an aggressive, dominating leader. The popularity of Reilly in the Charlie Chan Club is a case in point. McCandless (1942) found this tendency conspicuously present in a group of delinquent boys when the cottage in which they lived was autocratically controlled; Sanford (1950) showed that authoritarian personalities tend to regard an authoritarian leader as "better" than a democratic one; and Carter (1953) discovered that elected leaders were more self-assertive than appointed leaders. This tendency to admire a dominator can be plausibly explained, however, in either or both of two ways: the followers may enjoy identifying with a "strong," dominating individual, and they may feel that the group's task is likely to be performed most effectively when there is an energetic, powerful leader. But neither hero worship nor a strong desire to get a job done is necessarily inconsistent with a desire to participate in some way in decision making. The truth seems to be that, on the whole, the most acceptable leader is *both* strong and, in some sense, democratic. He is strong in that he has plenty of energy, foresight, and willingness to make decisions on his own when others are not ready to make them. At the same time he is usually willing to listen to the ideas of others and even to submit cheerfully when a majority clearly wants something other than what he wants. In other words, what most people seem to want is a democratic—not a laissez-faire —leader.

The distinction between democracy and laissez-faire will in fact go far to account for many of the instances in which a more authoritarian leader is preferred to a less authoritarian one. Wherever the less autocratic one is in actual fact not democratic but laissez-faire, he is of course likely to be rejected. For instance, this explanation can be readily applied to the striking finding of Berkowitz (1953) that, in decision-making groups in business and government, the satisfaction of the group is ordinarily greater when the chairman takes greater control of the group's discussion and does more of the talking himself. Probably few of these groups, if any, were highly autocratic. They probably varied primarily along the dimension from laissez-faire to democracy as defined in this book— from relatively passive, do-nothing behavior, with no clear agenda and no effort to keep the discussion on the main track, to an energetic, planful, responsible type of discussion leadership. When these are the alternatives, most groups choose the more responsible and active leader.

Similarly, it is understandable that students who are anxious about passing an examination will tend to prefer a definite, well-structured teaching method rather than a less structured, more "student-centered" approach (M. J. Asch, 1951; Wispe, 1951; McKeachie, 1951). "Progressive education" is not necessarily what the students themselves want. But when it is not, the chances are that it verges on laissez-faire; that is, in a situation in which there is a clear goal wanted by most of the group, the leader fails to measure up to the expectation of the group that he will help them get results.

Consideration promotes satisfaction. A leader's consideration for the welfare of his followers is not by definition an exclusively democratic thing. The "benevolent despot" is a familiar idea—perhaps most despots believe that they are benevolent. It was for this reason that, in the Iowa experiments reported in this book, an attempt was made to keep the democratic and autocratic leaders as equal as possible in their degree of friendliness or considerateness. It follows that the greater satisfaction in the democratic groups cannot be explained by any greater considerateness on the part of the democratic leaders, but primarily by the larger amount of participation in group decisions and the larger amount of individual freedom that the group members enjoyed.

It is impossible, however, to separate completely the idea of democracy from the idea of concern for the welfare of the group. To Lincoln, democracy meant "government for the people" as well as by the people; and "respect for the individual" surely implies regard for the welfare of individuals as well as for their dignity and freedom.

As might be expected, most—though not all—of the available evidence supports the familiar idea that considerateness on the part of a leader tends to produce satisfaction on the part of his followers. The exceptions demonstrate that the principle is not absolute. Pelz (1951) found that, in large white-collar working groups, employees do not necessarily prefer the type of supervisor who takes their side and "goes to bat for them" in conflicts with higher echelons. In his data the opposite tendency was more frequent. The reason, however, was not any preference for inconsiderateness in a boss; it seemed to be, rather, that a supervisor who identifies with higher management is assumed to share in their power qualities and to be able, with his "pull" on the higher level, to look out for the interests of his group as a whole. This, then, is just one more example of the generalization that when effective performance is the decisive consideration, followers may put up with a good deal in order to get a leader they regard as efficient. Similarly, Scott (1952) finds that among naval crews morale is higher when officers are less friendly, in the ordinary sense, and insist on relatively formal relations with their subordinates. Again, this may be because such officers are seen by subordinates as more powerful, more in rapport with higher echelons, and more in accord with a code which prescribes aloofness as the correct behavior for superiors. Shils and Janowitz (1948) report a similar code, widely accepted by subordinates, in the Nazi German army, and Carter (1953) finds even in the United States an almost zero relationship between sociability and leadership.

None of this evidence, however, really counts against the common-sense idea that a kind person is normally preferred to one who is unkind or lacking in human feeling. The issue is not whether a buddy-buddy type of friendliness with subordinates necessarily enhances the prestige of a person placed in authority over others. Judging from the evidence it does not. The issue is whether those who give an impression of kindness and consideration—which can be part of a father-image rather than a brother-image—are normally preferred, other things being equal. And the evidence is overwhelming that kindness is preferred. It is enough to cite, without going into details, the research of Fillmore Sanford on the popular image of Franklin D. Roosevelt (1950), of Stouffer and others on the attitudes of privates as contrasted with those of higher officers (1949), of Shils and Janowitz on the wartime German image of Hitler (1948), of Katz and Kahn (1951), Roff (1950), Reid and Ehle (1950), Hemphill, Siegel and Westie (1952), and Halpin (1954).

Freedom—especially free communication—promotes satisfaction. Here, too, there is enough negative evidence to show that the main conclusion cannot be taken for granted. Scott (1952) found morale higher in those naval units in which the officers were not only more formal in relations with subordinates, as indicated above, but also more strict in their discipline. Again, however, the probability is that this is due to counterbalancing factors, which may be characteristic of military organizations as such, and does not by any means show a general lack of appreciation of freedom.

In addition to the Iowa experiments, the evidence that freedom is preferred includes the experiments of Mowrer (1939), Adams (1943–1946), and Robbins (1952). Many studies of larger groups, especially industrial groups, have brought out the importance of communication, including communication upward in a hierarchy. There are experiments indicating the inhibiting or distorting effect of status consciousness upon communication (Hurwitz, Zander, and Hymovitch, 1953; Kelley, 1951), and much observational testimony to the same effect (Roethlisberger and Dickson, 1939; W. F. Whyte, 1948). There is also some corroboration in the factor analysis of Hemphill and Westie (1950). The nature of their first factor, "task-focused agreeable cooperativeness vs. disagreeable control," supports the idea that control—or at least excessive control—is disagreeable.

But clearness of roles—including authority relationships—also promotes satisfaction. The evidence indicates that when a person is clear about his role and the role expectations of others—when he knows just what he is expected to do—he is usually more easy in his mind as well as more efficient. Scott (1952) and also Stogdill and Koehler (1952) present evidence that a danger to morale lies in large differences between the formal organization of a working group and its informal organization. The experience of "seeing double" with regard to human relationships is a disturbing one, both directly and because of the disappointed expectations and bad blood that it tends to create. Stouffer and others (1949) demonstrate the importance of "helping and advising" subordinates and "explaining things clearly" as elements in enlisted men's ratings of the leadership qualities of their noncoms. Roff (1950) confirms this. Probably the most interesting findings on this point are those of Heinecke and Bales (1953), who discovered that in experimentally created discussion groups satisfaction was higher in those groups in which there was a stable, well-agreed-upon status hierarchy. Heinecke and Bales suggest that when the problem of relative statuses is settled there is less need to waste time on disguised attempts to change status positions; when people know where they stand in relation to each other, they are more ready to get down to business on the main job. This is not, of course, an argument for an emphasis on status. It means, rather, that, with a given level of status consciousnness in a group, it is better to have status relationships clear than to have them ambiguous and unsettled.

This strongly suggests that when an organization is in some respects autocratic—whether rightly or wrongly—it is better to have clear lines of authority than to gloss them over with a pretense of being equalitarian and "democratic." When a superior acts sometimes as if his authority does not exist and sometimes as if it obviously does exist, he may cause his subordinates to "see double" in a most disturbing way. This is not a count against democracy, but against pseudo-democracy, in situations in which the real thing does not and perhaps cannot exist. Whether a given degree of democracy really "cannot" exist in a given situation is always a separate question, but if it does not exist, morale is apparently served better by frankness than by pretense.

Effective performance promotes satisfaction. There is ample evidence, too, corroborating the finding of the Iowa experiments that an effective democracy is likely to be more enjoyed than an ineffective laissez-faire atmosphere, and that even autocracy may be cheerfully accepted if it gets results. A leader who is seen as strong may be preferred to one who is seen as weak, perhaps partly because it is pleasanter to identify oneself with strength than with weakness, and partly because, when a group is seen as a means to some end, the prime consideration is whether it is led effectively toward that end.

The preference for democracy as against laissez-faire is confirmed, for example, by the findings of Fouriezos, Hutt and Guetzkow (1950) that, in seventy-two decision-making conferences, in business and government, general satisfaction was lowered when a competitive laissez-faire atmosphere prevailed—that is, when many group members were concerned with the satisfaction of ego-related or "self-oriented" needs, more than with solving the group's problem. This means, presumably, that a leader who is active in helping the majority to get on with its main task, rather than being too much distracted by the more self-assertive, ego-inflating individuals in the group, is likely to make the group more productive and also pleasanter for most of its members. Similar corroboration comes from the experiments of Deutsch (1949) and of Mintz (1951).

Bales (1952) shows that attempts to control a group are likely to meet with resistance if the group has not yet arrived at a common definition of its task. By the same token, if it has arrived at a common feeling about what needs to be done, "control" that helps it to accomplish that task is presumably, in general, acceptable. A number of studies (e.g., Reid and Ehle, 1950) have found "strength" and other similar qualities to be prominent in determining who becomes a leader. Naturally, this depends on what the group wants. As Wolman (1956) discovered, when the group is "instrumental"—when it is seen by its members as a way of reaching specific goals—a disliked but "powerful" person is more likely to be endorsed as leader than a more friendly person who is perceived as less effective. This is a common-sense idea, but it is often ignored in practice by the sentimental pseudo-democrat who forgets the frequent necessity for a leader to get things done, and the frequent desire of the group itself to get things done, with a leader's help in coordinating their efforts.

Cultural norms influence, but do not determine, reactions to democracy. The question has often been asked about the Lewin-Lippitt-and-White experiments: "Would it turn out very differently in an autocratic culture—Nazi Germany, for instance, or Japan?" Fortunately, it is now possible to answer this question on the basis of experimental facts. Four experiments similar to our own have been conducted in postwar Japan. Naturally the results are not identical with those obtained in America, but the significant finding is that the similarities outweigh the differences, in spite of Japan's authoritarian traditions.

These experiments have been well summarized by Misumi (1959). They include, first, a modest experiment by Kobayashi (1947) in which a democratically led group was found (as in America) to develop more friendliness and more interest in work than a parallel autocratically led group. In contrast with the American results, however, satisfaction was at least as great in the autocratic group.

A more extensive experiment conducted by Mizuhara (1950) used eight democratic and eight autocratic groups of fifth-grade boys. Again the democratic groups showed stronger motivation.

The most extensive experiments, however, and those most closely paralleling our own, were conducted under Misumi himself. His first experiment (Misumi, Nakano, and Ueno, 1958) involved 6 groups of 5 boys each; the task was to make an embossed map of Fukuoka Prefecture. As in our experiments,

the group morale was higher in the democratic groups than in the other two. They frequently exchanged friendly remarks and showed more concern and satisfaction with the work and more willingness to continue it. . . . As to the quantity of the work, the democratic groups obtained the highest rating; the autocratic groups were next, and the laissez-faire groups last. As to the quality, the autocratic groups did the best work, the democratic groups were next, and the laissez-faire groups last.

His second experiment (Misumi, Nakano, and Okamura; unpublished) involved 72 children in 12 groups. They worked on two tasks: (a) "An interesting task which children would do spontaneously, that is, without need of much guidance or advice from leaders"—to paint a picture of a fish pennant traditionally used in Japan at the Boys' Festival. (b) "A more difficult task, requiring more help from a leader"—to construct a model of the children's primary school. The work was evaluated by a committee of 40 members. On both tasks the laissez-faire group did the poorest work, but as between democracy and autocracy the results depended on the nature of the task. In the more interesting task, the work done in democracy was superior; in the less interesting task, the work done in autocracy.

Comparing his results with ours, Misumi comments:

We found that our children are more dependent upon the leader than the American children. The American children showed more direct aggressive behavior than ours. Consequently we may speculate that the emotional expression of our children is more strongly controlled or suppressed, while they are also leader dependent. . . . However, in spite of such differences, our experiments revealed similar tendencies, or "dynamics," under similar situational conditions. This means, it seems to us, that the socio-cultural determinants were not so strong as the situational determinants of the group atmosphere under these experimental conditions.

It would be a mistake, evidently, to assume without specific evidence that results would be radically different in countries that are politically more autocratic than America. In particular, it would be dangerous to assume that Russians are, as individuals or as small-group members, less "democratic" than Americans; Hanfmann and Beier (pp. 134–142 in Bauer, Inkeles, and Kluckhohn, 1956), in a systematic comparative study of Russians and Americans, find the Americans more conformist and prone to stereotypic thinking than the Russians. Nevertheless, there is ample evidence that the values inculcated in a particular culture or subculture are important in influencing how any leader is judged (Reid and Ehle, 1950; Sanford, 1950; Shils and Janowitz, 1948, p. 568).

SUMMARY

Most of the evidence covered by this chapter supports a major finding of the Iowa experiments: *if democracy is really democracy and not laissez-faire*—i.e., if it emphasizes strong leadership and other factors that make for efficiency—*it is usually more satisfying than autocracy.* This is true at least in our own culture and probably also in most of the other cultures of the world, including the Russian and the Japanese.

The two major factors that sometimes make autocracy more satisfying, in the experimental literature, are clearness of roles and efficiency of group performance. Both of them can sometimes be achieved in a democracy, and if they are achieved it has a clear superiority, since the other major factors in satisfaction—participation, consideration, and freedom—all favor democracy.

This is also consistent with the material presented in Chapter 9, "Autocracy without Frustration." That chapter discussed three "narcotic, frustration-reducing factors" in autocracy: resignation to the inevitable, lack of experience with freedom, and vagueness about democracy, as compared with anarchy. Each of these, however, operates only to cushion the impact when autocracy is painful; they are not active satisfactions. Two other factors mentioned in that chapter, a "need for dependence" and "satisfaction in identifying with a leader's power," do need to be considered as active satisfactions in autocracy, but neither of them looms large in the experimental evidence. The "need for dependence" is perhaps largely satisfied if there is economic security, clearness of roles, and personal consideration of subordinates by their immediate superiors—none of which are impossible in a democracy. As for "satisfaction in identifying with a leader's power," it too can be found, though probably not in the same pathological form, in a democracy led by vigorous, forward-looking individuals. Hero worship is not by any means confined to autocracy. One comes back once more, then, to the basic conclusion: *If democracy is really democracy it is usually more satisfying than autocracy.* Human beings do not ordinarily try to "escape from freedom" unless freedom is linked, unnecessarily, with other things that they dislike.

18

How Efficient Is Democracy?

THE efficiency advantages of democracy are less familiar than its disadvantages. The more traditional assumption is that democratic methods, whatever their moral value may be, are not too effective from a practical standpoint. When it was reported that Mussolini had at last "made the trains run on time" in Italy, probably few were surprised. Even among good democrats the most frequent reaction probably was: "Naturally a dictator can make trains run on time—but at what price in terms of other values?"

In sharp contrast with this is the apparent belief of many modern "liberal" educators and students of industrial management—a belief based, in some cases, partly on a misreading of the Iowa experiments—that democracy has actually been proved superior to autocracy in efficiency. The fact that in these experiments the democratic groups were more creative and better motivated, with work continuing when the leader was out of the room, has been widely publicized in some circles and has sometimes been focused upon to the exclusion of other ways in which the autocratic groups were more efficient.

Again it seems worthwhile to present first a bird's-eye view of the conclusions arrived at, and then go into details, including a review of the experimental evidence that has been accumulating during the past thirty years.[1]

The major *disadvantages* of democracy from the standpoint of efficiency appear to be these:

1. *Lack of authority to insure sustained, coordinated action.* It is perhaps self-evident that the possession of authority—that is, the socially accepted right to command, and the implied right to compel

---

[1] This outline owes much to the thinking of Cecil Gibb in his chapter on "Leadership" in the *Handbook of Social Psychology* (1954).

obedience if necessary—is an essential part of a number of relationships, including those of parent to child, teacher to pupil, employer to employee, and government to citizen. Whenever the thing that has to be done is dangerous, difficult, or even simply boring to the individual who is asked to do it, some element of explicit or implicit compulsion may be necessary to insure that he does it, and that his efforts are geared in with those of the others in the group.

Of course it can be argued, as we have argued in this book (pp. 129–137), that a weakening or denial of authority is a characteristic of anarchy rather than of democracy—that democracy, rightly conceived, is a form of authority, not a denial of it. But this does not eliminate the practical problem of whether the spirit of freedom does, in practice, necessarily undermine to some extent the vigor of authority. It is perhaps inevitable that, when freedom is highly valued, many parents and others in positions of natural authority will feel "autocratic" whenever they vigorously exert their authority, and that this feeling of guilt will partly paralyze their efforts. To whatever extent it does paralyze their efforts, "democracy" clearly falls short of a hard-boiled autocracy in ability to get things done.

2. *Confusion of purposes.* In autocracy the group's purpose is almost sure to be clear. Without autocracy the purpose may be clear (when there is "true democracy," with active and purposeful leadership) but also it may not (when there is laissez-faire, or some mixture of laissez-faire and democracy). To the extent that emphasis is placed on individual freedom and general participation rather than on vigorous democratic leadership, the result is often confusion of counsels rather than a single definite goal.

3. *"Talk, talk, talk."* Even the best led type of democratic discussion takes time, and poorly led laissez-faire discussion usually takes an inordinate amount of time. Firm decisions by a single boss have at least the advantage that action can begin immediately.

4. *Mediocre leaders.* The popular person who is elected to office is not necessarily the most competent man for the job, and fear of becoming unpopular may keep him from doing his best work after he takes office. It is often contended, therefore, that elections are a poor way of insuring either ability or integrity in the leaders of a group.

The major *advantages* of democracy from the standpoint of efficiency are apparently the following:

1. *Full involvement.* Participation in the group's decisions (including the setting of group goals) normally means stronger identification with the group, and greater commitment to jointly held goals. As a motivating force, the power of democratic participation is often very great.

2. *Spontaneous cooperation.* In contrast with laissez-faire and with some forms of autocracy, true democracy is characterized by genuine friendliness, good will, and a relative absence of "self-oriented needs" which impair group efficiency. Free and spontaneous absorption in the group task also promotes the best sort of communication within the group on what ought to be done and how it ought to be done.

3. *Creativity.* While "groupism" sometimes actually inhibits originality of thought, individual freedom seems absolutely essential if originality is not to be confined to one or a few persons at the top. Both laissez-faire and democracy clearly surpass autocracy in this respect.

4. *Wiser decisions.* While democratic discussion takes time, the pooled and sifted thinking of a number of diverse individuals is apt to be more inclusive, more critically examined, and therefore wiser, than what emerges from the limited vision of one individual. Democratic thinking, in comparison with autocratic, is likely to be slower but sounder.

FOUR DISADVANTAGES

Now let us review in more detail the four *disadvantages* of democracy from an efficiency standpoint.

1. *Lack of authority to insure sustained, coordinated action.* As stated above, the crucial issue is: To what extent does a strong spirit of freedom necessarily undermine the firmness of legitimate authority? As an exercise in definition the problem is easy; all that is needed is to define "democracy" as a social climate in which a strong spirit of freedom *is* combined with firm (though judicious and limited) use of legitimate authority—"natural" authority in the case of parents, teachers, and employers, and delegated authority in the case of elected representatives of the group. But this does not solve the practical problem, which is: To what extent is this actually possible? To what extent, and under what circumstances, is it possible to have a spirit of freedom that is strong and yet so

rational and circumscribed that it does not undermine the necessary uses of authority?

This is the rock-bottom question. Unless we first tackle it, and somehow come to terms with it, it will not be possible to make sense about the lesser problems of creating a viable democracy. It will be worthwhile, therefore, to look at the available evidence in some detail, including the evidence of history as well as our own and others' experimental data.

The evidence of the Iowa experiments (pp. 64–5) is encouraging as far as it goes. The democratic groups did combine a fairly large amount of freedom and participation with a fair amount of efficiency. It should be noted, though, that the circumstances were rather favorable for achieving this and that, even under these favorable circumstances, democracy was not always feasible. Twice, a group that was intended to be democratic, or wanted to be democratic, broke down and became anarchic.

The Charlie Chan Club, which started out with the leader intending and trying to create democracy, disintegrated and became laissez-faire. Voting became impossible because a majority could not be achieved—the psychological situation could not be organized in terms of clear-cut alternatives—and even if a vote had occurred and a majority had been able to agree on something, the outvoted minority members would almost certainly have gone their own sweet way and left the majority to fend for itself. A similar thing happened in the Law and Order Patrol under laissez-faire leadership, and in this case, unlike that of the Charlie Chan Club, the breakdown was clearly not wanted by the boys themselves. They spontaneously organized themselves around Bill as a leader, and all of them except Finn were eager to forge an integrated group when the table broke down, the group disintegrated, and all further attempts at organization proved abortive.

POLITICAL COMMENTARY

Of these two instances, the second is more like what happens in a large group such as a nation. In a nation it is almost certain that a large majority will hate anarchy, and yet, like the Law and Order Patrol, they may not be able to summon the wisdom and the cooperative skills and attitudes necessary to transform anarchy into democracy. This is an evil in itself; it is also an evil if, as often happens, hatred of anarchy provides the motive force for a pendulum swing from anarchy into autocracy. A "strong man" is called in "to bring order out of chaos."

Other experimental evidence on this particular question is somewhat meager, perhaps because those who have seriously thought about it usually have decided that the need for authority in a working group is self-evident. There is ample evidence, however, that a mild relaxation of authority, in order to achieve higher "morale," does *not* normally lead to heightened efficiency.

The evidence shows that it is necessary to distinguish clearly between a satisfied group and an effective group. A group can be having a good time—it can have "high morale" in this sense of the word "morale"—without accomplishing what it is supposed to be accomplishing. If a boss tries to make his subordinates happy by being highly "democratic" and permissive, he may put too little effort into seeing that they do their jobs. As Likert put it, in companies in which human-relations programs have been emphasized:

> Some supervisors interpret the training to mean that the company management wants them to keep employees happy, so they work hard to do so. The result is a nice country-club atmosphere in which the leadership function has been abandoned to all intents and purposes. Employees like it and absences and turnover are low, but since little production is felt to be expected they produce relatively little. (Quoted by Whyte, 1956, p. 64.)

Likert probably had in mind the work of Kahn and Katz (1953), who conclude, after surveying much experimentation, that a satisfied group is not, on the average, more productive than an unsatisfied one. Horsfall and Arensberg (1949) find, not unnaturally, that an excessive amount of sociability and pleasant conversation can detract from efficiency. Of four work groups in industry, the least productive devoted most time to social activity. Consequently the evidence presented in the previous chapter, indicating that on the whole democracy is the most satisfying of the three atmospheres considered, proves nothing about whether it is also the most efficient.

POLITICAL COMMENTARY

This is perhaps the best point at which to take a brief, inadequate glance at the evidence of history on the relative efficiency of autocratic, democratic, and anarchic governments.

On the one hand, it is possible to point to a number of countries that have been reasonably successful in combining a fairly high degree of individual freedom and political participation with a fairly high degree of efficiency, as indicated by ability to maintain a high living standard or to win wars. Ancient Athens comes to mind (though its glory was short-lived), and a number of modern countries, such as the Scandinavian, Switzerland, most of the British Commonwealth, and the United States. There have also been a number of miserably *inefficient* autocracies, such as the decaying Turkish, Chinese, and Czarist Russian empires. The German, Italian, and Japanese autocracies lost World War II, not only because they were outnumbered but also because of certain elements of inefficiency that have been fully disclosed only since 1945.

On the other hand, it is equally possible to find historical examples of countries in which "democracies"—less mature and seasoned democracies, perhaps, than those of Britain or the United States—have broken down, like the Law and Order Patrol, and have become miserably inefficient anarchies. There are Russians who will say that in 1917 when Lenin took over the government from the nerveless hands of the "democratic" Kerensky, Russia was saved from internal weakness no less than from economic chaos and from the quixotic continuation of a hopeless war. There are Italians who will say that Mussolini saved his country not so much from communism as from economic anarchy, since the workers had seized hundreds of factories and, without coordinated planning or experience in management, had only driven the national economy further toward disaster. There are Germans who will say that Hitler was a necessity in view of the economic straits in which a weak democratic Germany found itself during the disastrous years of 1929–1932. There are Chinese who will say that the rule of Chiang Kai-shek was far better than the chaos of the period before 1927, and there are other Chinese who will say that even the Communist strait jacket of Mao Tse-tung is preferable to the civil wars out of which he emerged.

In contrast with these examples of democratic breakdown, recent history offers several examples of notably effective autocracy, at least in the field of warfare. Napoleon was no democrat. Hitler, starting from scratch in 1933, by 1941 seemed close to conquest of all Europe and Africa—and what stopped him then was not chiefly the democratic West but the autocratic East. The Communists, starting with a backward and prostrate country after the revolution and the civil wars of 1917–20, suffered terribly again in the process of defeating Hitler, but by 1959 were beating America to and around the moon.

In the face of all this conflicting evidence only one thing is clear: the evidence of history gives no simple answer. If anything, the weight of the evidence seems on the side of autocracy, but the historical picture is complex enough to leave plenty of room for further analysis by both historical and experimental methods.

For a leader the chief problem takes a simple form: can I be firm without being *autocratic?*

What stands in the way of clear thinking on this issue is, as we see it, primarily a semantic obstacle: the taboo that still lingers around a whole group of words—not "firmness" (which was never tabooed) but "authority," "discipline," "obedience," "force," "compulsion," "coercion," etc. To those who care about freedom, all of these words usually have some flavor of evil; they are seen as, at best, necessary evils. What the semantic diagnosis implies is that— if democracy is to become as efficient as it can be—those of us who shudder at a word like "authority" should take ourselves in hand and try to divest ourselves of this shudder. We should force ourselves to discriminate and to say "Authority (discipline, force) is not inherently evil. Inherently it is morally neutral, and in any case inevitable. Under *these* circumstances the use of it is evil while under *these* circumstances it is good—not a necessary evil but good." Only after this kind of strenuous clarification will we be psychologically capable of preserving freedom where it is vital to preserve it and at the same time preserving an authority strong enough to compete with autocracy in vigor, unity, swiftness, and decisiveness of action.

2. *Confusion of purposes.* Unity of purpose is related to firmness of authority but not by any means identical with it. Like firmness of authority it is often attainable in a democracy. Through discussion a democratic group may arrive at a consensus that is as clear and unitary as the commands of a person in authority. More frequently, such a group may achieve singleness of purpose on all necessary practical matters by delegating to an individual or to a small group the decisions as to how the group as a whole will work toward its major objectives.

The advantage of autocracy lies in the fact that it nearly always has unity of purpose (at least on the surface) while democracy has it only sometimes. An autocratic boss decides what the group will try to do, and no one dares to dispute him. In a democracy such unity and clearness are often lacking. Perhaps the typical situation is neither wholly "democratic" nor wholly "laissez-faire" but something in between—a partial consensus, with some cross-purposes and some confusion still remaining as to what ought to be done.

This not-too-encouraging conclusion is supported, on the whole, by a large amount of further experimental evidence.

In the field of business and industry perhaps the best available evidence is the research of Schlesinger, Jackson, and Butman (1958). These investigators conducted a large number of problem-solving discussions, in a realistic setting, on the middle-management levels of the Bell Telephone Company. They found that when the appointed leaders of these discussions were naturally self-assertive and directive they were definitely better liked than the less directive leaders, and that their groups were more effective in arriving at good solutions of the practical problems presented to them. This might be interpreted merely as evidence that "democracy" is better than laissez-faire. None of the leaders were actually autocratic. The differences appear to have been primarily in the leader's foresight, energy, and clearness as to what he wanted the discussion to accomplish, rather than in any autocratic readiness to dominate or keep others from expressing themselves. This is not the whole story, however. The more directive leaders, who proved so effective, were apparently somewhat more directive, more "autocratic" in a sense, than the "democratic" leaders in the Iowa experiments. The Bell Telephone experiment makes it look as if the ideal group leader, from the standpoint of getting good results in a practical business meeting, is neither purely democratic nor purely autocratic (as these terms are defined by the Iowa experiments) but perhaps—in terms of the triangle on p. 135—something like a third of the way from democracy to autocracy.

Another important experiment indicating autocratic efficiency is that of Shaw (1955). An earlier experiment by Leavitt (1951), using techniques developed by Bavelas, had shown that a centralized pattern of communication—the "wheel" pattern, with one person in the center and spokes radiating to the others—resulted in the group's solving problems with exceptional speed and accuracy. Presumably, the person at the center took over a certain organizing role and a degree of individual responsibility which in this type of problem was appropriate. This does not prove, of course, that he behaved in an "autocratic" way. Shaw, however, using similar communication nets, discovered that when the centrally placed person behaves in an "authoritarian" way the group solves arithmetic problems faster, and with greater average correctness, than when he behaves in a "nonauthoritarian" way. "Authoritarian" here means that a leader to which this term was applied was instructed to give orders (not suggestions) to the others, never to accept suggestions uncritically, and in general to make it clear that he was the boss. The "nonauthoritarian" leaders were instructed to offer suggestions (not orders), to be hospitable to the suggestions of the others, and in general to behave in a cooperative manner.

In this particular situation the problem could be most readily solved if all of the bits of information possessed by various group members at the outset were collected in one place, in the mind of one person, and if he then solved the problem alone, on the basis of this collected information. The superiority of the authoritarian groups, according to Shaw's own interpretation, lay largely in the fact that the authoritarian leaders were apt to say, early in the game, "You all give your information to me and I'll work out the problem"—with the result that these groups started immediately to work according to the most efficient procedure. In the nonauthoritarian groups the same procedure was usually hit upon eventually, but only after much over-polite, time-consuming discussion of what the procedure ought to be. Orders brought fast action in accord with the centralized plan which in this particular situation was the best one; "suggestions" did not. It follows that the findings in this situation cannot necessarily be carried over to other situations in which there is no one definitely best procedure, or in which the best procedure is not a highly centralized one, or in which the best procedure is clear to the whole group at the outset even without orders from an autocrat.

It should also be especially noticed that in Shaw's "nonauthoritarian" groups the central person was not instructed to be passive; his role resembled that of a democratic leader more than that of a laissez-faire leader. Like the Bell Telephone research, this experiment suggests that the most efficient procedure, in a particular situation, may be a rather directive form of democratic leadership. Like the successful leaders in the Bell Telephone experiment, the successful leaders in this one were prepared to step in and play a very actively structuring, directive role *when the situation called for it* (see also Gibb, 1951; McCurdy and Eber, 1953).

Most of the other research related to this point merely demonstrates again the great efficiency advantage of democracy as compared with laissez-faire, and since this point is not likely to be disputed the evidence can be reviewed more briefly. Carter (1951) found that the behavior of good leaders was especially likely to be characterized by "diagnosing the situation" and by "giving information on how to carry out action." They were not especially characterized by sociability (Couch and Carter, 1952). In other words, active communication (if not active direction) is definitely part of the role of a good leader (Borgatta, Couch, and Bales, 1954). Hemphill, Siegel, and Westie (1952) have evidence that, of all types of behavior, effective communication may be the most important in distinguishing between good and poor leaders. Stogdill and Koehler (1952) found that the group atmosphere is most likely to be a healthy one when the leader devotes much time to consulting with his associates (especially those on his own level) and to inspections of organization. Gibb (1949) and Cattell and Stice (1953) obtained tentative indications that "autocratic" leadership is associated with orderliness of performance, goal direction, and group cohesiveness, and Gibb (1951) later elaborated these indications. Gekoski (1952) finds greater group productivity when a supervisor "structures the interactions" of members of the group.

As might be expected, perhaps, the case for a strongly "structuring" leadership is especially strong in a military setting. For example, Halpin and Winer (1952) find that under combat conditions the effectiveness of airplane commanders, as rated by instructor teams, is greater when they are rated highly on "initiating structure." Similarly, Torrance found that aircraft crews perform better when given well-structured critiques (1953), and that, under conditions of "survival," strongly structuring leadership is more effective (1954).

3. "Talk, talk, talk." It would be hard to find two personalities as different as Adolf Hitler and our own boy Finn, but they would agree on one thing: that democracy wastes entirely too much time on talking. Finn's expression was "talk, talk, talk," while Hitler's was "babble," but the meaning was the same.

In clubs and committees as well as in parliaments this is an ever-present possibility. Most of the rest of us would probably agree with Finn and Hitler if we stop to think of the hours we have spent in unproductive meetings, some of which were probably not very different from those of the Law and Order Patrol. It will be remembered that even in democracy the Law and Order Patrol took a great deal of time out for talking (e.g., for the long scene quoted on pp. 101–6), and that the proportion of time they devoted to hard work, as distinguished from talking, was much higher in the apathetic reaction to autocracy than in democracy. The experiments also contain hundreds of examples of unproductive verbal self-assertion. It took unusually skillful leadership to bring about any integrated creative discussion in the Charlie Chan Club, distracted as it was by Reilly's bumptious bickering ("No, you guys are going to use green"), Fred's joking ("Look, I have a rocking chair instead of a stool"), and Leonard's silliness ("Oh, eek! Scram, the G-man! April fool!"). Even Finn, though he protested against wasting time in talking, did his bit to make the talking unproductive ("Blah! . . . The meeting will now come to order. I want a meeting.").

Even when the group members are adults and quite serious about wanting to accomplish something, their efforts may be balked by the difficulty of arriving at agreement. In Shaw's experiment (1955) the nonauthoritarian groups spent an inordinate amount of time deciding on their own plan of procedure.

Apart from the Iowa experiments and that of Shaw there does not seem to be much experimental evidence directly on this point, but there is a great deal on the closely related question of the relative efficiency of group thinking and individual thinking. Probably the chief upshot of these experiments (reviewed in more detail on pp. 289–291) is that in the majority of situations group thinking seems to be somewhat better than individual thinking. "Many heads are better than one"—not always, but usually. From the present standpoint, however, the most relevant fact is that in most situations groups are *not much* better than individuals. They are frequently slower than individuals (Gurnee, 1937a; Klugman, 1944) even when they are wiser or more accurate. And this means that if a not-too-important decision is thrashed out in time-consuming group discussion, when a single individual could have reached almost as good a decision by himself, the time lost in man-hours or man-minutes is considerable.

The clearest experimental evidence is probably that of Taylor and Faust (1952). They studied the performance of single individuals, groups of two and groups of four in a problem-solving situation (the game of "Twenty Questions") which lends itself to objective observation of the problem-solving process, and also to group as well as individual thinking. They found that the groups of two were somewhat better than the single individuals, in both speed and percentage of successful problem solution, but not twice as good; and the authors point out that from the standpoint of accomplishment per man-hour this implies superiority of the single individuals. As for the four-man groups, they were only very slightly better than the two-man groups, which means that in terms of efficiency per man-hour the two-man groups were almost twice as efficient as the four-man groups.

One practical conclusion, then, seems to be this: There is no need to make a fetish of discussion. It always takes time, and whether its advantages outweigh this drawback is a question that has to be answered according to the circumstances.

In principle, of course, there is nothing necessarily "undemocratic" about delegating many decisions to single individuals, as long as the group retains ultimate control. A maturely democratic group can realistically adapt to circumstances in a great many ways, sometimes using the device of individual investigation and decision, sometimes the device of individual decision briefly reviewed by one other person, sometimes that of individual spade work and recommendations to persons in authority or to a larger group, and sometimes that of full group discussion.

Here, as in other contexts, an underlying efficiency-advantage of autocracy is, perhaps, a comparative freedom from taboos and fetish-words. While a democratic leader is often afraid of being "undemocratic" an autocratic leader is seldom afraid of being "unautocratic." It would be a wholesome thing if many super-conscientious democratic leaders were to relax and focus on the practical question, "What is the best way to do what has to be done?"

4. *Mediocre leaders.* "If you had tuberculosis would you go out into the street and consult an average man with no special training or competence? If you wanted a bridge built would you consult the nearest clerk, or barber, or longshoreman? Certainly not; you would consult a doctor or an engineer. All right, now suppose you want to preserve the freedom of the human race or its prosperity or its peace. You want a man to share in the governing of your country. Is intelligence any less necessary than in medicine or engineering? Are specialized training and experience any less necessary? They are not. In our present intricately interdependent world, the profession of statesman—if it is to become what it must become for the preservation of our freedom, our prosperity, and our peace—must re-

cruit men who are not less able and not less specifically trained for their job than a doctor or an engineer is for his. We must discard the utterly nonsensical notion that 'all men are created equal' and deliberately see to it that we are governed not by the average but by the best."

The reader has probably heard this line of argument more than once. It is the classical argument for aristocracy, expressed by men of uncommon common sense since the time of Plato. And, even though we have found almost no research evidence bearing on it, it seems to us to be unanswerable—as an argument for certain improvements within democracy, rather than for throwing over the democratic philosophy itself. For the sake of the efficiency on which the survival of democracy may depend, it *is* important to find ways to bring the best men to the top, and to develop their best qualities. The question of how this can be done is discussed at some length in the next chapter, pp. 294–310.

FOUR ADVANTAGES

Now to turn to the positive side—we have suggested four possible *advantages* of democracy from the standpoint of efficiency.

1. *Full involvement.* Again the most important experiments are from the field of business and industry, and again the pioneer work consists of the Hawthorne studies of Elton Mayo and others (Roethlisberger and Dickson, 1939). While the girls in the first of these studies were coming to feel that they were participating members of an important group, they were not only beginning to enjoy work much more than before but also—a much more interesting fact from the standpoint of their employers—they were becoming more hard-working and productive.

Since that time a number of important experiments in industry have shown a similar relation between participation and productivity. Coch and French (1948) found that, whereas a change in factory techniques normally led to a prolonged drop in productivity, participation in group planning for adaptation to the change resulted in an unusually rapid recovery of efficiency. Bavelas (reported in Maier, 1946) has had striking success in getting factory groups to agree to increase their output; after deciding, they then proceed to do so. Marquis, Guetzkow and Heyns (1951) found that a sense of participation increases not only satisfaction with a conference session as such, but also satisfaction with the decisions arrived at. Wickert (1951) found that turnover, as well as low morale, was related to a lack of feeling of involvement in decisions on the job, and lack of a feeling of contribution to the company. Haire (1954), summarizing major findings in the field of industrial social psychology, says: "There is a good deal of evidence that participation is the most powerful technique available for modifying the behavior of a group"; according to him the increases of production that have often followed the introduction of profit-sharing plans are probably not so much due to new economic incentives as to the psychological effect of participation in labor-management committees.

In the military field, Stouffer and others (1949) found that discussion sessions led by elected individuals were more effective as well as more satisfying than those led by appointed ones. And, in the field of education, the paradoxical finding has turned up, more than once, that a "student-centered" approach, stressing full student participation, is more effective in producing testable improvement than the students think it is. Wispe (1951) found that students in student-centered groups, while worrying for fear they were not getting as good preparation for examinations as they should, actually did as well in examinations as those who had been taught by more directive methods. M. J. Asch (1951) got what seemed to be quite different results; his students performed better in examinations after being taught by a directive teaching technique. His nondirective group may have verged on laissez-faire, however, since in it even the subject matter of discussion was determined by the students. And, while the students of Faw (1949) felt that they had gained less information from the student-centered teaching technique, they were wrong; they actually did better than the others in objective examinations. Somewhat similar results were obtained by Perkins (1950). It looks as if the greater meaningfulness and personalness of knowledge that is gained through a more spontaneous type of learning are among the more important factors determining the effectiveness of education.[2]

A sub-problem, with psychological characteristics of its own, is the importance of participation as a factor in changes of attitude.

[2] For an excellent theoretical analysis of the psychology of participation, see Gordon Allport (1945).

How effective is a democratic, as compared with an autocratic, method of persuasion?

Here the accumulated evidence of superior democratic efficiency is perhaps more impressive than anywhere else. It now seems clear: (a) that a change of attitude is likely to be more real and lasting if a person arrives at it at least partly on his own, rather than entirely by pressure from outside, and (b) that when individuals have been led, by at least partly spontaneous psychological forces, to a changed attitude, the change can be clinched and carried further if the individuals are in a group that decides "This is what we think and this is what we are going to do."

The emphasis of Lewin (1952) on the power of group decision is well known. He was greatly impressed by the above-mentioned success of Bavelas in getting groups to set higher production quotas, and by the experiments of Radke and Klisurich (1947) on getting groups to change their food habits. Willerman's (1943) experiment on changing food habits forms part of the same tradition, and the well-known work of Preston and Heinz (1949), confirmed by Hare (1953), shows a similar value of "participatory" leadership in establishing agreement within a group. In industry, Levine and Butler (1952) found that foremen's standards for rating workers could be changed more by a discussion than by a lecture, and Torrance and Mason (1956) discovered the same thing in a military context, in which the objective was a change in attitude toward the acceptability of survival rations in the Air Force.

While group decision is not a factor in the classical experiments of Hovland, Lumsdaine and Sheffield (1949) on "two-sided" vs. "one-sided" types of persuasion, these experiments do involve the question of whether some element of spontaneity is involved on the part of the listener. The "two-sided" approach, which more candidly brings up opposing arguments and allows the listener to form his judgment on the basis of a more inclusive view of the facts, is a more democratic form of persuasion than the approach which seeks to overpower the listener by a one-sided presentation of the case. In the original Hovland-Lumsdaine-and-Sheffield experiment there was no general superiority of this more democratic approach; its relative effectiveness depended on other factors, such as the intelligence of the listener, and whether he was initially in agreement with the point of view presented. The same was true in the very similar experiment of International Research Associates and the Institut für Sozialforschung (Dinerman and Kaufman, 1960) on the effectiveness of candor in Voice of America broadcasts to Germany. Apparently another factor is the position of the listener on the scale from "authoritarian" to "equalitarian" personality. Sarnoff, Katz, and McClintock (1954) present evidence that authoritarian presentation of an argument in relatively effective with authoritarian personalities. On the other hand, the experiment of Lumsdaine and Janis (1953) showed a decisive superiority of the more democratic "two-sided" type of persuasion when resistance to later counterpropaganda is taken into account. It has also been argued by White (1952–1953) and others that, under present conditions of heightened skepticism about international "propaganda," the democratic "two-sided" philosophy of propaganda is decidedly more practical and effective than the autocratic "one-sided" philosophy.

2. *Spontaneous cooperation.* The virtues of competition as an incentive have been extolled so often that it may seem like sentimentality to talk about its drawbacks from the standpoint of efficiency. Actually, those drawbacks can be very great. Basically, it is a simple matter of the direction of attention. If the attention of group members is focused mainly on where they stand as individuals, it cannot be focused mainly on the goals of the group. In many situations, a status orientation is the enemy of a problem orientation.

The experimental evidence on this point is overwhelming.

In the Iowa experiments it is illustrated by the inefficiency of laissez-faire, which flowed not only from a general lack of clarity and order but also from the fact that group purposes were continually becoming lost in the perpetual inane struggle of individuals for attention and prominence. More decisively, the dangers of competition were illustrated by the important experiment of Deutsch (1949), who found that groups motivated by rewards given to them as groups were superior in many ways to groups motivated by individual rewards. Deutsch's cooperative groups proved superior in degree of involvement in the group task, in open-mindedness in listening to each other's ideas, in effectiveness of communication, in spontaneous division of labor, in friendliness, in productivity per unit of time, and in quality of group products. Similarly, Haythorn (1953) found that striving for individual prominence reduced the amount of friendliness in his experimental groups.

Hemphill, Siegel and Westie (1952) showed the same thing for "dominating" behavior, and Husband (1940) found that pairs of close friends worked faster than pairs of strangers. (See also Mintz, 1951; Maller, 1929; Stendler, Damarin, and Haines, 1951.)

In the field of business and government there is an outstanding study of seventy-two actual decision-making conferences by Fouriezos, Hutt and Guetzkow (1950). They found that when group members were concerned mainly with the satisfaction of ego-related or "self-oriented" needs, the productivity of the group was significantly lowered. Such groups had longer meetings but completed fewer of their agenda items than groups that were less characterized by self-oriented needs. Similarly, Patterson and Willett (1951) found that in the British mining industry a number of policies designed to increase the cohesion of working groups led to a very marked increase of carefulness and decrease in the rate of accidents. (See also Goodacre, 1953; Flanders, 1951.)

None of this evidence implies that group cohesion necessarily increases productivity; in fact, Marquis, Guetzkow and Heyns (1951) show that it does not. There is always the danger that friendliness will lead to spending too much time in "socializing" when the situation calls for hard work (Horsfall and Arensberg, 1949; Bos, 1937). There is also much evidence that—in our culture—individual competition is likely to be a stronger incentive for hard work, on individual tasks, than group competition (Sims, 1928; Sorokin et al., 1930). It would be a mistake to conclude that cooperative groups are, without regard to the circumstances, more productive than competitive ones. What does seem clear is that friendliness which does not lead to time wasting is all to the good, and also that, in *highly interactive* functions such as group discussion, the prevalence of "self-oriented needs," including competition for individual status, is likely to do more harm than good.

Perhaps the chief reason why a friendly atmosphere is good for productivity (other things being equal) is that communication is better between friends than between rivals. There is strong evidence that good communication is important in group functioning; as has already been mentioned, the research of Hemphill, Siegel and Westie (1952) has led them to the belief that good communication is more important than any other single thing in distinguishing good leaders from poor ones. And unresolved status rivalry in any group, large or small, certainly tends to interfere with good communication. The Hawthorne studies show this in a factory setting, and William F. Whyte's study of the restaurant industry (1948) leads to similar conclusions. Back (1951) has confirmed the common-sense observation that a friendly attitude promotes open-minded, receptive listening to another person's ideas, and the distorting effects of status differences upon the flow of communication have been studied in some detail by Kelley (1951) and by Hurwitz, Zander, and Hymovitch (1953). The evidence of Heinecke and Bales (1953) may seem to count against this conclusion, but actually it does not. What they found was that the gradual establishment of a clear status hierarchy led to heightened effectiveness in group discussion; this demonstrates, not that status hierarchies as such are good for communication or for productivity, but that an unclear, unstable, unresolved status situation is more distracting and distorting than a stable one.

Taken altogether, then, the evidence suggests that whatever promotes an atmosphere of mutual good will in a group, as distinguished from dog-eat-dog competition, is likely to increase the ability of the group to focus single-mindedly on what it is doing, and the ability of the members to communicate effectively with each other about how to achieve the goals of the group.

What does this mean with regard to the desirable behavior of leaders?

The clearest implication is that when a leader shows friendliness and consideration—provided he does not also let down in his demands on the group, when his legitimate role is to be "boss"—he promotes a friendly atmosphere throughout the group. His friendliness is contagious; it spreads to the others. And a friendly atmosphere in the group as a whole often shows itself in terms of tangible performance. In industry this applies at least to turnover and absenteeism, and often also to performance while on the job.

Commonplace as it may sound, this point is not universally admitted. For example, army officers, in contrast with enlisted men, often disapprove of a noncom who "pals around with his men off duty," or who helps them in their work (Stouffer and others, 1949, Vol. I, Chap. 8). Halpin and Winer (1952) found that instructor teams rated airplane commanders slightly lower, on the average, when their behavior showed more than average consideration for their subordinates. And, it will be recalled, Scott (1952) found morale (not performance) to be higher in naval units in which officers were less permissive and more formal in their relationships with their men.

The evidence in favor of at least being considerate is, however, very strong. Presumably, if the case for a formal, dignified aloofness has any validity, it is most valid in a military context, in which it can be maintained that impersonality promotes absoluteness of discipline, and discipline is a matter of life and death. Yet even in a military context—an American military context—Roff (1950) found that concern for the welfare of fellow group members, lack of rank consciousness, ability to mix with subordinates, and willingness to pass on information to subordinates were all related to good, not poor, combat leadership. Campbell (1953) obtained similar results with submarine officers.

As for business and industry, the evidence of Katz, Maccoby, Gurin and Floor (1951) is strongly in favor of the generalization that "punitiveness" in a boss usually impairs the productivity of his unit, while "employee-centered" supervisors get the most work out of their subordinates. These results were obtained both with manual workers (section gangs of the Chesapeake and Ohio Railroad) and with white-collar workers (in the Prudential Life Insurance Company). There seems little doubt that, while formality and impersonality may at times be desirable (especially in military organizations where the tradition is ingrained), and while the right of a boss to demand hard work should not be questioned, both morale and productivity are likely to be enhanced if, within these limits, he shows a great deal of consideration for the individuals who work under him, and natural friendliness in his social contacts with them.

3. *Creativity.* It is not contended here that "democratic discussion" is usually good for creativity. But individual freedom is. According to William H. Whyte:

> The most misguided attempt at false collectivization is the current attempt to see the group as a creative vehicle. Can it be? People very rarely *think* in groups; they talk together, they exchange information, they adjudicate, they make compromises. But they do not think; they do not create. . . . Fast becoming a fixture of organization life is the meeting self-consciously dedicated to creating ideas. It is a fraud. Much of such high-pressure creation—cooking with gas, creating out loud, spitballing and so forth—is all very provocative, but if it is stimulating, it is stimulating much like alcohol. After the glow of such a session

has worn off, the residue of ideas usually turns out to be a refreshed common denominator that everybody is relieved to agree upon—and if there is a new idea, you usually find that it came from a capital of ideas already thought out—by *individuals*—and perhaps held in escrow until someone sensed an opportune moment for its introduction (1956, pp. 57–59).

Probably Whyte does not do full justice to the virtues of group thinking (see pp. 290–1). As far as creativity is concerned, however, the experimental evidence on the whole supports him. While groups may be more creative than their average member, they apparently are not more creative, in general, than their most competent members would be if left to their solitary, undistracted selves. Group discussion often does have a distracting effect (Sengupta and Sinha, 1926; Burri, 1931) which seems to impair especially the more complex, intellectual thought processes (Allport, 1924; Kelley and Thibaut, 1954, p. 750), and therefore tends to divert an individual from pursuing any one creative line of thought to its conclusion (R. L. Thorndike, 1938). In a group there is also likely to be a conformity tendency that inhibits the more unusual, individualistic lines of association (Allport, 1924), or brings about a passive acceptance of what seems to be the prevailing opinion of the group (Sherif, 1935; Thorndike, 1938a; Bovard, 1951).

Since democracy is almost by definition a group affair in which group consensus is sought, all of this is in a sense an argument against resorting to general "democratic" discussion when the alternative is to let the most creative individuals work alone. But, it should be noticed, the question of the creativity of group discussion has no bearing at all on the question of whether individual freedom promotes creativity. In the light of history, plus some experimental evidence (p. 65), there appears to be no doubt whatever that it does. This is a virtue which both democracy and laissez-faire have in common and which autocracy can never share. To the extent that autocracy permits completely untrammeled creative thinking by persons other than the autocrat, it is no longer, in that respect, autocratic.

4. *Wise decisions.* When a boss takes time to be "democratic" and discuss a problem with his subordinates or his colleagues, is he likely to add to, or subtract from, the over-all effectiveness of his work?

Two elements in this situation have already been considered:

the motivating value of participation, and the time-wasting possibilities in excessive or inappropriate discussion. A third should now be considered: the sheer efficiency of group thinking. It has been discussed from the standpoint of creativeness, but not from the standpoint of wisdom. Is a group more likely to arrive at wise, mature decisions than its members would arrive at if thinking separately? Do experiments support the proverb that "many heads are better than one," or the proverb that "too many cooks spoil the broth"?

On the whole, with many exceptions depending on the nature of the situation and the nature of the group, the "many heads" seem to be wiser. Not faster, and not more creative, but wiser.

On this question there is a fairly large experimental literature, most of which does not use the word "democracy" but simply compares the problem-solving efficiency of groups and of individuals. Since this literature has been ably summarized by Dashiell (1935) and by Kelley and Thibaut (1954) it will be only briefly summarized here, with some attention to its bearing on the problem of democracy.

As far as speed is concerned, groups have no clear superiority. Some experiments (e.g., Husband, 1940) have indicated that in some situations groups are faster, while others (e.g., Gurnee, 1937; Klugman, 1944) indicate that in other situations they are slower.

As far as accuracy or correctness of problem solving is concerned, however, the answer is far more clear-cut. Group thinking, in the course of genuine discussion—that is, democratic discussion—usually leads to conclusions that are truer and sounder than those of a single individual, such as an autocratic leader. This is conspicuous in the pioneering experiment of Marjorie Shaw (1932), who showed how often a group discovers and corrects the errors made by individuals. A single individual is often too much identified with his own idea to be able to see its defects, fully and clearly, without help from the outside; another person, approaching the proposed idea with detachment and a fresh point of view, can see errors to which the originator of the idea is blind. This testing and winnowing process can be more or less relied upon to occur if discussion is democratic—that is, if it is cooperatively pursued by individuals thinking independently, listening open-mindedly, and holding themselves to the main subject of discussion.

To some extent, as experiments have shown (Kelley and Thibaut, 1954, p. 739), this gain in wisdom is due to the simple fact that average judgments are more likely to be correct than deviant judgments. If there is any realistic basis for judgment at all, opposite extremes of error tend to cancel out, leaving a mean or composite judgment that is usually not too far from the "truth," as defined by independent criteria. There is also, however, a "plus" or "extra" value in group thinking that is not derived from the mere process of averaging. (Watson, 1928; Gurnee, 1937a, 1937b; Timmons, 1939, 1942; R. L. Thorndike, 1938a; Klugman, 1944; McCurdy and Lambert, 1952; Perlmutter and de Montmollin, 1952). And this superiority is nothing mystical; it is evidently based on one or more of three quite identifiable factors.

Probably the most important factor is the sifting and winnowing described above. Another is that by and large—with many conspicuous exceptions—those who are most right also *feel* most right and are most ready to advance their ideas self-confidently and persuasively. Still another is that the sheer variety of opinions in a group gives everyone more ideas to choose from than he would be likely to hit upon by himself. This is especially likely if everyone in the group feels free to speak when he thinks he has something new and worthwhile to contribute. A well-organized group in which no one feels strange and shy may be better in this respect than a newly formed, unorganized group (French, 1944), and a well-led group, in which the leader makes a point of drawing out the opinions of quiet, unassertive group members, is clearly better than one in which a too-quickly-achieved consensus inhibits those who have atypical ideas (Maier and Solem, 1952).

POLITICAL COMMENTARY

One of the clearest illustrations of the efficiency value of free speech consists of the blunders committed by totalitarian rulers whose subjects do not dare to tell them the full truth. Realism at the top of any political structure is promoted by a healthy atmosphere of free criticism on the part of those below. For instance, Hitler's blunder of attacking Russia and his later blunders as self-appointed commander of the war in the East were examples of a disastrous pigheadedness that would have been less possible if criticism of him by his subordinates had been more free.

THE UPSHOT

What does it all add up to? Which is more efficient, autocracy or democracy?

Our own reading of the evidence indicates that pure autocracy is seldom very efficient, since it lacks the motivation-giving and wisdom-giving values of broad participation. Pure laissez-faire is usually conspicuously inefficient, since it lacks the guiding and integrating values of active leadership, and also the ability of a democratic group to discipline itself. The most efficient procedure does appear to be, as a rule, democracy—if democracy is sharply differentiated from laissez-faire, with clear acceptance not only of active leadership but also of the firm use of authority when firmness is called for, and explicit delegation of authority to certain individuals when such delegation is appropriate.

Of course this means that, in order to be as efficient as possible, democracy must be a highly variable thing, with continual realistic adaptation of methods to circumstances. The members of a democratic group must be prepared to grant broad powers to an elected leader at one time and limited powers at another time. If they have a constitution it must be flexible enough to permit this. A leader or boss must be prepared at one time to exert authority so broadly and energetically that his opponents are sure to call him "autocratic," and at other times to let other people take all the initiative—or all the glory. A parent, teacher, or employer who wants to be "democratic" and also efficient should continually seek to broaden the base of participation in decision making, whenever participation is really functional and not too time consuming; yet he should usually (not always) exert active leadership and he should unhesitatingly, without the slightest feeling of guilt, use his natural authority whenever the situation calls for firm control or for swift, decisive, coordinated action.

To recognize democracy as the most efficient procedure is not, then, an easy formula for success. Both autocracy and laissez-faire are far less difficult and demanding, for leaders as well as for ordinary group members, than democracy in the sense in which that

---

[3] It seems to us that this position is actually very similar to the apparently different position of Cecil Gibb (1954, p. 911), whose excellent summary of the evidence includes a plea for a "variable leadership technique" that ranges

word is used here.[3] It is therefore appropriate for the last chapter of this book to take up in more detail some of the practical difficulties of this demanding task.

over the whole continuum between authoritarianism and democracy. We suspect that what he means by authoritarian in this context is very much like what we would call "democratic use of authority," while what he means by democracy is not far from what we would call "laissez-faire." Perhaps too, if words are carefully defined there is no contradiction between our position and Plato's critique of democracy in terms of the kind of people it produces (*The Republic*, Book VIII, 557C–561A). What he calls democracy seems very close to what we have called laissez-faire.

19

What Can Be Done About the Inefficiencies of Democracy?

THE sovereign remedy for the inefficiencies of democracy is to make it a genuine democracy (as distinguished from laissez-faire) in all of the ways that have just been summarized: emphasis on active leadership, elimination of the taboo against words like "authority" and "discipline," appeal to the majority only to the extent that such an appeal is feasible, continual realistic adaptation of methods to circumstances. But this leaves still unanswered a number of more concrete practical questions such as: What circumstances call for what adaptations? How can "authority" and "discipline" be reconciled with our most cherished freedoms? How can "strong leadership" prevent the wasting of time without dominating too much or impairing the quality of group thought? If elections put mediocre men in office, how can the process of election be made more intelligent?

These and other questions can be most systematically answered if the four major "inefficiencies of democracy" discussed in the last chapter are taken up in the same order.[1]

1, 2. *Lack of authority* and *confusion of purposes.* Although these two factors are psychologically distinguishable they are closely linked in practice. Both raise the question: What can be done, without abandoning the essentials of democracy, to achieve the

[1] In this chapter so much of the discussion applies to both small groups and large ones that the separation of political comment from the rest of the discussion has been discontinued.

294

realism in facing up to a necessary task, and the unity, swiftness, and decisiveness of action which autocracy claims as peculiarly its own?

Some of the answers are obvious—for instance, that freedom is not enough without an equal emphasis on responsibility, and that in general, once a majority has reached a decision, it is the responsibility of the outvoted minority to cooperate cheerfully with what the majority has decided.

It is somewhat less obvious—though, in our judgment, fundamental—that, while this obligation extends to nearly all matters of action, it does not extend to matters of thought or speech. The distinction between speech and action is crucial. A dissenter does not need to feel an obligation to keep quiet about his opinions, even after he is definitely outvoted. If dissenters stopped talking frankly just because they were outvoted, foolish decisions by the majority might never be reconsidered. But the obligation to go along with the majority in the realm of action (apart from questions of principle) should be as clear and universally accepted as the lack of obligation to go along in the realm of thought. Only by keeping this distinction clear can democracy compete with autocracy in vigor and unity of action, while surpassing autocracy in vigor of thought and adaptation to a constantly changing reality.

Certain other ways of achieving unity in a democracy are still less obvious:

Enforcing cooperation. To say that a dissenting individual should feel an obligation to cooperate is one thing; to say (as in the previous chapter) that the majority can legitimately *compel* him to cooperate is another thing and calls for more extended discussion. If freedom is part of the essence of democracy, does it follow that compulsion is inherently undemocratic and should be reduced to the lowest practicable minimum? Many think so. Many tend to identify democracy with freedom of the individual, object "on principle" to government coercion of any sort that custom has not sanctioned, and feel that in doing so they are defending democracy against autocratic encroachment. Many forms of compulsion have been opposed on such grounds: increased taxes, military service, price control, compulsory arbitration as a last resort in labor disputes.

In our judgment those who oppose such things "on principle" are fundamentally mistaken. Compulsion is not, as we see it, inherently undemocratic—provided it is on behalf of majority decisions, or in support of the basic values of the community, and provided it does not invade the realm of thought or speech. Compulsion is at best frustrating and unpleasant, but if it touches only the body and not the spirit it is not tragic. And the alternative may be anarchy. In this respect our experiments are in line with the experience of history. Those who pit themselves against a democracy's right to compel cooperation may actually be defending the principle of anarchy against the kind of vigorous and united democratic action that is needed in order to compete, in peace or war, with dictatorship.

Freedom of speech is, as we see it, a last-ditch essential of democracy. Freedom of action is not. Freedom of action is always desirable, other things being equal, but it should be relinquished gracefully, without a trace of moral indignation, whenever a majority has clearly decided that a certain kind of cooperation is more important.

After all, a certain kind of compulsion is an everyday experience, even with no external restraint. All of us have experienced frequently the problem of "having to force ourselves" to do something. We expect certain parts of "ourself" to take leadership in getting the other more reluctant parts of the self prodded into action and coordinated for appropriate action taking. A similar type of responsibility must frequently be one of the delegated leadership functions of an efficient democracy.

The art of compromise. Just as compulsion may be rejected even when it is actually necessary, so compromise may be rejected as morally unworthy, even when it is necessary. There is an element in the American tradition that scorns compromise; many Americans tend to see it as a sign of weakness, or as a giving up of the best for the mediocre. Actually, creative, artistic compromising is a necessary characteristic of most sound decision making. Without it there is likely to be a delay in decision making far beyond the point where discussion should stop and action should begin.

As has already been suggested the art of "deciding to decide" is an important part of the skill needed to prevent talk that frustrates action and reaches the point of boredom. "Deciding to decide" often means deciding to compromise. The art of compromise is important, therefore, in order to pass quickly enough from discussion to action, and also in order that what is agreed upon will be acceptable enough to both sides to serve as a good basis for united action. It involves creative thinking (based on creative listening) about ways of combining what one person wants most with what others want most, and it also involves cheerful resignation to the prospect of a decision that will not completely satisfy anyone.

New standards when action starts. A third not-so-obvious way of achieving unity is a drastic shift in standards once an action decision has been reached. At this point freedom and individuality, which have been paramount during the discussion phase, should bow to *unity and coordination.*

Here again the distinction between speech and action is appropriate. Democracy can compete with autocracy in efficiency only if it makes a sharp distinction between the standards appropriate to the conference room and those appropriate to the workshop or the battlefield. Hitler thought that "half measures" were an inherent curse of democracy. He was wrong; Churchill and others have demonstrated that the curse is not inherent. It is real nevertheless. The democratic readiness to see the other fellow's point of view, to suspend judgment, to focus on words and thoughts rather than on actions *is* psychologically at variance with the coordination and vigorous insistence on group unity which effective action in an emergency often requires. If the group does not by common consent change its standards about the appropriate type of leadership and the appropriate type of activity when the time for action comes, it may go down before rivals or enemies who cultivate, both in and out of season, standards appropriate to the production line and the battlefield.

Among other things, this often means a change of leaders. In both small and large groups there is usually a natural division of labor between leaders who are creative and effective in reflective exploration of possible actions and leaders who are effective in acting. When action starts, then, it is often necessary to get new leaders who are more decisive and action-oriented than those who were best in the pre-action phase.

3. *"Talk, talk, talk."* What can be done about the inordinate amount of time that "democratic discussion" often takes?

In many unproductive meetings little or nothing is done about it. Many of us have sat through innumerable wasted hours while muddleheaded and self-assertive individuals talked. In all probability, most of the others were feeling as impatient and as helpless as we did. But to "shut that fool up," they felt, would have violated democratic principles. And they were right; Finn's outspoken "Blah," refreshing as it might be, can become too easily the technique by which a tyrannical majority silences dissenting individuals. It smacks too much of the unanimity in Stalin's Supreme Soviet.

Perhaps, though, it is oversimplifying to think of only two alternatives: "shutting him up" and "letting him talk on and on." Perhaps, if the impatient majority could stop feeling guilty about the aggression implicit in wanting to "shut him up," and could fully realize that impatience to get the job done is legitimate and natural, it would be able to do more active thinking about the problem and find ways of arriving at a good practical decision in a reasonably short time *without* having to shut anyone up.

To say how this can be done is of course far more difficult than to say that it needs to be done. No rules of thumb will suffice. What matters most is tactful ingenuity in adapting to the innumerable different concrete situations that arise at the national and small group levels. Consideration of the following possibilities, however, may contribute something to the fertility of imagination that is needed:

Agreement on "what we are talking about." Even the most well-meaning groups, or intelligent members of a group, will waste time straying from the main topic if they do not see clearly what it is. Often there are unexpressed differences of opinion about the main purpose of a meeting or discussion. Often what seems irrelevant to some is very relevant to what some others conceive as the purpose. One way of preventing irrelevance is to discover the differences at the outset and achieve some common agreement on "what we are talking about." This makes the agenda an important part of the group task, often calling for its best thinking. If the agenda has not been talked through and clarified, or exists only in the mind of a leader, freedom of discussion is likely to have a large component of "babble." So many of us have had so many experiences with babble situations that we may have come to associate them with "being democratic." Actually, they represent not democracy but anarchy.

Staying on the beam. Agreeing on an agenda is the first step; sticking to it is the second. Often this is difficult—especially when interest is high and discussion is lively. One of the characteristics of any highly motivated interaction is that group members tend to lose themselves in what they are thinking and saying. This may lead to a wandering off the topic unless someone has been empowered to keep the discussion focused on the topic. In many large and small group meetings it has been found useful to delegate such a responsibility to a "group-procedures observer" so that the leader can pay attention to the substance of the discussion and everyone else can plunge thoroughly into the task with the assurance that there is a delegated responsibility of "watching for when we get off the beam."

One antidote to a talk-talk-talk atmosphere is shared knowledge of progress—of movement in a desired direction because of the collaborative efforts of all the individuals or subgroups. Unless the group can get clear information about the success or nonsuccess of its efforts, there is little chance for it to develop appropriate "group-impulse controls" against babbling. Therefore an important task for the leadership and membership in democratic groups is to face the question, How will we know we are getting where we want to go? The boys in the laissez-faire clubs could easily check by their own experience the fact that they were getting nowhere. Larger groups require the specialized technology of sample survey procedures and other recently developed ways of answering systematically the questions, Are we making progress? Are we moving in a satisfactory direction? "Babble-control," then, breaks down into two sets of practical problems, staying on the beam in decision-making processes, and evaluating action success during the post-decision phases of problem solving.

Limiting debate. The spectacle of the filibuster in the American Congress is well calculated to make American democracy ridiculous throughout the world. Actually it is not democracy, since the will of the majority is usually frustrated by it. If the majority were always prepared to act in its own interest, it would insist that discussion be both reasonably brief and related to the question at issue. There are few issues on which the most relevant facts and arguments cannot be summarized if an hour is granted to each side and if both sides have time to prepare in advance. To promote the most productive combination of influence and compromise, it is worthwhile to establish standards and procedures for a good distribution of listening and talking. This means finding ways of allowing time for the emergence of enough relevant information and enough variety of influence-attempts to make a sound decision possible, and yet to limit discussion after this point has been reached.

"Call for the question." Most of the decision-making in the democratic clubs in the experiment was relatively informal, for example:

> Mr. Rowe now tries to arrive at a final decision, "Shall we decide what we want to do today?"
>
> The decision is hard to get, however, since the boys begin to talk about a picnic. . . . Mr. Rowe quietly brings them back to the question in hand, "Well, what are we going to do today?" Leonard says, "Well, let's carve, that's what we want to do." Mr. Rowe pauses, senses the approval of the group for this proposal, and doesn't take time for a formal vote. . . .

One of the important functions of the leader, or any alert group member, is to identify the moment at which the group seems to have implicitly arrived at a decision, or to "call for the question" when he feels that all the really important points on the various sides have been brought out. There is always the possibility of a tyranny of the minority in pushing for a quick decision after its views have been presented, or of delaying a decision until the majority give up the struggle as hopeless; or there may be a tyranny of the majority in calling for a decision while some individuals feel deeply that their views have not yet been fully and fairly presented; or there may be the pathology of indecisiveness in which discussion is prolonged until no one has any further vital interest in the topic and there is boredom with what started out to be a significant task. The question whether "we are ready to make up our minds now" is important for every group to face frequently with the help of alert leaders and members.

Smaller working groups. Frequently a great deal of the "babble" can be prevented if a decision—or at least the preparation for a decision—is delegated to an individual or a small group.

In the extreme case of war or other national emergency, sweeping powers can be delegated to a Washington or a Churchill to cope with the emergency. In this way the speed of action which Hitler claimed as a unique advantage of autocracies can be achieved, and the procedure may be basically democratic *if* the majority keeps the right to recall the executive, and opposing minorities keep the right to criticize freely everything that the decision group does. In less extreme cases, too, where the majority does not want to be bothered by most of the day-by-day decisions, the power to make them can be usefully delegated to an executive committee or to some other small group.

When the decision has some importance, and speed is not imperative, a democratic group will often prefer to limit the role of the small committee to initial spadework, coming in to the larger group with analyses or recommendations. An example is the committee system of the American Congress, in which the power given to committees is ordinarily not the power to decide but the power to investigate, to discuss, and to make recommendations for the consideration of the larger body.

Such methods save an enormous amount of time. In addition, there is reason to think that the quality of thinking done by well-qualified individuals and small groups is clearer, better organized, often better informed, nearly always bolder and more imaginative, than the thinking of larger groups. The personalities and discussion skills of the individuals concerned are usually more important than group size. There is much evidence, however, that, other things being equal, discussion in a large group is usually less integrated and productive than discussion in a group of two or three to seven or eight persons.

There are a number of reasons for this. For one thing, a meeting of minds is more possible when there are not too many minds to meet. Even when there are only two people it is often hard enough for each of them to understand the other clearly and use each other's ideas creatively. For another thing, the atmosphere in a small group is likely to be more easy and informal. In small groups, more readily than in large ones, the more alert group members can achieve sensitivity to the "sense of the meeting" so that consensus can be developed and identified without formal procedures of voting and taking of sides. In a small group it is easier to keep on one subject; in a large group, when a large number attempt to be active, it very often happens that no one train of thought is followed far enough or evaluated thoroughly enough. Finally, there is the factor of self-advertisement; in a large group there is likely to be more self-assertive competition for attention and consequently less genuine absorption in the problem to be discussed.

A case in point is the dramatic change in the Charlie Chan Club in its third meeting under democratic leadership (see p. 126–8) when Fred and Leonard were both absent. In the absence of their competition Reilly quieted down and became really absorbed in his work, while Lyman blossomed as he had never blossomed before. Creative group thinking could easily occur in this atmosphere, while it certainly could not occur in the usual atmosphere of the group, with Reilly, Fred, and Leonard all competing for the spotlight. Lyman's coming out of his shell was partly because of the democratic leadership and partly because the group was small.[2]

Discussion in small committees may not always be more productive than in large groups, but if it is even as productive the economy of time—measured in man-hours—is considerable.[3] In some organizations and associations it often seems desirable to have a larger group participate in order to have "democratic" representation of the different interests or subgroups, or to avoid hurting the feelings of certain individuals by excluding them. Efficiency of decision making may in a given case seem less important than these other considerations. Nevertheless it does seem clear that decision groups should never be blindly enlarged without recognition of the probable penalty in disorganized discussion and waste of time. And certainly it should not be assumed that a larger group is *inherently* any more democratic than a small one. The subgroups whose representation is considered desirable may not actually care to participate except when their interests are at stake. Competent leaders can often see to it that these persons are consulted whenever appropriate without wasting their time in routine participation in meetings devoted mainly to discussions of subjects in which they are not really interested.

4. *Mediocre leaders.* There is no dispute about the need, in any society, to bring the best men to the top and to develop their best qualities. The only question is, how?

Every American who has learned well his high school lessons in citizenship has at least one simple answer to this profound and complex problem. Ours, he will tell you, is not a democracy in which the ordinary citizens directly decide all questions. It is some-

---

[2] Cf. Taylor and Faust (1952). South (1927) finds that small committees are better for the creative task of problem solution, and large ones for the critical task of rejecting wrong solutions.

[3] Borgatta and Bales (1953) have shown that when one person in a group talks more, others tend to talk less. Obviously, the amount of inhibition depends both on the number and on the behavior of others in the group.

thing better—a representative or republican form of government, in which the average man chooses those who are abler and wiser than himself to answer most political questions for him. He can vote every two or four years, and in the meantime remain a clerk or a longshoreman, while lawyers and statesmen in the Halls of Congress conduct the public business for him. The Vans and Hamils of the country willingly elect a Bill or an Eddie to represent them and serve their interests.

This is true up to a certain point. The cartoonists of America have failed to do justice to the dignity and wisdom of Congressmen. They are often able and honest men, better educated, more successful economically, more experienced in law and politics, and probably much better informed on most public questions than the average of their constituents. Similarly Bill was more imaginative and Eddie more sensible than Van or Hamil or Finn. Certainly the republican or representative form of government is a considerable improvement over direct democracy from the standpoint of efficiency. But the ones who are chosen are often not the most able, and not well informed enough for the immense tasks thrust upon them. Too often a Bill is elected and fails to measure up to his job; and too often an able leader gets scant support. He may resign, or be thrown out, because of the apathy of his followers, or unintelligent critical evaluation of his quality. A popularity contest alone is not necessarily a good measure of competence. The practical question comes back again: In a nation and in all of the smaller groups of which a nation is composed, what can be done to get—and keep—more competent leaders?

Here are some possibilities:

Education in humility. If the best are to become leaders, it is necessary that the average man should want to choose and actively follow someone who is very different from himself. But to recognize and prefer a type different from oneself is not a universal tendency. On the contrary many voters admire themselves, or feel safe with themselves, and prefer a candidate who is like themselves, or at least not too different. The ignorant man who does not have the perspective to perceive his own ignorance is likely to scorn "longhairs" and "eggheads"—if he notices their existence at all— while he dismisses the problems of Europe and Asia with a glib formula some demagogue has taught him.

Fred showed a similar conceit when he booed Sam's sensible

idea of a division of labor in painting the mural. In the Charlie Chan Club the one boy who might have led the group in constructive activity was Sam, but the "masses" in this group—Reilly, Fred, and Leonard—paid no attention to him. They were full of elbowing, bickering, status-minded egotism, and were in no mood to recognize that any other boy (or adult) could be superior to them in any respect. Hitler put the thing rather strongly when he said "The representatives of the majority, that is, of stupidity, hate nothing more ardently than a superior mind." (Hitler, 1939, p. 104). Actually it does not need to be hate, or even dislike. Fred, for instance, showed no dislike of Sam. He just ignored him and refused to open his mind to Sam's ideas. But ignoring those who are competent is harmful enough if the fate of a nation, or of any smaller organization, depends on the competence of its leaders.

What can be done about it—especially in America, where being "highbrow" is more often a liability than in most of the rest of the world, and where politicians have catered to bumptious equalitarianism since long before Andrew Jackson?

There is no short cut to getting competent leaders. In the last analysis it has to rest on thoughtful realism in the followers and voters themselves. The necessary thought processes do not demand high intelligence. They do demand a certain freshness of common sense, a certain basic self-confidence that makes it easy to admit inferiority in many fields, a certain ability to forget preconceptions of either equality or inequality and to look at the world with eyes that see.

This freshness of perception is one of the things that parents and teachers would do well to cultivate in children if they want to promote workability in the democracy of the future. How to do it is another question. There is an inherent paradox in trying to promote simultaneously both humility and self-confidence. How, for instance, can realistic humility be encouraged without at the same time encouraging passivity and uncritical hero worship? One answer is that the emphasis should be far more on realism than on humility as such. If there is enough realism, there will be humility where it is appropriate and self-confidence where it is appropriate. This would seem to imply a non-status-minded attitude on the part of the adult leader (teacher, parent), a focus of attention not on the child's status or his idea of it but on the reality situation.

Most of the time the adult would be looking with the child at the world around him. The adult could for instance set an example of realistic humility by readiness to say "I don't know" or "Let's ask somebody who knows." While listening open-mindedly and never ridiculing, the adult might often point out facts of which the child has shown ignorance in his jaunty snap judgments. When political matters are discussed with children the adult might often condemn the pretended omniscience of demagogues and show respect for leaders who defer to the knowledge of experts in specialized fields.

Long-range as this line of attack may be, it is more fundamental than any of the other measures which are suggested below for getting competent leaders. If we in the democracies are to be governed not by the average but by the best, the people themselves must become emotionally able to recognize and support competence.

The location and assessment of leaders. The task of locating competent persons for positions of responsibility is a continual one in a nation and also in small groups. The committee must select a chairman, the club must elect a president and other officers, the school board must select a teacher for the classroom group, the city must select a mayor and council members, the political party must seek out and decide on its candidates, and the nation must decide on a President, a Prime Minister, or other members of its government. In all of these cases the first problem is to become aware of the potential leader resources within the group, the party, or the nation. The fact that someone has become visible through the performance of some previous public role is often a helpful clue but often misleading. In large groups, as a rule, many of the most competent men have not come to general attention. A location procedure, or nomination process, is needed to improve the chances that the best candidates will come up for consideration. Several industries have strengthened their location process by involving all members of the work group in nominations for promotion to the job of foremen, and the British Army developed a very successful procedure for locating candidates for officers' training through nomination by enlisted men. A Hitler or Stalin usually locates his governmental assistants from the relatively narrow range of acquaintances who have come to his attention as ardent followers. An efficient network procedure of nominations within a democracy has the great advantage of more thoroughly seeking out and calling to attention the potential leadership resources of the group. To make such a system efficient, the nominators must use appropriate criteria and take their nomination opportunity seriously. This they will do if they have had previous successful experiences with the procedure and there is clear public visibility of just how it works so that everyone knows his participation is genuine rather than a façade for the self-perpetuating activities of a small clique in power.[4]

Once candidates have been identified, there is still the problem of their assessment. Just as a lawyer has to pass a bar examination and a doctor, medical examinations, so a candidate for political responsibility might be fairly expected to pass examinations in the profession of statesmanship. On the things which can be more or less objectively measured (such as general intelligence and relevant information) objective tests could be given. Minimum standards could be set, and, above this minimum, voters might have the privilege of using test data as one of the many criteria of competence. The public needs a sort of Consumer's Research on the fitness of candidates for elective office.

The valiant efforts of the League of Women Voters and other citizens' groups represent a long step in the direction of filling this need, and so do certain efforts to gather and publish the opinions of persons who are especially well-informed—for instance, a poll of Washington correspondents on the qualifications of Congressmen. In the United States, however, such efforts are clearly not widespread enough. The ordinary citizen is continually urged to "get out and vote" when, if he is honest, he realizes that he has little or no knowledge on which an intelligent vote could be based. In small groups such as the five-boy clubs in the experiments every voter can judge candidates for office on the basis of personal observation. Hamil has direct knowledge of Bill's impractical grandiosity and of Van's corruptibility. In a large city or a nation, however, such directness of contact is usually impossible; the voters are helplessly ignorant—with a resulting loss of morale and feeling of participation—unless they cooperatively undertake to get from

---

[4] Another promising method of locating potential leaders is the "leaderless group discussion"; see, for example, Bass and Coates (1952). On the use of role playing in the selection of foremen, see Symonds (1947). The very broad subject of what constitutes leadership actually lies outside the scope of this book. For a review of the literature, see especially Gibb's article in the *Handbook of Social Psychology* (1954).

those who are well informed the kinds of information on candidates that they really need.

The rewards of leadership. From personal acquaintance and from the public press, many of us are familiar with examples of competent people who avoid leadership responsibility, or who resign from positions of public responsibility because they "can't stand it any longer." For a variety of reasons, high-level jobs in the American government are often not attractive to men of high caliber. This suggests another major element in obtaining competent leaders. If any large number of men who are wanted in top government posts voluntarily refuse to accept them because of insufficient rewards or excessive penalties, the nation itself is impoverished.

Sometimes the reasons are financial; the money returns for certain government jobs are not such as to draw top men from better paid jobs in the law, business, etc. Sometimes there is a distaste for humiliating security checks, or a fear—justified or not—of being unable to investigate objectively and report facts honestly. Sometimes there are penalties in the form of criticism and insecurity of tenure.

These same negative aspects of leadership responsibility are found at the level of the local community. The teacher, the committee chairman, the candidate for City Council are likely to experience or to anticipate expressions of critical distrust, and therefore to avoid leadership responsibility or to inhibit imaginative leadership actions.

There is no easy solution to a problem as deeply embedded in our culture as this one. Nevertheless, there have been times and places in which public service has been more rewarded and rewarding than it is in the United States today. There is hope, therefore, of at least making progress on it if the nature of the problem is clearly seen and its importance recognized.

The division of labor and leadership requirements. A consistent and disturbing finding from studies of groups of children and of adults is that in most groups the same few individuals seem to be looked up to as the appropriate leaders regardless of the particular group task or group activity. This is true even though shifts of task and situation often require new persons in positions of responsibility if efficiency is to be achieved and maintained.

The epoch-making industrial and technological advances of the past few hundred years would have been quite impossible without an enormous expansion in the division of labor. Walter Lippmann has called division of labor "the great revolution" of our times. The cave man, the medieval peasant, and the American pioneer were jacks-of-all-trades; modern man is a specialist. Yet in the field of democratic government, we in America still expect our Congressmen to be jacks-of-all-trades. We act as if we think they can be experts simultaneously in economics and international diplomacy, in labor relations and in finance, in the problems of France and those of China, in military strategy and in the complex, time-consuming art of getting reelected. Hitler had a point when he said that in a democratic parliament all questions are decided by a "majority of ignoramuses and incompetents, since the composition of this institution remains unchanged, while the problems to be dealt with extend to nearly all fields of public life, and therefore would require a continuous change of the deputies who have to judge and decide them" (Hitler, 1939, p. 114).

The specialization represented by the committee system is one approach to solution. The members of the Senate Foreign Relations Committee, for instance, can specialize more or less on foreign affairs, and the others in the Senate then often show a certain amount of deference to their recommendations. But the members of the Foreign Relations Committee are not yet trained and seasoned and up-to-date in world affairs as they might be if they did not have to pose as experts also in domestic affairs and run errands for their constituents. The appalling lack of direct knowledge of other countries in most of the chiefs of the Soviet government has some parallel on our side of the Atlantic. Yet this committee must play a significant part in decisions which might make the difference between war—atomic war—and peace. Or between the survival and the destruction of the free world.

One path of advance in national government would seem to lie through an expansion of the committee principle. This might mean, for example, relating committee membership and chairmanship more to competence and less to seniority; smaller committees and less overlapping of committee membership; more relief from other nonessential duties; more deference of the larger group to the findings of the committees; and, perhaps most fundamental, a revised set of expectations for division of labor on the part of the general public. It would be a wholesome thing if the public could respect those leaders who do not pretend to know everything about everything, and could learn to look in different directions for leadership at different times and on different problems.

"Mary is the one to ask for help on this, and Joe is the one to listen to on that" is an attitude and a skill which can be taught in the classroom and the family. This would promote efficiency in getting things done, and also improvement in the mental health of many ignored and frustrated individuals who have competence which now is never called for, and so not developed.

The training of leaders. Hitler put it rather well when he said, "The most important economic measures are brought before a forum, while only one-tenth of its members can evidence any economic training. This means nothing short of placing the final decision of affairs into the hands of men who entirely lack all qualifications for this task" (Hitler, 1939, p. 114). The same might be said of parents and other leaders on all levels of group size.

If training is what our leaders lack, training is what they should get—both pre-service and in-service training. For political leaders, Plato's remedy seems like plain common sense: political education and apprenticeship, under the guidance of experts, which would give would-be statesmen both the kind of book learning and the practical experience that they need most. On the basis of a careful job analysis there could be a description of the kinds of knowledge most needed in various legislative and administrative positions; the list would probably include certain aspects of not only economics but also law, political science, history, sociology, social psychology, international relations, etc. Varied practical experience is equally needed. The schools of public administration and of foreign service which have recently begun to flourish are steps in the right direction, but it is not enough merely to have such training available; it is not likely to be in great demand unless the voters themselves come to realize its importance and insist on it, as they now insist on the proper training of physicians and engineers.

In-service training is as important as pre-service training. The international and the national situation are in constant flux. The research which is relevant to the improvement of leadership performance is going on constantly at an accelerated rate. Therefore, it would make for greater effectiveness if all leaders had time for study as well as for decision making and action. A small but increasing number of our national leaders are now participating in seminars and other types of study groups where they are brought into contact with new research and have opportunity for leisurely analysis and integration of the new information. It is a step in the right direction.

Currently there is much attacking of our public schools for cluttering up the curriculum with courses which are not part of the basic "hard core." The real difficulty comes in deciding what is basic and should be regarded as part of the "hard core." An excellent case can be made for the proposition that it should include training in the skills needed by parents and community citizens. The form that such training should take is a large question, but there is an evident need to answer it if we are to overcome the major inefficiencies of current democracy, and replace them with productive action of responsive followers—thinking independently and participating actively—under creative leaders at all levels of society.

These are some of the ways in which efficiency can be sought without losing sight of the essentials of democracy.

It is often an arduous task, and often even the essentials of democracy are necessarily slow in coming. The majority of the people in a politically underdeveloped country, like the children in a family or classroom, may be relatively lacking in the values and skills described here as the psychological core of democracy. When they are, a believer in democracy who is also a realist makes whatever compromises are necessary.

To recognize such practical limitations, however, is only the beginning of wisdom, in large groups or in small ones. A deeper realism would recognize also the danger of rationalizing the *status quo* and of moving too slowly in the direction of greater freedom and greater participation. Along with efficiency in reaching tangible goals it would give due weight to the direct satisfactions of freedom and of participation, and to their probable value in developing the kinds of individuals—self-confident, fair, friendly—that most of us would like to see increasingly populate the earth. Above all, it would give due weight to the experimentally demonstrated efficiency values of democracy—real democracy as distinguished from laissez-faire—and to the likelihood that, if enough thought and effort are given to making democracy real, it can evolve into something more practical and effective than any autocracy that ever existed.

Bibliography

ABEL, T. Why Hitler Came to Power. New York: Prentice-Hall, Inc., 1938.

ACKERSON, L. Children's Behavior Problems. Chicago: University of Chicago Press, 1942.

ADAMS, R. G. The behavior of pupils in democratic and autocratic social climates. Abstracts of dissertations, Stanford University, 1943–1946, 19–20, 83–86.

ADORNO, T. W., FRENKEL-BRUNSWIK, ELSE, LEVINSON, D. J., and SANFORD, R. N. The Authoritarian Personality. New York: Harper & Brothers, 1950.

ALLPORT, F. H. Social Psychology. Boston: Houghton Mifflin Co., 1924.

ALLPORT, G. "The Psychology of Participation." Psychol. Rev., 1945, 53, 117–132.

ASCH, M. J. "Nondirective Teaching in Psychology: An Experimental Study." Psychol. Monogr., 1951, 65, No. 4 (Whole No. 321).

ASCH, S. E. "Effects of group pressure upon the modification and distortion of judgments." In G. E. SWANSON, T. M. NEWCOMB and E. L. HARTLEY (eds.), Readings in Social Psychology (2nd Ed.). New York: Henry Holt & Co., Inc., 1952, pp. 2–11.

BABCHUK, N., and GOODE, W. F. "Work Incentives in a Self-determined Group." Amer. Sociol. Rev., 1951, 16, 678–687.

BACK, K. "Influence through Social Communication." J. Abnorm. Soc. Psychol., 1951, 46, 9–23.

BALDWIN, A. L. "Socialization and the Parent-Child Relationship." Child Development, 1948, 19, 127–136.

——. "The Effect of Home Environment on Nursery School Behavior." Child Development, 1949, 20, 49–61.

BALES, R. F. Interaction Process Analysis: A Method for the Study of Small Groups. Cambridge, Mass.: Addison-Wesley Publishing Company, Inc., 1950.

——. "Some Uniformities of Behavior in Small Social Systems." In

G. E. Swanson, T. M. Newcomb, and E. L. Hartley (eds.), *Readings in Social Psychology*. New York: Henry Holt & Co., Inc., 1952.

Barker, R., Dembo, T., and Lewin, K. "Frustration and Regression: An Experiment with Young Children." *Univ. of Iowa Stud. Child Welf.*, 1941, *18*, No. 1.

Bass, B. M., and Coates, C. H. "Forecasting Officer Potential Using the Leaderless Group Discussion." *J. Abnorm. Soc. Psychol.*, 1952, *47*, 321–325.

Bauer, R., Inkeles, A., and Kluckhohn, C. *How the Soviet System Works*. Cambridge: Harvard Univ. Press, 1956.

Bavelas, A. "Morale and the Training of Leaders." In G. Watson (ed.), *Civilian Morale*. New York: Reynal & Hitchcock, 1942, pp. 143–165.

Berkowitz, L. "Sharing Leadership in Small, Decision-making Groups." *J. Abnorm. Soc. Psychol.*, 1953, *48*, 231–238.

Bird, C., Monachesi, E. D., and Burdick, H. "Infiltration and the Attitudes of White and Negro Parents and Children." *J. Abnorm. Soc. Psychol.*, 1952, *47*, 688–699.

Block, J. "Personality Characteristics Associated with Fathers' Attitudes Toward Child Rearing." *Child Development*, 1955, *26*, 41–48.

Borgatta, E. F., and Bales, R. F. "Interaction of Individuals in Reconstituted Groups." *Sociometry*, 1953, *16*, 302–320.

Borgatta, E. F., and Cottrell, L. S., Jr. "On the Classification of Groups." *Sociometry*, 1955, *18*, 665–678.

Borgatta, E. F., Cottrell, L. S. Jr., and Myer, H. J. "On the Dimensions of Group Behavior." *Sociometry*, 1956, *19*, 223–240.

Borgatta, E. F., Couch, A. S., and Bales, R. F. "Some Findings Relevant to the Great Man Theory of Leadership." *Amer. Sociol. Rev.*, 1954, *19*, 755–759.

Bos, M. C. "Experimental Study of Productive Collaboration." *Acta Psychologica*, 1937, *3*, 315–426.

Bovard, E. W. "Group Structure and Perception." *J. Abnorm. Soc. Psychol.*, 1951, *46*, 398–405.

Burri, C. "The Influence of an Audience upon Recall." *J. Educ. Psychol.*, 1931, *22*, 683–690.

Burt, C. *The Young Delinquent*. New York: D. Appleton Company, 1925.

Campbell, D. T. "A Study of Leadership among Submarine Officers." Columbus, O.: The Ohio State Univ. Res. Found., 1953.

Carroll, W. *Persuade or Perish*. Boston: Houghton Mifflin Co., 1948.

Carter, L. "Leadership and Small Group Behavior." In M. Sherif and M. O. Wilson, *Group Relations at the Crossroads*. New York: Harper & Brothers, 1953.

CARTER, L., HAYTHORN, W., SHRIVER, E., and LANZETTA, J. "The Behavior of Leaders and Other Group Members." *J. Abnorm. Soc. Psychol.*, 1951, 46, 589–595.

CARTWRIGHT, D., and LIPPITT, R. "Group Dynamics and the Individual." *Int'l J. of Group Psychotherapy*, 1957, 7, 1, 86–102.

CARTWRIGHT, D., and ZANDER, A. (eds.). *Group Dynamics: Research and Theory*. Evanston, Ill.: Row, Peterson & Company, 1953.

CATTELL, R. B. *Personality: A Systematic Theoretical and Factual Study*. New York: McGraw-Hill Book Co., 1950.

——. "New Concepts for Measuring Leadership in Terms of Group Syntality." *Hum. Rel.*, 1951, 4, 161–184.

CATTELL, R. B., SAUNDERS, D. R., and STICE, G. F. "The Dimensions of Syntality in Small Groups." *Hum. Rel.*, 953, 6, 331–336.

CATTELL, R. B., and STICE, G. F. *The Psychodynamics of Small Groups*. Urbana: Laboratory of Personality Assessment and Group Behavior, Univ. of Illinois, 1953.

CASS, L. K. "Parent-Child Relationships and Delinquency." *J. Abnorm. Soc. Psychol.*, 1952, 47, 101–104.

COCH, L., and FRENCH, J. R. P. "Overcoming Resistance to Change." *Hum. Rel.*, 1948, 1, 512–532.

COUCH, A. S., and CARTER, L. "A Factorial Study of the Rated Behavior of Group Members." A paper read at Eastern Psychol. Assn., Atlantic City, April, 1952.

DASHIELL, J. F. "Experimental Studies of the Influence of Social Situations on the Behavior of Individual Human Adults." In C. MURCHISON (ed.), *Handbook of Social Psychology*. Worcester, Mass.: Clark Univ. Press, 1935, pp. 1097–1158.

DEMBO, T. "Anger as a Dynamic Problem." *Psychol. Forschung*, 1931, 15, 1–144.

DEUTSCH, MORTON. "An Experimental Study of the Effects of Cooperation and Competition upon Group Process." *Hum. Rel.*, 1949, 2, 199–231.

DINERMAN, HELEN, and KAUFMAN, HELEN. "The Effectiveness of Candor in Voice of America Broadcasts to Germany." 1960.

DOLLARD, J., DOOB, L. W., MILLER, N. E., MOWRER, O. H., and SEARS, R. R. *Frustration and Aggression*. New Haven: Yale Univ. Press, 1939.

FAW, V. "A Psychotherapeutic Method of Teaching Psychology." *Amer. Psychologist*, 1949, 4, 104–109.

FESTINGER, L. *A Theory of Cognitive Dissonance*. Evanston, Ill.: Row, Peterson & Company, 1958.

FLANDERS, N. A. "Personal-Social Anxiety as a Factor in Experimental Learning Situations." *J. Educ. Res.*, 1951, *45*, 100–110.

FLEMMING, E. G. "A Factor Analysis of the Personality of High School Leaders." *J. Appl. Psychol.*, 1935, *5*, 596–605.

FOURIEZOS, N. T., HUTT, M. L., and GUETZKOW, H. "Measurement of Self-Oriented Needs in Discussion Groups." *J. Abnorm. Soc. Psychol.*, 1950, *45*, 682–690.

FRENCH, J. R. P., JR. "Organized and Unorganized Groups under Fear and Frustration." *U. of Iowa Stud. Child Welf.*, 1944, *20*, No. 409, 231–308.

FRENKEL-BRUNSWIK, ELSE. "Interaction of Psychological and Sociological Factors in Political Behavior." In KATZ, D., CARTWRIGHT, D., ELDERSVELD, S., and LEE, A. M. (eds.), *Public Opinion and Propaganda*. New York: Dryden Press (Holt), 1954, pp. 363–380.

——. Further explorations by a contributor to "The Authoritarian Personality." In R. CHRISTIE and MARIE JAHODA (eds.), *Studies in the Scope and Method of "The Authoritarian Personality."* Glencoe: The Free Press of Glencoe, Illinois, 1954.

FRENKEL-BRUNSWIK, ELSE, and HAVEL, JOAN. "Prejudice in the Interviews of Children: I. Attitudes Toward Minority Groups." *J. Genet. Psychol.*, 1953, *82*, 91–136.

FREUD, S. *The Ego and the Id.* London: Hogarth Press, 1927.

FROMM, E. *The Sane Society.* New York: Rinehart & Company, Inc., 1955.

——. *Escape from Freedom.* New York: Farrar & Rinehart, 1941.

GEKOSKI, N. "Predicting Group Productivity." *Personnel Psychol.*, 1952, *5*, 281–292.

GIBB, C. A. "The Emergence of Leadership in Small Temporary Groups of Men." Unpublished doctoral dissertation, Univ. of Ill., 1949.

——. "An Experimental Approach to the Study of Leadership." *Occup. Psychol.*, 1951, *25*, 233–248.

——. "Leadership." In G. LINDZEY (ed.), *Handbook of Social Psychology.* Cambridge: Addison-Wesley Publishing Company, Inc., 1954, pp. 877–920.

GLUECK, S., and GLUECK, ELEANOR. *Unraveling Juvenile Delinquency.* Cambridge: Harvard Univ. Press, 1950.

GOODACRE, D. M. "Group Characteristics of Good and Poor Performing Combat Units." *Sociometry*, 1953, *16*, 168–178.

GORDEN, R. L. "Interaction between Attitude and the Definition of the Situation in the Expression of Opinion." *Amer. Sociol. Rev.*, 1952, *17*, 50–58.

GUETZKOW, H. (ed.). *Groups, Leadership and Men*. Pittsburgh: Carnegie Press, 1951.

GURNEE, H. "Maze Learning in the Collective Situation." *J. Psychol.*, 1937a, *3*, 437–443.

GURNEE, H. "A Comparison of Collective and Individual Judgments of Facts." *J. Exper. Psychol.*, 1937b, *21*, 106–112.

HAIRE, M. "Industrial Social Psychology." Chapter 29 in G. LINDZEY (ed.), *Handbook of Social Psychology*. Vol. 2. Cambridge: Addison-Wesley Publishing Company, Inc., 1954.

HALPIN, A. W. "The Leadership Behavior and Combat Performance of Airplane Commanders." *J. Abnorm. Soc. Psychol.*, 1954, *49*, 19–22.

HALPIN, A. W., and WINER, B. J. *The Leadership Behavior of the Airplane Commander*. Columbus: Ohio State Univ. Res. Found., 1952.

HARE, A. P. "Small Group Discussions with Participatory and Supervisory Leadership." *J. Abnorm. Soc. Psychol.*, 1953, *48*, 273–275.

HARE, A. P., BORGATTA, E. F., and BALES, R. F. *Small Groups: Studies in Social Interaction*. New York: Alfred A. Knopf, Inc., 1955.

HARRIS, D. B., GOUGH, H. G., and MARTIN, W. E. "Children's Ethnic Attitudes: II. Relationship to Parental Beliefs." *Child Develpm.*, 1950, *21*, 169–182.

HART, I. "Maternal Child-Rearing Practices and Authoritarian Ideology." *J. Abnorm. Soc. Psychol.*, 1957, *55*, 232–237.

HARTSHORNE, H., MAY, M. A., and MALLER, J. B. *Studies in Service and Self-Control*. New York: The Macmillan Co., 1929.

HAYTHORN, W. "The Influence of Individual Members on the Characteristics of Small Groups." *J. Abnorm. Soc. Psychol.*, 1953, *48*, 276–284.

HAYTHORN, W., COUCH, A., HAEFNER, D., LANGHAM, P., and CARTER, L. F. "The Behavior of Authoritarian and Equalitarian Personalities in Groups." *Hum. Relat.*, 1956, *9*, 57–74.

HEIDER, F. "Attitudes and Cognitive Organization." *J. of Psychol.*, 1946, *21*, 107–112.

———. *The Psychology of Interpersonal Relations*. New York: John Wiley and Sons, Inc., 1958.

HEINICKE, C., and BALES, R. F. "Developmental Trends in the Structure of Small Groups." *Sociometry*, 1953, *16*, 7–38.

HEISE, G. A., and MILLER, G. A. "Problem Solving by Small Groups Using Various Communication Nets." *J. Abnorm. Soc. Psychol.*, 1951, *46*, 327–336.

HEMPHILL, J. K., and WESTIE, C. M. "The Measurement of Group Dimensions." *J. of Psychol.*, 1950, *29*, 325–342.

HEMPHILL, J. K., SIEGEL, A., and WESTIE, C. M. An exploratory study of relations between perceptions of leader behavior, group characteristics, and expectations concerning the behavior of ideal leaders. Unpublished staff report. Ohio State Univ. Personnel Res. Board, 1952.

HEWITT, L. E., and JENKINS, R. L. *Fundamental Patterns of Maladjustment; the Dynamics of Their Origin.* Illinois: D. H. Green, 1946.

HITLER, A. *Mein Kampf.* New York: Reynal & Hitchcock, 1939.

HOMANS, G. C. "The Western Electric Researches." Chap. 4 of *Fatigue of Workers: Its Relation to Industrial Production,* by the Committee on Work in Industry, Nat. Res. Council. New York: Reinhold Publishing Corporation, 1941.

HORSFALL, A. B., and ARENSBERG, C. M. "Teamwork and Productivity in a Shoe Factory." *Hum. Organization (Applied Anthrop.),* 1949, 8, 13–25.

HOVLAND, C. I., LUMSDAINE, A. A., and SHEFFIELD, F. D. *Experiments in Mass Communication.* Princeton: Princeton Univ. Press, 1949.

HOWELL, T. H. "An Experimental Study of Persistence." *J. Abnorm. Soc. Psychol.,* 1933, 28, 14–20.

HURWITZ, J. I., ZANDER, A. F., and HYMOVITCH, B. "Some Effects of Power on the Relations among Group Members." In D. CARTWRIGHT and A. F. ZANDER (eds.), *Group Dynamics: Research and Theory.* Evanston, Ill.: Row, Peterson & Company, 1953, 483–492.

HUSBAND, R. W. "Cooperative vs. Solitary Problem Solution." *J. Soc. Psychol.,* 1940, 11, 405–409.

JACOBSON, E., CHARTERS, W. W., JR., and LIEBERMAN, S. "The Use of the Role Concept in the Study of Complex Organizations." *J. Soc. Issues,* 1951, 7, 18–27.

JENNINGS, H. H. *Leadership and Isolation.* New York: Longmans, Green, & Co., Inc., 1943. Revised Ed., 1950.

KAHN, R. L., and KATZ, D. "Leadership Practices in Relation to Productivity and Morale." In D. CARTWRIGHT and A. F. ZANDER (eds.), *Group Dynamics: Research and Theory.* Evanston, Ill.: Row, Peterson & Company, 1953, 612–628.

KATZ, D., and KAHN, R. L. "Human Organization and Worker Motivation." In L. R. TRIPP (ed.), *Industrial Productivity.* Madison, Wis.: Indust. Rel. Res. Ass., 1951.

KATZ, D., MACCOBY, N., GURIN, G., and FLOOR, LUCRETIA. *Productivity, Supervision and Morale Among Railroad Workers.* Ann Arbor: Survey Research Center, 1951.

Kelley, H. H. "Communication in Experimentally Created Hierarchies." *Hum. Relat.*, 1951, 4, 39–56.

Kelley, H. H., and Thibaut, J. W. "Experimental Studies of Group Problem Solving and Process." In G. Lindzey (ed.), *Handbook of Social Psychology*. Cambridge: Addison-Wesley Publishing Company, Inc., 1954, pp. 735–785.

Kelman, H. C. "Attitude Change as a Function of Response Restriction." *Hum. Relat.*, 1953, 6, 185–214.

Klugman, S. F. "Cooperative vs. Individual Efficiency in Problem-Solving." *J. Educ. Psychol.*, 1944, 35, 91–100.

Kobayashi, S. "Problems in Group Guidance—Democratic Leadership and Autocratic Leadership" (in Japanese). Child Study, 2, pp. 117–126.

Köhler, W. *The Place of Value in a World of Facts*. New York: Liveright Publishing Corp., 1938.

Kremer, A. H. "The Nature of Persistence." *Stud. Psychol. & Psychiat.*, 1942, 5, 40.

Leavitt, H. J. "Some Effects of Certain Communication Patterns on Group Performance." *J. Abnorm. Soc. Psychol.*, 1951, 46, 38–50.

Leavitt, H. J., and Mueller, R. A. H. "Some Effects of Feedback on Communication." *Hum. Relat.*, 1951, 4, 401–410.

Lesser, G. S. "Maternal Attitudes and Practices and the Aggressive Behavior of Children." Unpublished doctoral dissertation, Yale Univ., 1952.

Levine, J., and Butler, J. "Lecture vs. Group Discussion in Changing Behavior." *J. Appl. Psychol.*, 1952, 36, 29–33.

Levy, S. "Experimental Study of Group Norms: The Effects of Group Cohesiveness upon Social Conformity." Unpublished doctoral dissertation, New York Univ., 1953.

Lewin, K. *A Dynamic Theory of Personality*. New York: McGraw-Hill Book Co., 1935.

———. "Group Decision and Social Change." In T. Newcomb and E. Hartley (eds.), *Readings in Social Psychology*. New York: Henry Holt & Co., Inc., 1947, pp. 330–344.

———. *Resolving Social Conflicts*. New York: Harper & Brothers, 1948.

———. *Field Theory in Social Science*. New York: Harper & Brothers, 1951.

———. "Group Decision and Social Change." In G. E. Swanson, T. M. Newcomb, and E. L. Hartley, *Readings in Social Psychology*, New York: Henry Holt & Co., Inc., 1952, pp. 459–473.

Lewin, K., Lippitt, R., and White, R. K. "Patterns of Aggressive Behavior in Experimentally Created Social Climates." *J. Soc. Psychol.*, 1939, *10*, 271–279.

LINDEMAN, E. C. *The Democratic Man.* Boston: Beacon Press, 1956.

LINDZEY, G. (ed.). *Handbook of Social Psychology.* Cambridge: Addison-Wesley Publishing Company, Inc., 1954.

LIPPITT, R. "An Experimental Study of Authoritarian and Democratic Group Atmospheres. Studies in Topological and Vector Psychology." I. *Univer. Ia. Stud. Child Welf.*, 1940, *16*, No. 3, 44–195.

———. "An Experimental Study of Three Social Climates." Ph.D. thesis, Univ. of Iowa, 1940a.

———. *Training in Community Relations: A Research Exploration toward New Group Skills.* New York: Harper & Brothers, 1949.

LIPPITT, R., GOLD, M., and ASSOCIATES. Experiments in improving classroom mental health. (Ms. in preparation.)

LIPPITT, R. GOLD, M. "Classroom Social Structure as a Mental Health Problem." *Journal of Social Issues,* 1959, vol. *15*, pp. 40–50.

LIPPITT, R., POLANSKY, N., and ROSEN, S. "The Dynamics of Power." *Hum. Relat.*, 1952, *5*, 37–64.

LIPPITT, R., WATSON, JEANNE, and WESTLEY, B. *The Dynamics of Planned Change.* New York: Harcourt, Brace & Co., 1958.

LIPPITT, R., and WHITE, R. K. The "Social Climate" of Children's Groups. In R. G. BARKER, J. S. KOUNIN, and H. F. WRIGHT (eds.), *Child Behavior and Development.* New York: McGraw-Hill Book Co., 1943, pp. 485–508.

LIPPITT, ROSEMARY, and HUBBELL, ANNE. "Role Playing for Personnel and Guidance Workers: Review of Literature with Suggestions for Application." *Group Psychotherapy,* 1956, IX, 2, 89–114.

LOVELL, C. "A Study of the Factor Structure of 13 Personality Variables." *Ed. & Psychol. Meas.*, 1945, *5*, 335–350.

LUMSDAINE, A. A., and JANIS, I. L. "Resistance to Counterpropaganda Produced by a One-Sided vs. a Two-Sided Propaganda Presentation." *Pub. Opin. Quart.*, 1953, *17*, pp. 311–318.

LYLE, W. H., JR., and LEVITT, E. E. "Punitiveness, Authoritarianism, and Parental Discipline of Grade School Children." *J. Abnorm. Soc. Psychol.*, 1955, *51*, 42–46.

MACARTHUR, R. S. "An Experimental Investigation of Persistence and Its Measurement at the Secondary School Level." Doctor's dissertation, London: Univ. London Lib., 1951.

MCCANDLESS, B. R. "Changing Relationships Between Dominance and Social Acceptability during Group Democratization." *Amer. J. Orthopsychiat.*, 1942, *12*, 529–535.

McCloy, C. H. "A Factor Analysis of Personality Traits To Underlie Character Education." *J. Educ. Psychol.*, 1936, 27, 375–384.

McCurdy, H. G., and Eber, H. W. "Democratic vs. Authoritarian: A Further Investigation of Group Problem-Solving." *J. Pers.*, 1953, 22, 258–269.

McCurdy, H. G., and Lambert, W. E. "The Efficiency of Small Human Groups in the Solution of Problems Requiring Genuine Cooperation." *J. Pers.*, 1952, 20, 478–494.

McDonough, M. R. "The Empirical Study of Character." *Stud. in Psychol. & Psychiat.*, 1929, 2, No. 3.

McKeachie, W. J. "Anxiety in the College Classroom." *J. Educ. Res.*, 1951, 45, 153–160.

Maier, N. R. F. "The Quality of Group Decisions as Influenced by the Discussion Leader." *Hum. Relat.*, 1950, 3, 155–174.

Maier, N. R. F. *Psychology in Industry.* Boston: Houghton Mifflin Co., 1946.

Maier, N. R. F., and Solem, A. R. "The Contribution of a Discussion Leader to the Quality of Group Thinking: The Effective Use of Minority Opinions." *Hum. Relat.*, 1952, 5, 277–288.

Marquis, D. G., Guetzkow, H., and Heyns, R. W. "A Social Psychological Study of the Decision-Making Conference." In H. Guetzkow (ed.)., *Groups, Leadership and Men: Research in Human Relations.* Pittsburgh: Carnegie Press, 1951, pp. 55–67.

Miller, N. E., and Dollard, J. *Social Learning and Imitation.* New Haven: Yale Univ. Press, 1941.

Mintz, A. "Non-Adaptive Group Behavior." *J. Abnorm. Soc. Psychol.*, 1951, 46, 150–159.

Misumi, J. "Experimental Studies on 'Group Dynamics' in Japan." *Psychologia*, 1959, II, No. 4, 229–235.

Misumi, J., Nakano, S., and Okamura, N. "A Cross-cultural Study of the Effect of Democratic, Authoritarian and Laissez-faire Atmosphere in Japanese Children (II)," (in Japanese). Unpublished paper.

Misumi, J., Nakano, S., and Ueno, Y. "A Cross-cultural Study of the Effect of Democratic, Authoritarian and Laissez-faire Atmosphere in Japanese Children (I)," (in Japanese). *Res. Bull. Fac. of Educ., Kyushu Univ.*, 1958, (in English), 5, pp. 41–59.

Mizuhara, T. "Management of Group Activities and Motivation" (in Japanese). *J. of Child Study & Mental Hygiene*, 1950, 1, No. 3, pp. 37–41.

Moreno, J. L. *Who Shall Survive?* Washington, D.C.: Nervous & Mental Disease Monograph, No. 58, 1934.

Mowrer, O. H. "Authoritarianism vs. Self-Government in the Management of Children's Aggressive Reactions as Preparation for Citizenship in a Democracy. *J. Soc. Psychol.*, 1939, *10*, 121–126.

NATIONAL TRAINING LABORATORY. "Manual of Human Relations Skill Practice Exercises." Mimeographed in preparation for publication, 1958.

ORWELL, G. *Nineteen Eighty-Four*. New York: Harcourt, Brace & Co., 1949.

OSGOOD, C. E., and TANNENBAUM, P. H. "The Principle of Congruity in the Prediction of Attitude-Change." *Psychol. Rev.*, 1955, *62*, 42–55.

PATTERSON, T. T., and WILLETT, E. J. "An Anthropological Experiment in a British Colliery." *Hum. Organization*, 1951, *10*, 19–23.

PELZ, D. C. "Leadership within a Hierarchical Organization." *J. Soc. Issues*, 1951, *7*, 49–55.

PEPITONE, A. "Motivational Effects in Social Perception." *Hum. Relat.*, 1950, *3*, 57–76.

PERKINS, H. V., JR. "The Effects of Climate and Curriculum on Group Learning." *J. Educ. Res.*, 1950, *44*, 269–286.

PERLMUTTER, H. V., and DE MONTMOLLIN, GERMAINE. "Group Learning of Nonsense Syllables." *J. Abnorm. Soc. Psychol.*, 1952, *47*, 762–769.

PIGORS, P. *Leadership or Domination*. Boston: Houghton Mifflin Co., 1935.

PINARD, J. W. "Tests on Perseveration: I. Their Relation to Character." *Brit. J. Psychol.*, 1932, *23*, 5–19.

PLATO. *The Republic*. E.g. trans. by W. H. D. RANSE. New York: Mentor Books, 1956.

POLANSKY, N., LIPPITT, R., and REDL, F. "An Investigation of Behavioral Contagion in Groups." *Hum. Relat.*, 1950, *3*, 319–348.

PRESTON, M. G., and HEINTZ, R. K. "Effects of Participatory vs. Supervisory Leadership on Group Judgment." *J. Abnorm. Soc. Psychol.*, 1949, *44*, 345–355.

RADKE, MARIAN J. "The Relation of Parental Authority to Children's Behavior and Attitudes." *Univ. Minn. Inst. Child Welf. Monogr. Ser.*, 1946, No. 22.

RADKE, MARIAN, and KLISURICH, D. "Experiments in Changing Food Habits." *J. of Amer. Dietetic Assoc.*, 1947, *23*, 403–409.

REDL, F. "Group Emotion and Leadership." *Psychiatry*, 1942, *5*, 575–596. Also in A. P. HARE, E. F. BORGATTA, and R. F. BALES (eds.), *Small Groups*. New York: Alfred A. Knopf, Inc., 1955, pp. 71–87.

Reid, I. D., and Ehle, Emily L. (now Krueger, Emily L.). "Leadership Selection in Urban Locality Areas." *Pub. Opin. Quart.*, 1950, *14*, No. 2, 262–284.

Richards, T. W., and Simons, W. P. "The Fels Child Behavior Scales." *Genet. Psychol. Mon.*, 1941, *24*, 259–309.

Riesman, D. *The Lonely Crowd.* New Haven: Yale Univ. Press, 1950.

———. *Individualism Reconsidered.* Glencoe, Ill.: The Free Press of Glencoe, 1954.

Robbins, Florence G. "The Impact of Social Climates upon a College Class." *Sch. Rev.*, 1952, *60*, 275–284.

Roethlisberger, F., and Dickson, W. J. *Management and the Worker.* Cambridge: Harvard Univ. Press, 1939.

Roff, M. A. "A Study of Combat Leadership in the Air Force by Means of a Rating Scale: Group Differences." *J. Psychol.*, 1950, *30*, 229–239.

Roseborough, Mary F. "Experimental Studies of Small Groups." *Psychol. Bull.*, 1953, *50*, 275–303.

Sanford, F. H. *Authoritarianism and Leadership.* Philadelphia: Inst. for Res. in Hum. Relat., 1950.

Sanford, R. N., Adkins, M. M., Muller, R. B., and Cobb, E. "Physique, Personality and Scholarship." *Mon. Soc. Res. Child Dev.*, 1943, *7*, Ser. No. 34.

Sarnoff, I., Katz, D., and McClintock, C. "Attitude-Change Procedures and Motivating Patterns." In D. Katz et al., *Public Opinion and Propaganda.* New York: Dryden Press (Holt), pp. 305–312.

Schlesinger, L., Jackson, J., and Butman, Jean. "The Effect upon Decisions of Experimentally Varying the Degree of Control Exercised by Chairmen of Management Committees." Paper read at meeting of Amer. Psychol. Assoc., Washington, Aug. 29, 1958.

Scott, E. L. *Perceptions of Organization and Leadership Behavior.* Columbus: Ohio State Univ. Res. Found., 1952.

Sears, R. R., Maccoby, Eleanor E., and Levin, H. *Patterns of Child Rearing.* Evanston, Ill.: Row, Peterson & Company, 1957.

Sengupta, N. N., and Sinha, C. P. N. "Mental Work in Isolation and in Group." *Indian J. Psychol.*, 1926, *1*, 106–110.

Shaw, Marjorie E. "A Comparison of Individuals and Small Groups in the Rational Solution of Complex Problems." *Amer. J. Psychol.*, 1932, *44*, 491–504.

Shaw, Marvin. "A Comparison of Two Types of Leadership in Various Communications Nets." *J. Abnorm. Soc. Psychol.*, 1955, *50*, 127–134. Reprinted in C. G. Browne and T. S. Cohen (eds.), *The Study of Leadership.* Danville, Ill.: The Interstate, 1958.

SHERIF, M. "A Study of Some Social Factors in Perception." *Arch. Psychol.*, New York: 1935, No. 187.

SHILS, E. A., and JANOWITZ, M. "Cohesion and Disintegration in the Wehrmacht in World War II." In D. KATZ, D. CARTWRIGHT, S. ELDERSVELD, and A. M. LEE, *Public Opinion and Propaganda*. New York: Dryden Press (Holt), 1954, pp. 553–582. Reprinted from *Pub. Opin. Quart.*, *12*, 1948, No. 2, 280–315.

SIMS, V. M. "The Relative Influence of Two Types of Motivation on Improvement." *J. Educ. Psychol.*, 1928, *19*, 480–484.

SOLOMON, D. "Influences on the Decisions of Adolescents." Ph.D. thesis, Univ. of Mich., Dec. 1959.

SOUTH, E. B. "Some Psychological Aspects of Committee Work." *J. Appl. Psychol.*, 1927, *11*, 348–368, 437–464.

SOROKIN, P. A., TANQUIST, MAMIE, PARTEN, MILDRED, and ZIMMERMAN, MRS. C. C. "An Experimental Study of Efficiency of Work under Various Specified Conditions." *Amer. J. Sociol.*, 1930, *35*, 765–782.

STENDLER, CELIA, DAMRIN, DORA, and HAINES, ALEYNE C. "Studies in Cooperation and Competition: I. The Effects of Working for Group and Individual Rewards on the Social Climate of Children's Groups." *J. Genet. Psychol.*, 1951, *79*, 173–197.

STOGDILL, R. M., and KOEHLER, K. *Measures of Leadership Structure and Organization Change*. Columbus: Ohio State Univ. Res. Found., 1952.

STOUFFER, S. A., et al. *The American Soldier*, Vol. I. Princeton: Princeton Univ. Press, 1949.

SYMONDS, P. M. "Role-Playing as a Diagnostic Procedure in the Selection of Foremen." *Sociatry*, 1947, *1*, 43–50.

TAYLOR, D. W., and FAUST, W. L. "Twenty Questions: Efficiency in Problem Solving as a Function of Size of Group." *J. Exp. Psychol.*, 1952, *44*, 360–368.

THELEN, H. *The Dynamics of Groups at Work*. Chicago: U. of Chicago Press, 1954.

THIBAUT, J. W. "An Experimental Study of the Cohesiveness of Underprivileged Groups." *Hum. Relat.*, 1950, *3*, 251–278.

THIBAUT, J. W., and COULES, J. "The Role of Communication in the Reduction of Interpersonal Hostility." *J. Abnorm. Soc. Psychol.*, 1952, *47*, 770–777.

THORNDIKE, R. L. "The Effect of Discussion upon the Correctness of Group Decisions, When the Factor of Majority Influence Is Allowed For." *J. Soc. Psychol.*, 1938a, *9*, 343–362.

THORNDIKE, R. L. "On What Type of Task Will a Group Do Well?" *J. Abnorm. Soc. Psychol.*, 1938, *33*, 409–413.

Timmons, W. M. "Decisions and Attitudes as Outcomes of the Discussion of a Social Problem." *Contrib. Educ.*, No. 777. New York: Teachers College, Columbia University, Bureau of Publications, 1939.

Timmons, W. M. "Can the Product Superiority of Discussors Be Attributed to Averaging or Majority Influences?" *J. Soc. Psychol.*, 1942, *15*, 23–32.

Titus, H. E., and Hollander, E. P. "The California F Scale in Psychological Research: 1950–1955. *Psychol. Bull.*, 1957, *54*, 47–64.

de Tocqueville, A. *Democracy in America*, Vol. I. New York: Alfred A. Knopf, Inc., 1945. (Original publication, 1835.)

Torrance, E. P. "Methods of Conducting Critiques of Group Problem-Solving Performance." *J. Appl. Psychol.*, 1953, 37, 394–398.

———. "The Behavior of Small Groups under the Stress of Conditions of Survival." *Amer. Sociol. Rev.*, 1954, *19*, 751–755.

Torrance, E. P., and Mason, R. "The Indigenous Leader in Changing Attitudes and Behavior." *Int. J. Sociometry*, 1956, *1*, 23–28.

U. S. Information Agency, *Khrushchev and Stalin as Seen by the Soviet Public*. Repatriate Reports, No. III, 1958.

Wagman, M. "An Investigation of the Effectiveness of Authoritarian Suggestion and Non-Authoritarian Information as Methods of Changing the Prejudiced Attitudes of Relatively Authoritarian and Non-Authoritarian Personalities." Ph.D. Dissertation, Univ. of Michigan, 1953.

Watson, G. B. "Do Groups Think More Efficiently than Individuals?" *J. Abnorm. Soc. Psychol.*, 1928, 23, 328–336.

Webb, E. "Character and Intelligence." *Brit. J. Psychol.*, *Mon. Supp.*, 1915, *I*, 3.

White, R. K. "The Meaning of Democracy as Inferred from Soviet and American Writers." Unpublished paper read at meeting of Amer. Psychol. Assoc., 1950.

———. "Hitler, Roosevelt, and the Nature of War Propaganda." *J. Abnorm. Soc. Psychol.*, 1949, *44*, 157–174.

———. "The New Resistance to International Propaganda." *Pub. Opin. Quart.*, 1952–1953, *16*, No. 4, 539–551.

Whiting, J. W. M., and Child, I. L. *Child Training and Personality: A Cross-Cultural Study*. New Haven: Yale Univ. Press, 1953.

Whyte, W. F. *Human Relations in the Restaurant Industry*. New York: McGraw-Hill Book Co., 1948.

Whyte, W. H., Jr. *The Organization Man*. New York: Simon and Schuster, Inc., 1956.

Wickert, R. "Turnover and Employee's Feelings of Ego-Involvement in the Day-to-Day Operation of a Company." *Personnel Psychol.*, 1951, *4*, 185–197.

WILLERMAN, B. "Group Decision and Request as Means of Changing Food Habits." Washington: Committee on Food Habits, Nat. Res. Council, 1943. (Mimeo.)

WISPE, L. G. "Evaluating Section Teaching Methods in the Introductory Course." *J. Educ. Res.*, 1951, *45*, 161–186.

WITTENBORN, J. R. "The Development of Adoptive Children." New York: Russell Sage Found., 1954.

WOLMAN, B. "Leadership and Group Dynamics." *J. Soc. Psychol.*, 1953, *43*, 11–25.

ZUCKER, H. J. "Affectional Identification and Delinquency." *Arch. Psychol.*, N.Y., 1943, No. 286.

Index

Accomplishment, under autocracy, 142–143
under democracy, 260, 285–288
under laissez-faire, 129–130
Activity, in autocracy, 151
Adult behavior, status in, 235–236
Aggression, in autocracy, 53–55, 66–73, 119–122
contagion of, 154–155, 157
on day of transition, 76–77
and emotional tension, 171–172
and frustration, 147–148, 161–167
habit of, 153–154
in laissez-faire, 151
major factors in, 57
vagueness of alternative, 141
Ambiguity, in democracy, 227
Analysis of conversations, 30
Anarchies, political, 137, 275
Apathy, in groups, 228
as obstacle to democracy, 246–253
Apprenticeship for politics, 309
Ascendance, dominating, 66–68
friendly, 68
objective, 68
Attention, demands for, 68–69, 167–168
Authority, needed in democracy, 270–276, 276–279, 294–296
Autocracy, activity in, 150–151
aggression in, 66–73
aggressive reaction meetings, 53–55, 119–122
aura of invincibility, 156
compared with democracy, 64–65, 134–136
conscience and, 201–202
creative thinking in, 65
discontent in, 73–78

"dominating ascendance," 66–68
friendliness in, 82–83
and frustration, 73, 147–148, 161–167
giving information, 39
guiding suggestions, 36
hostility in, 68
idealism in, 145
inefficiency of, 275
inevitability in, 139–141
lack of respect for members' goals, 49
leisure in, 151
loss of individuality in, 79–80
nonobjective criticism in, 34–36
open communication in, 45
order-giving in, 31–34
paths to status in, 169–171
praise in, 35–36
preferred by "good boys," 132–133
psychological defense of, 138–173
resignation in, 151–153
satisfying needs, 73
submissive reaction to, 140, 141
submissive reaction meetings, 51–53, 92–93

Beaumont, 52, 74, 145, 166
Becker, 114–115, 162, 163, 164, 165, 168
Behavior, study of human, 7–8
Bell Telephone Company, 277, 278
Ben, 52, 53, 75
Bill, 34, 35, 36, 37, 40, 41, 42, 49, 55, 56, 57, 58, 59, 60, 62, 63, 79, 80, 83, 90, 91, 92, 93, 94, 95, 96, 97, 98, 99, 100, 102, 103, 104, 105, 106, 129, 130, 131, 137, 146, 154, 233, 234,

325